cobra road

Other books by the author

WALES AND THE WELSH
TALKING OF WALES
AMERICANS AND NOTHING ELSE
INDIA FILE
THE STATE OF AMERICA
OUT OF RED DARKNESS
MY FOREIGN COUNTRY

cobra road
An Indian Journey

TREVOR FISHLOCK

JOHN MURRAY
Albemarle Street · London

*To the memory
of
Barney and Iris*

© Trevor Fishlock 1999

First published in 1999
by John Murray (Publishers) Ltd,
50 Albemarle Street, London W1X 4BD

The moral right of the author has been asserted

All rights reserved. No part of this publication may be reproduced in any material form (including photocopying or storing it in any medium by electronic means and whether or not transiently or incidentally to some other use of this publication) without the written permission of the copyright owner, except in accordance with the provisions of the Copyright, Designs and Patents Act 1988 or under the terms of a licence issued by the Copyright Licensing Agency, 90 Tottenham Court Road, London W1P 9HE. Applications for the copyright owner's written permission to reproduce any part of this publication should be addressed to the publisher.

A catalogue record for this book is available from the British Library

ISBN 0-7195-5516 7

Typeset in Photina by Servis Filmsetting Limited, Manchester

Printed and bound in Great Britain by the University Press, Cambridge

Contents

Map vi

1. A Ripping Yarn   1
2. To the Khyberees   7
3. War and Champagne   31
4. The Point of the Bayonet   51
5. The Palace Theatre   73
6. The Duty Baby   93
7. Where the Coconut Goes   105
8. Walking on Stilts   127
9. Shouting at India   143
10. The Poisoned Garden   165
11. To the Spinning Water   181
12. In the Carnatic   205
13. The Centre of the World   225
14. The Road to Panagarh   251

Index   260

IRAN
AFGHANISTAN
Malakand
Khyber Pass
Peshawar
Kohat
KASHMI
Srinagar
HIMACHAL
PRADESH
R. Jhelum
R. Indus
Lahore
Amritsar
Simla
PUNJAB
PAKISTAN
Delhi
Alwar
Vrindavan
Jaisalmer
RAJASTHAN
Udaipur
Bhuj
GUJARAT
Ahmadabad
Rajkot
Palitana
Somnath
Diu
Gulf of Cambay
R. Narmada
MADHYA
Bombay
MAHARASHT
ARABIAN
SEA
I N D
KARNATAKA
Goa
Bangalore
Mercara
Seringa
Mysore
KERALA
Laccadive Is. (INDIA)
Calicut
Cochin
Minicoy I. (INDIA)
Cape Comorin
N
W
E
S

Cobra Road

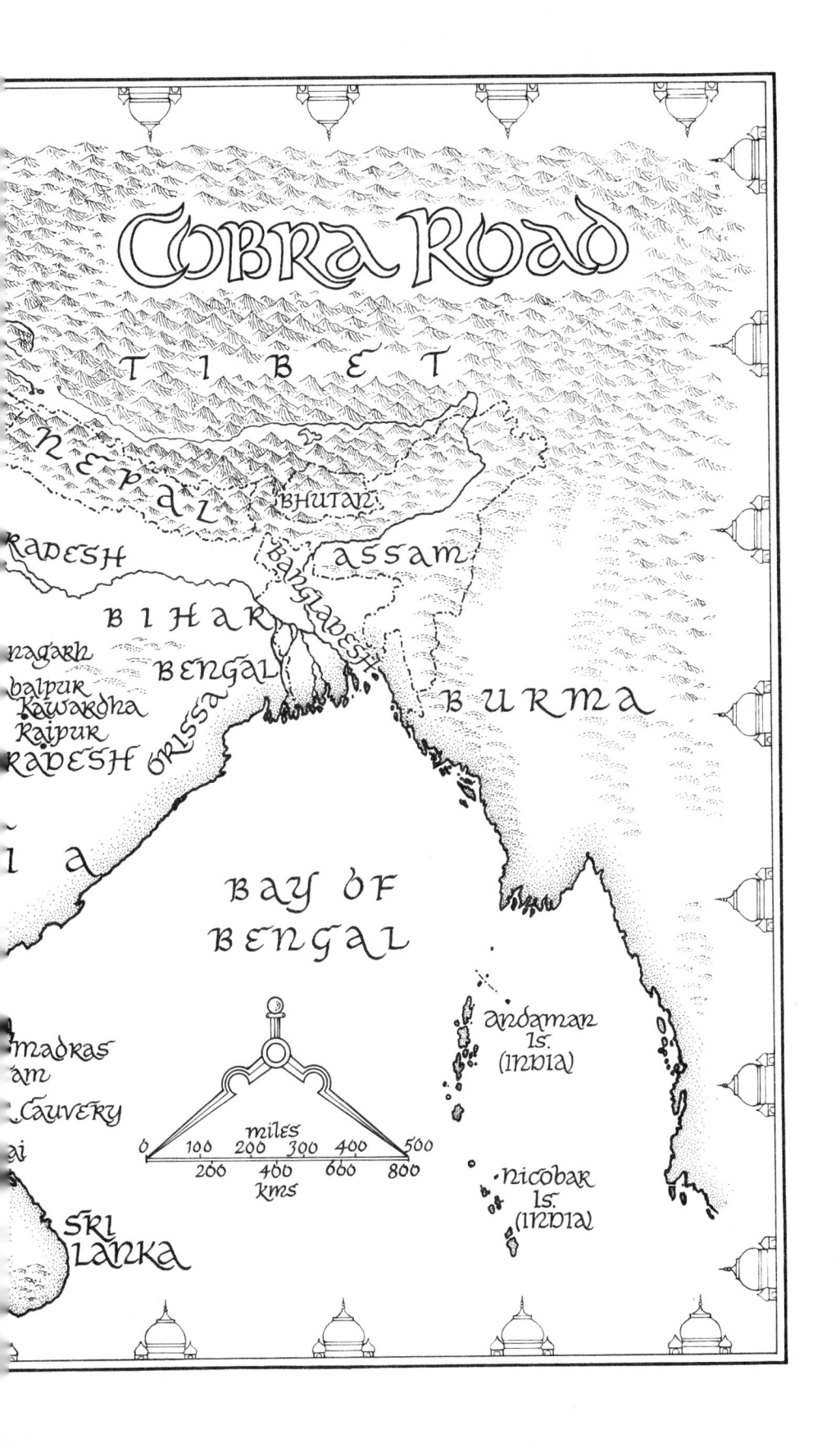

TIBET

NEPAL

BHUTAN

...RADESH

ASSAM

BANGLADESH

BIHAR

...nagarh
...balpur
Kawardha
Raipur

BENGAL

ORISSA

BURMA

...RADESH

...ia

BAY OF BENGAL

...madras
...am
...Cauvery
...ai

```
 miles
0  100  200  300  400  500
   200  400  600  800
        kms
```

Andaman Is.
(INDIA)

Nicobar Is.
(INDIA)

SRI LANKA

1

A Ripping Yarn

HOUSES IN THE VILLAGE in which I grew up had names rather than numbers, sturdy English announcements like The Limes and The Willows, and whimsical invitations like Bide-a-Wee and Restawhyle. Not far from us, Dorothy and Ernest King linked their names and destinies in redbrick Dorern.

Of all of them, none was more gratifyingly exotic than ours.

Panagarh.

I wrote it with a curlicued flourish on the flyleaves of my books. When I gave my address people wrinkled their noses and said: 'Eh? How do you spell that?'

'Definitely Eastern,' my father pronounced. 'Somewhere far away and hotter than hell.'

'China,' someone suggested.

Foreign, anyway, everyone agreed.

I do not remember how I discovered it was a town in India. Perhaps Uncle Herbert knew. He had served with the Royal Artillery on the North West Frontier for seven years in the 1930s. In a photograph in the family album he perched on a rock, wearing shorts and puttees, reading his home town newspaper, the *Hereford Times*. He showed my mother and father photographs of British soldiers gathered around the corpse of a warrior on the Frontier. The man had been decapitated and his head was balanced on his chest.

The souvenirs Uncle Herbert brought home were like all the other gewgaws from the bazaars that reminded many British families of an experience of India. He gave my parents two engraved brass cobras. They reared up beside the clock on our mantelpiece, on the coils of their tails, their hoods spread and their eyes glittering, like Nag and his wicked wife Nagaina in their great war with Rikki-Tikki-Tavi.

Half a mile from Panagarh, on the bend of the road, a gravel drive curved through pine trees to Pond Head, a white mansion commanding a lawn that ran down to a tidal creek. A friend lived there. We played cricket on the lawn. My friend's father was a retired colonel, with a standard-issue military moustache, and his mother an elegant creature who looked down her nose at us scruffy boys. At weekends they sat in front of the house and drank Pimms from a jug while sunshine sparkled on their large car. They were a picture of English country ease, like a scene from a film at the Regal down the road.

'Nevil Shute used to live at Pond Head,' my mother said. Some of his novels were on her shelves. *No Highway* and *A Town Like Alice*, I remember; and because he had lived at Pond Head I was drawn to read them. He was not the only writer who had starred in our neighbourhood. W.T. Stead had lived in a cottage nearby, although to us children he was notable only for having perished, with stoic British dignity, in the *Titanic*.

I imagined Shute sitting at his typewriter at Pond Head and smoking a pipe, as proper authors did, in the large room overlooking the lawn. Through the trees to the right, he would have seen a small cottage. On Sunday afternoons it housed a private scripture class run by an earnest retired officer, Wing-Commander Woofferton. I mourned the penal hours spent in Sunday best in that claustrophobic room, the time subtracted

A Ripping Yarn

from freedom, the waste of sunlight and snow. I directed my resentment at the heaving shoulders of the Wing-Commander as he wrung 'All Things Bright And Beautiful' from a wheezing harmonium.

In this little room, though, I launched the only commercial venture of my life, a capitalist lending library. I carried a bag of my books to the cottage and encouraged the other inmates to borrow one for a penny a week. At first, Wing-Commander Woofferton smiled benignly. At least I thought so; but after a few Sundays of watching me trade beneath the little oak cross on the harmonium, he cleansed my business from the temple.

I still have one of the books. Its stained green covers, with the name of my library written inside in blue pencil, evoke the afternoons in that Christian mission to the natives of distant Hampshire. *The Slave of the Khan*, by Michael Trevor, is an imperial ripping yarn. Set among the brown hills of the North West Frontier during the sunset of the British Raj, it describes the kidnapping and subsequent adventures of Jack Bray, a boy of fourteen, the spoilt son of a general. It has echoes of Rudyard Kipling's *Kim*, for one of the characters is a lama, a wandering holy man, and another is a resourceful Pathan boy. The dialogue is in the ornate 'Whither goest thou?' vernacular. 'O Lion of the hills', say the grovelling tribesmen in salute to their Khan. Even a camel is addressed as 'O Prince of the desert'.

Jack is seized by one of the Khan's men in the bazaar in Peshawar – 'the City of a Thousand and One Sins . . . its dark warrens a refuge for every cut-throat and ruffian from the border hills'. Doped and slung on a camel's back, he is taken through the Khyber Pass to a tribal fortress and dragged before the Khan, a man of fierce gaze with a nose 'curved out like a scimitar'. The Khan has had Jack kidnapped in revenge for the death of his own son at the hands of the British and, in order to terrify him, forces him to witness a barbaric execution. A prisoner is staked out on the ground, a metal pot lashed to his naked stomach. The pot has two chambers. In the upper one is a fire and in the lower part a starving rat. The Khan's words – 'Bring me a rat, a starving rat!' – chill me now as they did when I first read them years ago. To escape the fire's heat, the rat burrows into the prisoner's stomach.

In those days adults believed that the new American horror comics would make us wicked. Teachers rummaged in our pockets and desks and confiscated all transatlantic trash. No one thought to look behind the respectable hard covers of a boys' adventure book in which there was horror enough, the screaming of the Khan's writhing prisoner, the fountain of blood as the rat did its work.

The Slave of the Khan, like *Kim* and other stories, planted in my mind a notion of the vividness and swirl of India; and so did films at the Regal like *Gunga Din* and *Mowgli* and other melodramas of topi and turban. I did not see an Indian in the flesh, however, until the day a genial Sikh, wearing a red turban and a long belted raincoat, knocked at our door and smilingly introduced himself to my mother.

He knelt in the threshold and sprang the locks of his capacious leather suitcase. There in front of us was a treasure chest from a Silk Road caravan, spilling gorgeous brocades, silks and threads, a cascade of vermilion, peacock and gold. An enthralling perfume rose into the damp air and lodged itself in my memory. When I landed in India years later, I smelt it again and knew it, the scent of sandalwood and spice uncorked by the beaming Sikh on the doorstep of Panagarh, his soft persuasions matching the rustle of slippery silk in his long fingers.

No ink ran in our family veins, but newspapers and magazines were plentiful at home, and I thought that *Picture Post* and the *Daily Express*, then in its Beaverbrookian heyday, were full of the glamour and adventure of newsgathering. When our

A Ripping Yarn

evening newspaper ran an advertisement, 'Wanted For This Newspaper, Junior Reporter', I wrote for the job and got it. My father worried that life on a newspaper was insecure and my headmaster said bleakly that journalism was not a proper job, which may have been one of its attractions.

I went to Fleet Street eventually, and *The Times* set me to the coverage of the west of England and all of Wales, a foreign assignment, a gift of independence. I went to America for a while and then worked in London. One cold day in Gray's Inn Road, the Foreign Editor called me in and said: 'We'd like you to do India for us. The chap who's there now doesn't want to go through another monsoon. Could you possibly be there before it breaks?'

This was the second gift of independence, the vastness of the subcontinent, an involvement in the narrative of events and the fortunes of personalities against the background of history and culture. A foreign correspondent's life is often irregular and sometimes lonely; but for all its anxieties and discomforts, I preferred the rewards of the road and roamed India and its neighbours more or less as I wished, following the main stream of news and the tributaries of my curiosity. My portable typewriter still stands in a corner of the attic, a scarred relic, the reporter's equivalent of the Lee-Enfield. I took it everywhere and it doubtless made my right arm longer than the left. Perhaps the closest I came to losing it was at Delhi airport once when a customs officer confiscated it, to levy some sort of tax I suppose, and when I protested, he shouted: 'Sir, it is being taken for your own good.'

Of course, I shall never use it again as I used to. When I first travelled the subcontinent, communications were poor. Portable computers, satellite links and fax machines lay in the future. The telephone service was so bad that it was necessary to take a plane or to drive long distances to reach a large city to

Cobra Road

send a report. I typed my dispatches and handed them to a telex operator at a telegraph office or hotel; or I operated the telex machine myself. There were many times, in Punjab, or central India, or Baluchistan, or Kashmir or Kandy, in the Chittagong Hill Tracts or on the North West Frontier, when the telex stuttered and died, the operator spread his hands in a gesture of helplessness, the fans sighed to a stop, sweat ran down my back and anxiety took hold. But there were other times when the old machine stirred from its coma into creaking life. It whirred and hummed and the lights glowed and the keys stammered out the answering code from London, a pleasure and relief that now belongs in the museum of thrills.

Panagarh, I discovered, was not famous or notable. Indeed, it was rather obscure, appeared in no history or guide book I consulted and was not marked on many maps. In the years I lived in India I never found the time to go there. In any case, I rather liked having it gather dust in the attic of my imagination, an object of curiosity, a place I would see one day.

And then, years later, I decided to contrive a way of getting there, to see what it was like, to make a bagatelle ball progress towards it, to discover why someone should give its name to a house in England, to complete a circle. I thought I would start in the Khyber Pass and the City of a Thousand and One Sins, in the country of *The Slave of the Khan*, the story which first seared India into my imagination as I read it, over and over, as a boy in Panagarh.

2

To the Khyberees

IN DELHI, JUST BEFORE I boarded the evening plane to Pakistan, a security man removed the batteries from the pocket torch in my bag and took away my boarding pass. When the flight was called I found myself with two other passengers whose passes had been taken from them because they, too, had articles that contravened the security rules. One was a European woman whose offending item was a pretty pebble, the size of a gull's egg, that she had found on a beach in Goa. The other was a grey-haired woman wearing a sari, from whom the security men had seized a plastic bag containing half a dozen small coconuts.

After we had waited for a while a team of officials in uniform arrived. One gave us our boarding passes, a second carried my batteries in a plastic bag, a third had the pebble and a fourth the coconuts. A fifth produced some white string and tied a label to the batteries, another to the bag of coconuts and, with some difficulty, because the string kept slipping, yet another to the pebble.

'These items will be kept by the purser', we were told, 'and returned to you when you arrive in Lahore.'

As we joined the queue of passengers at the aircraft steps, the officers bent their heads in discussion over the coconuts. One of them selected a nut, knelt and banged it hard on the edge of the steps. After a few blows it shattered, spattering his shoes. He then selected a second nut, but his superiors directed him away from the steps and towards the steel towing bar attached to the Boeing's nosewheel. Under the blows of the coconut, the bar bonged like a temple bell. The nuts had passed through an X-ray but there was obviously some suspicion that one of them might be an ingeniously fashioned coconut bomb. If that were so, I thought, surely the last thing these men should do was hammer them to pieces under the nose of an airliner; and if they did not suspect a bomb, what was breaking them but vindictiveness? They knew, of course, that coconuts have a sacred and symbolic function for Hindus and that the elderly woman probably intended to use them in a religious ritual. Coconuts have been used in ceremonies for thousands of years and millions are cracked every day in rites of worship. They are broken on ships' bows at launchings, smashed at the inauguration of new buildings, the beginning of business ventures and before the shooting of new films. Fishermen break them before putting out to sea, to propitiate the god of the waves and the wind. Perhaps most importantly, the milk is poured as a chrism over the lingam found in temples and other sacred places. This phallic pillar symbolizes Shiva, one of the greatest of the Hindu gods, who is considered the essence of life, and who in one of the innumerable paradoxes of Hinduism, represents sexual energy while never shedding his semen. Coconuts are used in wedding ceremonies as emblems of fertility, a metaphor for the womb; and women anxious to conceive visit shrines where they pray and are given coconuts. A nut is not broken in the presence of a pregnant woman for fear that the baby's head might subsequently be broken. Indeed, the coconut is considered a substitute for the human head in rites which are vestiges of ancient blood sacrifice. Its tuft is thought of as hair and the three distinctive dark spots on the shell, lending it the crude appearance of a

To the Khyberees

human face, are seen as the Three Eyes of Shiva: the left is the moon, the right the sun, and the central eye casts the sharp glance of truth. Sometimes a figure is fashioned from straw, with a coconut for a head, and is worshipped as Shiva.

With an expression of blank resignation, the elderly lady watched as her coconuts were broken one by one beneath the Boeing. It seemed a bizarre version of puja, the act of worship, an offering to the gods. The shards were put into the plastic bag. As I entered the plane, the sweet southern aroma of coconut mingled with the sharp sniff of jet fuel.

❖

I changed at Lahore and took a plane to Peshawar, an old F27 workhorse. As it bounced over cobbles of turbulence my two neighbours across the aisle stuck their index fingers in their ears, screwed their eyes tightly shut like children and prayed hard. My immediate neighbour in the window seat, a bulky and bushy-bearded man, prayed and then slept peacefully, his head coming to rest on my shoulder. When he awoke he noted that I had not consumed the banana and cake in my airline snack box and asked if he could have them. I said yes and he pushed the food into his bag.

'I am well known in Peshawar,' he said. 'I can arrange anything. Car trip, hotel, change money.' But he did not offer his name.

It was late when we landed. I stayed near the airport at the best hotel in town. I appreciated its comfort, but for me it was the wrong place. True, there was a proper Frontier notice in the lobby: 'Personal Guards Or Gunmen Are Required To Deposit Their Weapons With The Hotel Security'. But the hotel was expensive and shiny, with paper strips over the toilet seats attesting to cleanliness, and it was characterless. It did not feel right to eat croissants at breakfast under the intensely watchful eyes of waiters wearing bow ties and black jackets. A couple of my friends were of the romantic tendency and I knew I would not be able to face their disdain if they discovered that I had stayed here. Of course, this hotel was no less 'real' than any other place on the Frontier and these computer-tapping denizens of the lobby, well-groomed men in dark suits, were as full-bloodedly Pathan as any rifle-toting warrior with toenails like shoehorns. Still, I was here, up to a point, to look into the old foxed mirror of history; and the Khyber Pass itself seemed to demand something more in keeping with its spirit. I called a taxi and moved to Dean's.

It had barely changed. I had stayed here many times and my shabby suite was familiar: a small veranda, a gloomy sitting-room with a sofa and table, a brown-painted bamboo screen and a narrow bed beneath a clunking ceiling fan. A handsome grey and pink gecko scuttled across the wall of the large bathroom, keeping the insect population under control.

I set down my bags and took off my shoe to flatten a well-polished cockroach patrolling the frayed green carpet. The air-conditioner in the sitting-room drowned the sound of the room's only innovation, a battered vintage television set. All the channels offered a fizz of static, except one which showed blurred Pakistani melodramas featuring squeaking heroines and pantomime villains with cruel moustaches and rolling eyes.

Shrubs and flowers brightened the hotel's dusty walled compound. Waiters ferried trays of tea and snacks to the bungalow terraces of rooms. If I wanted to drink alcohol I could go to the permit room and fill in a large buff form attesting to my foreign and non-Muslim status. The idea was not attractive. I remembered previous visits and a disapproving waiter serving bottles of slightly warm and soapy beer which came from a brewery founded in the 1860s by the father of Brigadier-General Reginald Dyer, the notorious slaughterer of Amritsar in 1919.

To the Khyberees

Dean's is a redoubt. It has been serving mulligatawny soup and roast chicken and potatoes for more than a hundred years. When I used to ask the managers at the reception desk how old it was they would look at me as if to say: 'How old would you like it to be?' It is a remnant of the Frontier that Rudyard Kipling chronicled and romanticized. Kipling made only one short visit to Peshawar, in 1885, as a nineteen-year-old reporter on assignment for the *Civil and Military Gazette* of Lahore. It did not matter that his stay was brief. The Frontier was part of his larger Punjab beat; and Kipling's India was, essentially, Punjab. In any case, he was a young man astonishingly sensitive to his surroundings and he grasped very quickly the drama of Peshawar and the Khyber, the harsh land studded with forts, the military bustle and sweat-blackened khaki, the rumours of war. He breathed the peppery dust of the bazaar and understood the warrior codes of honour and vendetta, the pitilessness beneath the picturesque. He drew on these fermenting images in many of his best stories and poems, not least in *Kim*, his masterpiece, published fifteen years after he left India.

No Frontier war was raging while he was there. But when he walked to sniff the air of the Khyber Pass near Jamrud Fort, a tribesman fired a bullet in his direction. 'I was shot at,' Kipling recalled, 'but without malice.' As he knew, the musketry of Frontier snipers was such that had the man wished to hit him he would certainly have done so. No doubt it was a warrior's mischief. It was, however, a personal experience of the 'bullet whistling down the Pass' that he described in his poem 'Arithmetic on the Frontier'. Part of that poem, the verse on the death of a young British officer – 'Two thousand pounds of education/Drops to a ten rupee jezail' – is inscribed on one of the marble slabs at Jamrud which relate the history of a region that was for a century the British Wild West. It is remarkable and fitting, a tribute by the authorities to the writer who, more than any other, evoked the atmosphere of the Frontier at a particularly dramatic time in its long history.

Kipling had been sent to Peshawar to report a crucial conference between Lord Dufferin, the Viceroy of India, and Abdur Rahman, the Amir, or ruler, of Afghanistan. At that time a Russian force was threatening to provoke war in Afghanistan, a move in the Great Game of British and Russian rivalry on the fringes of the Indian empire. The British sought to flatter the Amir so that he would keep his country as a buffer between India and Russia.

In his bluff appearance, Abdur Rahman reminded British soldiers and diplomats of Henry VIII. His passions were music, gardening, architecture and cruelty. He ordered tens of thousands of captives and criminals to their deaths. The fortunate were bayoneted or blown to bits from cannons – that was speedy and merciful – but most were boiled, strangled, cut to pieces, torn limb from limb, starved in iron cages hanging by the roadside or meticulously and slowly skinned alive. Compared with the Amir's sadism, the death-by-rat in *The Slave of the Khan* did not look horrifically far-fetched. Kipling knew that many of the rulers in this region savoured exemplary death agonies and enjoyed refinements of torture. In his 'Ballad of the King's Jest', a king lodges a captive in a tree. The man remains there for seven days, both he and his tormentor knowing that fatigue will eventually cause him to slip from the branches and be impaled on the bayonets embedded in the ground below.

Aboard a jolting tonga, a two-wheeled pony taxi that looks like a governess cart, I drove clip-clop to the cantonment that the British built to separate themselves from the noise, smells and dangers of the seething City of a Thousand and One Sins. This was their spacious garden suburb of bungalows, clubs, schools, military buildings, tennis courts and off-the-peg English country churches. Like the cool hill stations to which

To the Khyberees

they resorted in the hot weather, the cantonments they built outside Indian cities put a distance between them and the people they ruled and made them more remote.

Along The Mall and its sister avenues, military order prevailed, forever Sandhurst and Aldershot. Even the trees had been planted in disciplined ranks, and in their speckled shade the gateways of barracks and officers' messes formed a sergeant's paradise of gleaming cannon, white-painted stones, starched uniforms and heliographic bootcaps. The roads were painted with white lines. Police in smart uniforms supervised the traffic. Here the commonplace anarchy of the highways of Pakistan and India had been eradicated: those damned scruffy civilians were kept in order. A sign commanded: 'No Horns Please, Silence Is Gold'.

Another notice bore the single word: 'Smile'. In the 1840s that would have been especially good advice. At that time the city was part of the powerful Sikh kingdom of Punjab ruled by Ranjit Singh. Its governor was a mercenary soldier, General Paolo Avitabile, whose ruthlessness was observed by Lieutenant Greenwood, an English army officer passing through to fight in Afghanistan. 'At every corner', he noted, 'was erected a large treble gibbet, each of which had seventeen or eighteen malefactors hanging on it, as a gentle hint to the inhabitants to be on their best behaviour. I believe there was very little ceremony made with them. If a man looked sulky, he was strung up at once.'

The clerk at the bank where I went to change money kindly sent me to the bazaar. 'Go to the money changers there. They will give you a better rate than we can.' The labyrinth of the old city can hardly have changed since the thirty-year-old Mountstuart Elphinstone, the first Englishman to visit Peshawar, saw it in February 1809 while on a diplomatic mission. Through worn alleys chequered by sunlight and shadows, I moved from one trade to another, one smell to the next, from leatherworkers and coppersmiths to tailors and shoemakers and teashops, from burnt mutton and hot charcoal to scented fruit, horse dung and the fragrance of bread. This smoke-hazed warren was the stage for an immense and sprawling opera of beards, of oversized turbans, piecrust hats, filigree caps, loose smocks, shawls, waistcoats and pantaloons. A resolute and bristling masculinity prevailed. Shoulders were crossed by rifle straps and bandoliers, and large feet with strong splayed toes poked from stout sandals. The faces were eagle-beaked and thickly whiskered, and the eyes were as black as sloes or blue or feline amber. Ever since the first heavy cameras were hauled up to the Frontier these men have known how photogenic they are. You half-expect them, as they approach, to cock a glance at the light and suggest a hundredth at f.11.

Of course, only the men possessed faces. The women were almost invisible, painted from the picture, concealed in billowing burqas and navigating through latticed peepholes.

I went to the dark and dusty Peshawar museum which, at all times, seems permanently located in the depths of a Sunday afternoon, perfect for the pleasures of melancholy. The air itself seemed heavy, used and narcotic. I peered into the gloomy cases of old stone figures and fragments of pottery, of stained swords and mouldering costumes. An inscription tried to explain the script on a piece of ancient stone but gave up the struggle: 'It does not give connected sense but it impresses upon us the instability of everything.'

❦

I hired a car and a driver and set off on the crowded road out of the city. The heat was punishing. Skinny ponies were almost hidden beneath their loads of hay. Donkeys staggered under

To the Khyberees

heavy panniers. Camels walked by, as supercilious as sommeliers; but none was as smug as the camel kneeling in a pick-up truck, surveying the fray.

There was a fashion among car owners to sport on their rear windows a word or phrase in English: Love. Cool. Speed. My God. Truth. Terror. Mafia. A sign painted on the back of a bus declared: 'The Owner Of This Bus Is God'. The buses, named Flying Coach and Airbus, brilliant with chrome-work, art and Urdu slogans, poured loud music into the mêlée. The lorries had prows jutting over the cabs, like the caps that German officers used to wear; and every space and panel on their bodywork was filled with paintings of birds, lions, flowers, windmills, trees, boats, luscious female faces and intricate patterns. Sunlight glittered on hundreds of medallions and on the decorative chains jingling like horse harness beneath the bumpers. Hub caps had been polished to a mirror brilliance and in them were the distorted reflections of the roadside traders, the men brewing tea on charcoal fires, the sugarcane juicers grinding their mangles and the butchers in ragged singlets hacking the carcases of goats on bloodied blocks, all enveloped in rolling farts of sooty exhaust.

We called at the office of the Khyber Political Agent, a compound full of jeeps and gossiping police and militia. Here I bought a permit to travel through the Khyber. It cost £2 and, in contrast with the usual travellers' tales about encounters with subcontinental bureaucracy, it was swiftly issued by a smiling man with a long grey beard.

'The foreigners', it stated, 'should not travel before Sunrise and after Sunset . . . and are not allowed to make photography of the prohibited areas and Women Folk.'

With the permit came the obligatory services of a khassadar, a Khyber levy from the tribe predominant in this area, the Afridi. He was lean and gawky, with a yo-yo Adam's apple and the wispy rudiments of a beard, and he wore a beret with a red badge and a slate-blue uniform shirt and pantaloons. He sat in the front seat and caressed the curved magazine of his rifle.

❃

His presence underlined the principal human fact of the Frontier. It is mostly the territory of hill clans, twelve thousand square miles divided into autonomous agencies, the homes of Afridis, Khataks, Wazirs, Mahsuds, Orakzais, Mohmands and others who form the loose cousinhood of the Pathans. They call themselves Pakhtuns and speak Pushtu, an ancient dialect of Persian. They comprise more than half the population of Afghanistan. Their lands straddle the Frontier, so that for them the line between Afghanistan and Pakistan is not a barrier. They have occupied this region for more than twenty centuries and enjoy the conceit that they are not only a people apart, but are also invincible.

The rulers of India, first the Moguls, then the British, fought the Pathans but never defeated them, encapsulating rather than absorbing them. The writ of the British authorities did not run in the tribal territories and, similarly, Pakistan's jurisdiction is confined to certain roads. When I first went to the Frontier in 1980 and began to learn something of the Pathans, they and other tribesmen in Afghanistan were fighting Soviet forces which were trying to extend the Russian empire's Central Asian conquests of the nineteenth and twentieth centuries. In the end, in 1989, the invaders retreated across the Oxus, leaving Afghanistan to its traditions of intestinal warfare. Into the disorder, filling the vacuum of a devastated country, erupted the Taliban. The word means students and these young men, mostly Pathans, were educated in more than a thousand strict Islamic schools set up on the Frontier to teach the children of

To the Khyberees

refugees from the Russian–Afghan war. A zeal for the spreading of a pure Islamic faith was married to Pathan traditions. In the mid-1990s the Taliban set out to bring all of Afghanistan under their control.

The Pathans have survived as a distinct people because of the impenetrable nature of their territory, their mastery of the high ground and their devotion to traditions. For their defiance of any form of government, they have been called truly free, but their existence is hardly free of regulation and social sanction. They live by Pakhtunwali, 'the way of the Pathan', a code unwritten but bred in the bone; and adherence to it is their defining stripe.

While I was drinking tea in a restaurant one morning, a tall young man came over and asked politely if he could sit at my table. He wanted some conversation. He had learnt English at a mission school and had later gained a degree in international politics from the university in Peshawar.

'I am Pathan,' he said, 'Afridi. With us, traditions and identity are first and foremost. We have never been ruled. Never, ever. Everyone else has been ruled. Not us. So we want to keep our different way of living. We can never compromise on that. My country is Pakistan, my community is Afridi and my home is an autonomous tribal area. It is a balance of understanding. Pakistan, if you like, is the host nation. If the president of Pakistan wants to visit a tribal area it is not enough for him to ask the governor of the North West Frontier Province. He also has to seek the permission of the tribal chiefs. Pakistan's laws do not apply in our lands and if someone commits a crime he is not answerable for it in Pakistan. Once a fugitive is past the gate and into tribal territory the Pakistan police cannot touch him. They have to contact the tribal chiefs if they want to extradite him. That is the power of tribals.

'But our own laws are very strict and when there is a crime

the chiefs will call a jirga, which is like a court but without lawyers and prosecutors. The jirga asks the culprit: why? what happened? The whole story is told in front of everybody. The chiefs make a decision and perhaps award compensation. This system is binding and the sanctions are powerful. The guilty man's house and property can be confiscated, so every man knows that if he does wrong he can impoverish his whole family. He also knows that in a tribal area he cannot disappear, that there is nowhere he can hide. So it is ridiculous to say that tribal people have no values or morals. Our standards are better than the government's. Our laws are strict.'

He paused. 'Also, with our people, fathers get respect.'

Family and tribal honour, and not least the honour of women, are the heart of the code. The notorious characteristic of Pakhtunwali, the bloody thread in Pathan history, is badal, vengeance. Death is considered the proper punishment for most of the offences against honour and a man has no choice but to defend the good name of his family by killing any transgressor, in or out of his family. Brothers kill brothers and cousins kill cousins; and since marriage between cousins is widespread, boys and men are drawn inextricably into the coils of family, neighbourly and tribal feuds. Vendettas are pursued remorselessly down the years; and lest it be thought this is a purely male province, Pathans have always said they are urged on by their women.

Theodore Pennell, a remarkable English doctor and a muscular Christian missionary, who lived on the Frontier from 1892 to 1912, said that revenge was a sweet word to a tribesman's ear, and even sweeter 'if the fatal blow is so managed that the murdered man has a few minutes of life in which to realize he has been outwitted and to hear the words of exultation with which his enemy gluts his hatred'.

When I first reported from the Frontier I heard a graphic account of a vengeance killing. Two men who had murdered an old man in a village near Peshawar were seized and brought before the tribal council of elders. The victim's widow was offered a choice: she could be paid a large sum in blood money or she could demand the murderers' deaths. She chose to have them executed. The old man's grandson, as the senior male relative, was given a pistol. He advanced on the two killers, who were kneeling mutely in the dust before him, and shot them through the head. He was only ten years old. Around that time, a man who shot and killed another, in settlement of a feud, was fined by his tribal elders, not for the killing but for shooting so close to a road that a stray bullet might have endangered the life of any passer-by.

Rioting broke out in Karachi in 1998 when a Pathan family called on a court to hand over a young man who had eloped with a girl of eighteen. The girl was sentenced to death by her tribe for marrying for love and bringing dishonour on them. They insisted that the police should release her from protective custody so that they could deal with her. While the petitions were being heard in a courtroom, the girl's father and six other men drew guns from their clothing and wounded the young man and several policemen.

A century ago, the *Imperial Gazetteer* for the North West Frontier noted that 'a Pathan considers it due to his honour to kill an unfaithful wife and her paramour, though in certain circumstances he will be content with lopping the foot of the latter'. John Masters, the soldier and author who confronted tribesmen on the Frontier in the 1930s, said Pathans would punish an adulterer by pushing a knobbly thorn twig down his penis. Presumably, that was only a preliminary ritual. Theodore Pennell recalled the irritation of a chief who saw his wife speaking to another man. Drawing his sword, the chief sliced off her head and threw it to the man, saying: 'You are so enamoured of her, you can have her.'

In Pennell's time, so many husbands cut off their wives' noses as a punishment that Pennell often performed primitive plastic surgery, transplanting flesh to build a rough-and-ready nose. But in one case the injury was so bad that he told the woman's husband that only an artificial nose would do. This would cost thirty rupees. The husband hesitated, pondering the matter.

'I could get a new wife for eighty rupees,' he reasoned.

He paid in the end, however. Pennell reflected that if the wife annoyed her husband in the future, the man could always take her nose off and lock it up as a punishment.

These are tough people and the measures that the Taliban now employ in Afghanistan, the stoning of adulterers and the removal of the feet and hands of thieves, do not seem to them to be too severe. John Masters thought that one measure of the Pathans' legendary hardiness was the custom of cleaning themselves with jagged stones after defecation. If this sounds like soldierly apocrypha – why not a smooth stone? – a more seemly example was cited by Lillian Starr, a nurse in Peshawar in the 1920s. She remembered an old man, wounded by a bullet, who began to amputate his own leg but found the task hard going and ordered his son to finish it with the stroke of a sword.

Pennell wrote that Frontier women treated men injured in fighting by pouring boiling oil into their wounds. They plucked out their own hair to suture gashes and often made a neat job of it. Among the tribes there were two stock treatments for injury and illness. In the first, used in cases of fever, the patient was stripped and wrapped in the skin of a newly killed sheep or goat, with the raw side turned to his body. He was then covered in quilts so that he sweated profusely. If this failed, it was simply repeated. The second treatment was the placing of an oil-soaked wad of cloth on to the part of the body where pain was felt. The wad was set on fire and burned a hole in the flesh. An indiges-

To the Khyberees

tion sufferer was burnt on his stomach and a man with headaches had the wad applied to his temple or scalp. Lumbago called for a burn on the loins.

❉

During the Russian–Afghan war of 1979–89, hundreds of thousands of refugees spilled over the border into the Frontier districts of Pakistan. The Street of the Storytellers in Peshawar, where travellers once listened to tales, became an exchange for news of the war. The leaders of the mujahidin, the guerrillas fighting in Afghanistan, established their headquarters in houses in the city. There was a constant traffic of armed men, back from the fighting to rest, or readying to cross the border with fresh supplies and ammunition to resume the struggle. Correspondents sat for hours in these places, drinking green tea, talking to the political leaders and listening to men who murmured: 'We bring you news from the fighting front.'

The trouble was that it was impossible to verify most reports. The guerrillas exaggerated the numbers of Russians they had killed and vehicles they had destroyed; and they counted every skirmish a significant victory. Divided by tribal rivalry, ambition and ideology, they shared only a passion to drive out the enemy. Sometimes they broke off from fighting Russians to pursue their own blood feuds and it was difficult at times to distinguish between acts of war and brigandage. There was a benefit to this disunity, however. There was no central nervous system to destroy. It was impossible for the Russians to deliver devastating blows to a single united enemy. The mujahidin were masters of irregular warfare and had no massive war machine.

In Peshawar the evidence of war was abundant enough. The refugee camps teemed and there were numerous witnesses to the bombing and rocketing of villages. Warriors showed us the pay books of dead Russian soldiers. They jabbed their fingers at the identity photographs of pale and bewildered-looking teenage conscripts, newly shorn by the regimental barber.

Shot, and sometimes horribly burnt, the wounded reached hospitals in Peshawar after long journeys, racing against gangrene. In a dirty, fly-infested ward, two boys of fifteen sat up in bed and proudly showed me the bandages over the shrapnel wounds in their stomachs. Limbless men hopped on their new crutches. Many of the injured had had their feet blown off by small mines dropped from helicopters on to mountain tracks. One evening, a youth showed me a basketful of these bombs. He had picked them up, wrapped them in wool and carried them to Peshawar. 'Look,' he said, thrusting them at me, and he laughed when I urged him to take care.

I knew that if I travelled to Afghanistan I would see only a fragment of the war; but I would certainly get an idea of how it was being fought; and nothing beats going and seeing. A friend, an American reporter, wanted to go too. After some days of negotiation in a shabby office, one of the groups of mujahidin agreed to take us. We bought shirts and baggy trousers, authentically grubby, from guerrillas who were wearing them. We shopped in the bazaar for berets and thin brown blankets and also for the black dye we were told to put on our hair. Looking like grotesque pantomime pirates, and in a nervous backstage state, we waited for three days at Dean's until we were summoned by a knock on the door. We were hustled on to a bus bound for the Khyber and ordered to feign sleep under our blankets to avoid detection by Pakistani border guards. Near Landi Kotal we were transferred from the bus to a cattle truck crammed with Afghans and driven to a gully in the foothills. The men fell to their knees and prayed, then shouldered their loads of blankets, clothing, shoes and medicines. There were thirty-five of them and the leader was marked out by his intelligent face, his air of authority, the bankerly pinstripe jacket over his tunic and his Kalashnikov. He was the only one with a weapon. He knew very little English. His only vocabulary seemed to be the words: 'Walk, mister, walk.'

In single file, with no clear idea of our destination or of how long we would be away, in the dark in all senses, we started climbing the mountain.

The men loped with panther strides. I concentrated on the heels of the one ahead. After we had been climbing for some hours a whisper came down the line: 'Afghanistan'. Facing inwards on a narrow ledge, groping for handholds, we picked our way for fifty yards across a cliff. Brief flashes of torchlight guided us down fissures and steep watercourses. Stumbling and slipping, we came at last to a gorge and rested. The men nibbled fragments of bread and lumps of brown sugar. I think they had hoped to find water here, but there was only a stagnant puddle in the hollow of a rock. One of them gently broke the scum with his index finger and they dipped in their tongues, lapping like cats.

Hands shook me from my doze. 'Walk, mister, walk.'

We descended at dawn to a hamlet of mud-walled cottages. Smiling men emerged to shake our hands and give us glass after glass of sugary tea. We did not linger. We were soon on the move again close to the top of scrub-covered hills while a couple of men scouted far ahead of us. In the distance rose snow-draped mountains. Beneath us, in the valley, spread green terraces planted with corn and vegetables, dotted with sheep and goats. I ached to rest in the groves shading the tumbling streams.

Up here, though, we grasped the true nature of Afghanistan. We journeyed through a honeycomb pattern of enclosed valleys, of small self-reliant enclaves connected not by roads but by thin veins of pathways. The land matched the molecular structure of the tribes. It was difficult for any invader to conquer, let alone govern.

In the first twenty-four hours we walked for twenty-one, grateful for the brief stops for prayer. All day we heard artillery fire, like the rolling boom of surf on a distant beach. Occasionally, we met other small bands of armed men. They waved and grinned.

'May you never be tired,' they called.

We marched into a village. All of us were drooping with fatigue. Here the mujahidin were among friends, greeting villagers with hugs, gently tugging the grey beards of old men to show their respect. We shook hands with everybody. Small boys gathered to watch us drink the tea that was splashed into small cups. A youth tipped a jug and poured water over our hands, the prelude to a meal. A cloth was spread on the hardened earth floor of a house and a dozen of us squatted around it. Fire smoke pricked our eyes. Fresh flat loaves were dealt like playing cards. The aroma was ambrosial, the taste and texture wonderful. We tore the bread and dipped it into spinach and curd. Everyone had a savage hunger. After the meal, we two foreigners were shown to charpoys, rickety string beds, in a corner of the room and given pungent quilts. In the half-second of consciousness before sleep slammed down, I was aware of our companions murmuring around the fire and the crackle and hiss of their spittle in the embers.

We climbed rapidly out of the village next day and spread out along a high track. This was the hill fighter's way, seeking the highest possible ground. But the Russian helicopter gunships had changed the game. They always had the advantage of height and the mujahidin feared them more than anything else. Our column paused beneath every mountain crest and ridge to avoid making a silhouette while scouts ensured that the way ahead was clear. When we descended to the valleys and traversed rivers and open ground, we separated into knots of three or four, a hundred yards apart, to present a smaller target to any gunship.

To the Khyberees

That second morning, our forward scouts saw the insect-dot of a helicopter. The order came down the line. By the time we heard the chop of the rotors overhead we had gone to earth, squeezed into crevices and curled up in spiky scrub. Utterly still under our blankets we were indistinguishable from the mountain boulders. That evening, four armed men came up from a village to warn us, as far as we could understand, that enemy forces were active nearby. They led us for three hours through the dark to the shelter of a remote mosque. There was nothing to eat. We all fell asleep on the floor, huddled like puppies. Snores and rumbles woke me just after five and my nostrils were clogged with the odour of warrior. The men roused themselves and went out to pray. And then:

'Mister, walk.'

From the cover of a stone wall we watched a helicopter rocketing the village of Agam. It was not easy for the Russians to destroy a people whose lives were lived in such medieval simplicity, who had so little. The villagers dug holes in the hillsides as shelters. Our column made a long detour and, three days after leaving the Khyber, filed up a steep path into Torabora, a mujahidin base 2,000 feet above the Agam river. Around two hundred well-armed fighting men lived here in caves and shelters of stone and mud brick. It was a Spartan place. There were no women. Wives and children were in the refugee camps in Pakistan. The men were leathery and lean but weariness lay in their faces and they looked older than their years. They lived on bread, spinach, an occasional egg or potato, rice sprinkled with the juice of bitter oranges and tea and sugar. At night they listened to the BBC news in Pushtu. The only book in this stronghold was a Koran. A helicopter had recently fired on the camp but no one had been killed. When we arrived a young doctor was cleaning splinter wounds, washing them with water from a tea glass and swabbing them with iodine. I looked into his medicine chest. It held analgesics, vitamin B and some bandages.

The commander of Torabora greeted us courteously. He was a former geography teacher, aged thirty, and had some English. Two rifle magazines were jammed in his belt. He was pleased that we were there to see how he was fighting the war. He operated by sending commandos to ambush lorries and raid enemy bases to steal guns and ammunition. His force was augmented by deserters from the Russian-trained Afghan army who brought weapons, information and military skill. He thought the war might last twenty years but had no doubt that the Russians would be driven out in the end. 'They have not learnt the lessons of history and geography,' he said, adding with a gentle laugh: 'You British could tell them.'

We stayed three days in this eyrie, sleeping on the floor of the doctor's smoky hut, living on bread and tea. When it was time to leave the commander said he had a man who would lead us to Jalalabad, more than twenty miles distant, and there we would meet guides who would take us back to Pakistan. He introduced us to Arif, a thickset man who wore a white skull cap, a patterned jumper over a dark grey tunic and a cummerbund of ammunition pouches. His eyes had the glitter of anthracite. He looked at us keenly. He shook hands and a thin knife-slash of a smile creased his pocked and bearded face. Perhaps our own growths of beard now made us more worthy of respect.

'We walk.'

He slung his rifle and we followed him on the stony path threading down the mountainside. At the bottom we crossed a river with our arms linked through his, struggling against the rush of freezing water. On the plain we passed through shot-up villages and fields where men turned to look at us and waved before resuming their work of cutting poppy pods with razor blades to harvest the white ooze of opium.

To the Khyberees

Towards the end of the afternoon we rested in tall grass, waiting for a patrolling spotter aircraft to fly away. Arif grumbled that looking after us was a chore. 'I must fight Russians,' he said, stroking his rifle. 'I should stay here and fight them.'

We followed him into a village outside Jalalabad and through the gate of a house where we were welcomed and given tea. Arif fidgeted as we drank. He did not like being so close to the city and I could see that he did not like the responsibility of looking after us. He had expected to find someone in this village who would guide us to Pakistan. For the time being he was stuck with us; and more people knew of our presence. With a troubled look he led us along a path until, with daylight fading, he ducked into a house. Two men here looked rather frightened, but after a quarter of an hour they served us some bread and curd. As we ate, a boy entered the room and whispered a few words. The bread fell from Arif's hand. He jerked to his feet, snatched up his rifle, ordered us out and scuttled past our startled hosts. We followed his slipslapping feet for almost an hour. It is one of my starkest memories of Afghanistan, this frightening run through the dark, tripping and panting, wondering where it would end. When we thought we could not run another yard, we came to the high walls of a house. Arif took us into a low room, the atmosphere acrid with woodsmoke. A dozen men squatting on the floor regarded us curiously. One of them, white-bearded, rose and grasped our hands. Arif was visibly relieved. 'Here, safe,' he said. 'Other house not safe – soldiers coming.'

In the morning he resumed his wheedling. 'I must fight Russians,' he said. 'You can stay here.' No, we said, we needed to return to Pakistan so that we could write our reports. If enemy soldiers found us they would shoot us. If we tried to make our own way back to Pakistan we might be mistaken by mujahidin for Russians and killed. We might be taken for spies or mercenaries. Arif nodded. Our only hold on him was his obligation to guard those in his care, a matter of honour. He muttered into his black beard.

When we awoke at dawn the following day, we were dismayed to see Arif's charpoy empty. We debated the desperate step of finding our own way back, a bleak prospect. Morning had worn into afternoon when Arif arrived, exhibiting his gash of a smile. 'Here', he said, 'is your guide. I have found him. He will take you to Pakistan.' He indicated a small and scrawny rodent of a man with a twitching nose and bright eyes who looked for all the world like Ratty in *The Wind in the Willows*. His name was Saddaq. He wore a stained pale blue tunic and a loosely twisted turban. He was an opium smuggler and had a roundel of the stuff, like a large Brie, to sell in the Khyber Pass. He did not carry it himself. It was in a bag on the back of a gormless and grinning youth. Saddaq spoke no English, but through Arif he offered to take us to Pakistan for the equivalent of £15. He was our lifeline.

His obligation to Pakhtunwali discharged, the mightily relieved Arif adjusted his ammunition belt and shook our hands. 'Now', he said grandly, 'I fight Russians.'

Saddaq insisted on smoking a chillum, a pipe, before we set off. He squatted over it, inhaled deeply and was seized and bent double in a fit of coughing. His eyes streaming and cheeks shining, he launched himself briskly towards the hazy mountains, his legs like pistons, his pointed black shoes pattering on the ground. His loose-lipped boy galloped behind with the opium on his back, hooting. We hurried in his wake.

We looked back to wave farewell to Arif. He was laughing. He raised his rifle in salute.

'Walk, mister,' he cried, 'walk.'

About three miles up the track, Saddaq darted into a house and emerged in the embrace of half a dozen smiling men. They

To the Khyberees

brought him a pipe. Once again he inhaled and reeled, wheezing and coughing explosively. Then he sprang to his feet and rushed eastwards once more, rekindled, like Popeye after spinach.

Saddaq was solicitous and cheerful. He led us across rivers, moving nimbly over the rocks, and on one occasion he and his boy insisted on carrying us pick-a-back over a stream, although we were twice their size. He had a piece of paper, a *laissez-passer*, which he showed to the leaders of guerrilla groups we met. At the end of each day, he found a mud house whose occupants gave us shelter, an earth floor, a quilt, tea, bread and curds. We grew fond of Saddaq. On the final day, as we faced the mountain wall, he had his customary pipe and paroxysm, checked that the opium was secure on the back of his human donkey and began the long climb. It took several hours to reach the top and Saddaq's face twitched into a Ratty smile as he spread his arms proprietorially.

'Pakistan, Zindabad,' he said, 'long live Pakistan'; and knelt to pray.

We picked our way down the other side and in a few hours came to the end of a track where a bus was waiting to pick up smugglers and other travellers. I realized I had not seen a motor road for two weeks and the only wheels I had seen were on an upside-down Russian troop carrier, stolen and crashed by a defecting Afghan officer, upon which our relief column had scrambled and posed for pictures as if they had just captured it. We squeezed into the bus, but although it was full it did not move. The driver refused to start because the passengers would not pay the fare he had demanded. For their part, the passengers thought he was asking too much. We broke the stalemate by paying the difference on everybody's fare, satisfying the honour of both the driver and the obstinate Pathans. At Landi Kotal we gave Saddaq his fee and he laughed merrily, scuttling away with

Cobra Road

his boy into the swirling dust of the alleys to sell his opium. We folded ourselves into a gaily painted Khyber bus crammed with armed tribesmen, sacks, parcels and protesting chickens, and headed for Peshawar and the luxury of Dean's Hotel.

3

War and Champagne

OTHER PASSAGES TWIST THROUGH the ragged hems of Afghanistan. Alexander the Great used an easier route in his incursion in 326 BC. So did Babur, the first of the Mogul conquerors of India, who entered in 1523 on his way to Delhi. But of all the passes, the Khyber has the resonant name. It is shorthand for the Frontier itself.

Men of the Khyber Rifles, in brown uniforms, and Afridi khassadars in their blue, stood gossiping around their stacked rifles at Jamrud Gate where I stopped to have my permit checked. The gate was formed by an arch supported by two towers, rather like chess castles. Now the Khyber lay ahead. It is one of those places to which I could never be indifferent. It seizes the imagination. The thirty-mile road seemed to me a serpent seeking escape from a maze of brown reefs, crags and rubble. There was no respite anywhere from menace, no pleasing symmetry to the land. The geographer O.H.K. Spate mused that the political fragmentation of the tribes of the Frontier matched the broken terrain; and for John Masters there was 'little doubt that something of the harsh bitterness of the scenery entered into everyone who spent any time there'.

In this land of garrisons almost every building was fortified. The larger forts had the look of great sandcastles and I felt that sentries' eyes were looking down from the towers built on sphinxes of dark rock higher up. Family compounds, protected by high crenellated walls of brown clay brick, were fitted out with watchtowers, rifle slits, iron turrets and steel gates with fancy wrought-iron work. A builder designing a house in the Khyber or anywhere else on the Frontier considers both comfort and covering fire. When I asked my driver to stop beside a particularly impressive fortified mansion he looked horrified. 'Not possible,' he said, pressing the accelerator. A school, too, had high strong walls, as if it could do duty as a fort in emergency, and over its imposing gate was the stern injunction in English: 'Enter To Learn'. Lines of women, loaded with fodder and bundles of sticks, picked their way through scrub, completing their effacement by turning their backs at a stranger's approach.

British soldiers called the Frontier 'the Grim', although many of them enjoyed a spell of service here. The Frontier was a khaki theatre of empire, a stage of military triumphs, disasters, punitive expeditions and numerous minor fights. On the rocks beside the road through the Khyber, soldiers had left their regimental badges, moulded in cement and painted. I scrambled up through the rocks and scree to examine the crests of the Cheshire Regiment, the York and Lancasters, the Gordon Highlanders, the South Wales Borderers, the Essex Regiment, the Royal Sussex Regiment and others. The paintwork was kept bright and the badges were respected, not defaced. These were soldiers' marks that said 'We were here' and spoke of sweat and endurance, not of glory. As I looked down at the narrow road my mind's eye saw the soldiers marching, lumbered with haversacks, pouches, scabbards, bandoliers and rifles, their kilts, puttees and tunics grimed by dust and gun-oil. Before the nature of cholera was understood, they wore woollen belts that were thought to protect them from the disease; and to shield them from the sun they wore thick pads over the spine and topis as big as buckets. 'The worst o' your foes', wrote Kipling, 'is the sun over'ead.' Along the Grand Trunk Road from Calcutta to Peshawar, there were cemeteries at twelve-mile intervals where heat-stroke victims were buried.

Although the epitaphs in Frontier cemeteries tell of death by sunshine and swift disease, they also bear witness to the fighting. 'Killed in an engagement with the hill tribes', they say, 'Murdered by a Pathan', 'Murdered on the Frontier'. Pathans were snipers of legendary patience and with their jezails, their long-barrelled brass-bound muskets, or their Martini-Henrys or Lee-Enfields, they waited many hours for their prey, nibbling crumbs of bread and urinating silently down a length of straw. A sentry's headstone records: 'A flash, a report, then a silence, the ghastly deed was done.' Supposedly, a headstone in Peshawar records the death of Captain Ernest Bloomfield, 'Accidentally shot by his orderly. Well done, good and faithful servant.' It does not exist, for there was no Captain Bloomfield and no such epitaph; the inscription reflects the humour of the Frontier where death came in many curious and sometimes horrible ways.

Kipling's lines reminded soldiers to save the last bullet for themselves: 'When you're wounded and left on Afghanistan's plains/And the women come out to cut up what remains . . .' John Masters told of the excoriation of a British officer on the Frontier, his skin left pegged out on a rock some distance from his body. But barbarity was not a Pathan monopoly. In 1882 a British officer was shot dead in Peshawar by an assassin who was persuaded that the murder of an infidel was a ticket to paradise. The British entered into the brutal spirit of the deed and cancelled the ticket to heaven by burning the killer's body inside the skin of a pig.

❊

The Frontier was a gripping drama for the new journalism of the later nineteenth century. For reporters with an eye for colour, rattling good yarns lay in every rocky defile and border station. Into the narratives of arduous marches and desperate fights, writers worked the details of the new artillery, the signalling equipment, the up-and-coming military commanders. They evoked the reek of horses and cordite. They admired the bravery of native troops in the service of the Great White Queen. They were sentimental about soldiers' graves and wounded Tommies. They spared no adjective in descriptions of the fanatical savagery of the tribesmen.

Such stories had an avid audience in the popular newspapers and magazines that prospered in the newly literate Victorian age. Advances in newspaper production and telegraph and postal communications brought descriptions, artists' pictures and photographs of Frontier dramas more rapidly to the doorstep, all in the cause of empire and circulation figures. In 1879 Disraeli admitted that the government had not received a message confirming some news in Afghanistan, noting wryly: 'We cannot compete with the *Standard* which does not hesitate to spend £500 on a telegram.'

Winston Churchill was one of the ambitious adventurers who hurried to the Frontier when war broke out in 1897. A religious leader called Sadullah, better known to British readers of the infant tabloid press as the Mad Mullah, had declared a jihad, a holy war, to drive the British from the Frontier. Ten thousand Pathans attacked the British fort at the top of the Malakand Pass, north of Peshawar, and a thousand Sikh troops desperately held them off. The British army headquarters in Simla ordered a rescue force into action. Even G.A. Henty, the arch imperial storyteller, could hardly have invented the name of the British commander of this expedition: Sir Bindon Blood, a man who had shot thirty tigers.

War and Champagne

Churchill, a twenty-three-year-old subaltern of the 4th Hussars, wrote of warfare with a young man's vivacity: 'A single glass of champagne imparts a feeling of exhilaration. A bottle produces a contrary effect. So it is with war, and the quality of both is best discovered by sipping.'

As he was to do later in the Sudan and South Africa, on the Frontier he combined the roles of army officer and correspondent. In the Malakand action, writing anonymously as 'A Young Officer', he worked for *The Daily Telegraph* for £5 a column; and in those days editors did not say: 'Keep it short.' His mother got him the job. His brother officer, Lord Fincastle, reported for *The Times* and won the Victoria Cross in a skirmish. Another officer, doubling as *The Times of India* correspondent, was killed in the same action.

'Neither was employed officially with the force,' Churchill wrote of them. 'Both had travelled up at their own expense to see something of war. Knights of the sword and pen, they had nothing to offer but their lives, no troops to lead, no duties to perform. They played for high stakes . . .'

Churchill rode for a while with a cavalry captain who was also the Reuter correspondent and whose squadron, in one hectic action, skewered twenty-one tribesmen with their lances. Churchill, his pencil sharp – and 'my long cavalry sword well sharpened – after all, I had won the Public School fencing medal' – understood his readers' appetite for vivid and bloody detail:

'Lieutenant Cassells turned sharply and fell. Two Sepoys immediately caught hold of him. One fell shot through the leg. A soldier who had continued firing, sprang into the air, and began to bleed with strange and terrible rapidity from his mouth and chest. Another turned on his back kicking and twisting. A fourth lay quite still. Lieutenant Hughes, the adjutant, was killed. The bullets passed with a curious sucking noise, like that produced by drawing the air between the lips. A crowd of tribesmen rushed over the crest of the hill and charged sword in hand, hurling great stones. The subadar major stuck to Lieutenant Cassells, and it is to him the lieutenant owes his life. The men carrying the other officer dropped him and fled. The body sprawled upon the ground. A tall man in dirty white linen pounced down upon it with a curved sword. It was a horrible sight.'

Trying to put himself into the minds of 'the brave Sepoys', he imagined them thinking that 'the Government of the Queen-Empress would never desert them. Trust in the young white men who led them, and perhaps some dim half-idolatrous faith in a mysterious Sovereign across the seas, who would surely protect them, restored their fainting strength'.

He met a British soldier whose arm had been amputated at the shoulder and wrote of his stoical demeanour. He speculated that the man's future held only 'some miserable pension insufficient to command any pleasures but those of drink, a loafer's life and a pauper's grave, a wretched system by which the richest nation in the world neglects the soldiers who have served it well'.

Many of the correspondents who covered these Frontier battles, and other imperial wars, were studiedly colourful and glamorous, sometimes preposterous, usually resourceful. They were, as often as not, pistol-packing figures, not so much reporters as writers of real-life adventures in dangerous and exotic settings. Melton Prior, an artist who covered the Malakand action for the *Illustrated London News*, travelled with his vital supplies of champagne, wine, whisky and cigarettes. He put these in cases marked 'drawing material' to protect them not from the wily Pathan but from the equally wily and pilfering Tommy.

War and Champagne

Near Charsadda, on the road to Malakand, Mumtaz, my driver, stopped to scrump some fruit from an orchard. We were passing through fertile and prosperous countryside, rich with rice, bananas and sugar cane, and served by flour and sugar mills. The hot air smelled of the raw planks stacked in timber yards and furniture factories. An immense graveyard stretched from the road into the distance, as far as I could see, the graves in their thousands decorated with streamers, glittering threads and coloured stones. 'Biggest cemetery in Asia,' Mumtaz said; and he may have been right.

I had visited Charsadda, years before, to see Khan Abdul Ghaffar Khan. He was almost ninety years old then (he had been three when Churchill was at Malakand) and was the greatest living witness of the old Frontier. He was huge and impressive, about six feet three inches, with a magnificent nose. He sat on a couch, dignified and courteous, and waited until tea and biscuits were brought for me before he would talk. He had been educated by British missionaries and was so impressed by their ideas of service to others that he decided he would spend his life in the cause of improving the conditions of the Pathans.

In 1929, influenced by the example of Mahatma Gandhi, he founded a Pathan movement whose members promised to renounce violence and vendetta, a hard thing for Pathans to do. He was also supported by the example of his father, an extraordinary man who pursued no feuds and simply forgave his enemies. Journalists labelled Khan Abdul Ghaffar Khan 'the Frontier Gandhi' and he was jailed by the British for his part in the struggle for Indian independence. He and his followers dyed their shirts with brick dust and hence were known as 'Red-Shirts', which only emphasized in British minds the idea that Ghaffar Khan was a subversive. After Partition, Pakistan jailed him, too, and later he spent years in exile in Afghanistan. His aim of uniting all Pathans in an autonomous Pathan state was

Cobra Road

considered dangerous. For half a century he was the outstanding leader of the Pathans. He sought to make his people politically aware, more civilized and less brutal. He certainly went against the grain of a killing culture by embracing non-violence. Others had tried. The Pathan poet Khushal Khan Khattack endeavoured in the seventeenth century to forge a grand alliance of Pathan tribes. When he failed he concluded bitterly that 'all Pathans are evilly disposed', but consoled himself with the thought that 'they are not slaves but free-born men'. It seems a sort of curse that unending feud and vengeance are part of Pathan identity. Khan Abdul Ghaffar Khan suggested it need not be like that.

We talked for a while and then the old Khan fell into silence and his face became very sad. 'I have been a fighter all my life,' he said at last. 'I always wanted to knit the divided tribes into one brotherhood and I wish I could have done more. So if you want to know how I feel, in the last part of my life, ask yourself how you would feel.'

❖

The road to the Malakand Pass climbed steeply and spectacularly on the left side of an immense bowl. A palisade of peaks rose on our right, thrusting into the blue sky. Mumtaz added his trumpeting to the fanfaronades of buses and trucks jostling and overtaking recklessly on the edges of the cliffs.

I had been told in Peshawar that interested visitors could see something of Malakand Fort, and I had been given a letter of introduction to an officer serving there. At the fort's gateway, where a sign proclaimed: 'It Is Sweet And Right To Die For Your Motherland', a guard shook my hand and directed me to a room nearby. Here I was met by a stiffly courteous major who offered me a soft drink. He was plainly discomfited by the letter.

War and Champagne

'We are proud to have here at this fort', he began, 'a room occupied by Churchill.' This was something I did not know. 'However, you have no written permission to see it, so you must return to Peshawar for permission. Then I will be happy to show you. You see, not long ago, one of your countrymen, a British army major, came here, but he, too, had no permission; so he could not see it also. If I could not show it to a British major, how could I show it to you?'

From the fort we descended into the Swat valley, through a long nave of tall and graceful trees. Mumtaz was keen to have lunch and we stopped at a small restaurant a few miles from Chakdarra Fort. Truck drivers lounged on low beds, Mumtaz ate a large meal and I sat on the veranda with green tea and a round of fresh bread, watching the cook fan his charcoal barbecue.

In 1897, a small British force in Chakdarra Fort was besieged for a week by the Mad Mullah's forces; and famously relieved, too, in fighting that left hundreds of Pathan warriors dead across the valley where, as Churchill reported, 'great numbers of vultures disputed the abundant prey with odious lizards'. Mumtaz said he would find me a guide and went into the fort. A few minutes later he emerged with a soldier of the Swat Scouts, in khaki shirt and pantaloons, who had been deputed to lead us through the trees and up the steep path to Churchill's Picquet, a square white fortress high on a bluff. A plaque on the outside wall said the fort 'had the distinction of being 2/Lt Winston Churchill's abode from where he used to send despatches back to London as a war correspondent in 1897'. For no obvious reason, except as a general admonition, another plaque next to it quoted a line from the Koran saying that every rise has a fall.

The thick stone walls enclosed a single whitewashed chamber with narrow gun ports and a homely fireplace. A couple of rungs were missing in the rickety ladder to the roof. I had a sentry's view of the broad valley and the mountains. Below, where the trade route from China to central Asia crossed the broad Swat river, Alexander led 25,000 of his men in his brief foray into India. I imagined Churchill sitting up here with his binoculars and his pencil and pad, scribbling his copy for *The Daily Telegraph*; and I could not help imagining, too, the sub-editors in London asking in the battle-weary way of sub-editors: 'Is there much more of this Churchill stuff?'

❁

Driving south to Kohat, we were imprisoned in a jam of trucks and minibuses in Darra. The smell of forges, of hot metal and charcoal fires, mingled with dust and billowing exhaust fumes. The ring of hammers on steel augmented the racket of car horns and staccato bursts of gunfire. A couple of men pushed through the crowd and fired guns by the open window of my car, close to my head, and ran off grinning while my ears sang, a little Pathan mischief in keeping with the boisterous feel of the town. Darra's smiths have been making rifles, pistols, bullets, holsters and bandoliers for a hundred years. The British approved the manufacture as a trade-off, partly to secure for themselves a safe passage through Darra, partly to reduce the thieving of British rifles. Darra had always made good copies of stolen British rifles, although the barrels did not last. The gun-makers could not match the quality of the Lee-Enfield bolt, but they could build a rifle around one; and soldiers on the Frontier not only chained their rifles to themselves at night but removed the bolts as well.

We stopped on the crest of the hill where the Kohat Pass begins. Far below, the brown and sage plain trembled in the heat. Beside the curling ribbon of road there were drops of hundreds of feet down sheer cliffs.

'How many buses go over the edge?' I asked Mumtaz.

'Two or three a year,' he said with a shrug.

At the summit the road passes beneath a commanding white memorial arch inscribed in large black letters with the single word Handyside. The site is fitting. This was Handyside's territory; and Handyside was heroic.

'It is difficult', said Sir Percival Griffiths, in his history of the Indian police, 'to write about Eric Charles Handyside without appearing to exaggerate.' A photograph shows a stocky and muscular man in uniform, a Sam Browne belt and dark puttees. He holds a large sun helmet against his broad chest. The jaw is square, the lips thin and set in a determined line, surmounted by a moustache no wider than the nostrils. The hair is wavy, the eyes gaze frankly into the lens. The image exudes toughness. Had he been an American he would doubtless have commanded the Texas Rangers or pinned on a sheriff's star. On the Frontier he was a fighter of outlaws and catcher of bandits, a veteran of numerous gun battles and sieges. Sir John Maffey, a chief commissioner of the Frontier, described the enthusiastic Handyside setting off one night to raid an outlaw village. He wore shorts, Pathan sandals, a Balaclava cap, a Pathan's heavy fur coat, a holstered revolver and a full cartridge belt. He was as 'happy as a schoolboy, hard as nails and ready to walk for a week on Pathan bread and water'.

Handyside was posted to the Frontier in 1913 after twelve years in Punjab. He had looked forward to matching himself against the tribesmen and was dejected when his first night operation ended with the outlaws surrendering meekly, 'the most miserable, contemptible, gutless set of rats!'

But to his relief, Handyside soon found that 'the Pathan is a man and the Frontier red in tooth and claw'. He became Commandant of the Frontier Constabulary. Detesting administrative work, refusing to be office-bound, he allowed his desk to overflow with unopened letters and telegrams. He wanted only to fight bandits and hoped to die in a gun battle. 'What would the likes of me do in retirement?' he asked. 'I'd rather be outed on the Frontier.'

One of his colleagues, tempted into amateur psychology, thought that Handyside's occasional melancholy and his famous insight into the Pathan mind could be traced to his Cornish and Russian parentage, his 'queer Celtic-Slavonic twist'. Handyside was one of those serious colonial officers who steeped himself in the culture in which he moved. The Pathans were his world. He respected his foes, their code of honour, their faith and their women; and was respected in return. John Maffey wrote that 'for his friend the enemy Handyside had the greatest admiration'. When Lord Reading, the Viceroy, visited the Frontier, Handyside talked to him enthusiastically about his work and described notorious Pathan raiders as 'splendid fellows' and 'topping chaps'.

'Mr Handyside,' said Lord Reading, 'you must let me have your recommendations for the Birthday Honours List.'

In April 1926, Handyside led his police into a village ten miles from Peshawar to capture two armed bandits, and was shot through the heart as he ran across a square. He was such a renowned figure that some of the tribal leaders subscribed to the memorial arch above the Kohat Pass.

His death brought to an end the charming institution he had founded, the bears' picnics. He had always been distressed by the spectacle of dancing bears which were, and still are, led around by their noses, beaten, tortured and made to perform parodies of dances at fairs. Whenever he could, Handyside gave these wretched creatures what he called 'a bears' holiday'. He paid their owners some money and ordered them to clear off for the day. Then he took the bears into the garden of his bungalow, removed their chains and gave them food and clean water and

War and Champagne

allowed them to rest under his trees and play and roll on the lawn, as free as Pathans.

Three years before his death, Afridi tribesmen stole rifles from the cantonment in Kohat. Handyside raided their village and recovered many of the guns, but the Afridis complained that the police had molested their women. To avenge the insult, a gang of them broke into the bungalow of Major Archie Ellis in Kohat. He was away. The intruders stabbed his wife to death and abducted his seventeen-year-old daughter Mollie. They gave her a coat to cover her nightdress and a pair of leather-soled socks and walked her for five days into the hills. The English maiden in the hands of fanatical Frontier ruffians was a newspaper sensation.

There was no question of attemping rescue by force. It was not a job for Handyside. The kidnappers would have killed the girl at the first sight of a soldier or policeman. The tribal territory where she was held was so fiercely guarded that no foreigner had entered it for twenty-six years. Since a white man would have had no chance of negotiating the girl's release, John Maffey called in Lillian Starr, the Peshawar nurse who had personal, indeed harrowing, experience of danger on the Frontier. Her father, a missionary, had had several escapes from fanatics anxious to gain the merit attached to knifing a Christian; and she had been married only three years when she saw her husband, a surgeon at the Peshawar hospital, stabbed to death by a Pathan who blamed him for converting his son to Christianity.

Dressed in tribal clothing, accompanied by Afridi negotiators and with forty tribesmen for protection, Mrs Starr rode into hostile territory. The kidnappers warned her away with a note declaring: 'Absolutely, lady-doctor and her company are prohibited.' But Mrs Starr and the negotiators persisted. They put pressure on the kidnappers by exploiting tribal rivalries and threatening severe punishment. Eventually they did a deal, securing the release of Mollie, unharmed, in exchange for two thieves in Peshawar jail.

Mollie's mother lies in the old British cemetery, a place overgrown with weeds and thistles. Here, as in many such graveyards in India, lie the adventurers who came for wealth, the soldiers for their pittance, the black sheep for redemption, the women for love or duty and, always poignant, the innumerable graves of infants who died when only a few weeks or months old. Among the faded headstones of those who fell to bullet, spear or disease, the inscription on one of the tombs is still clear enough to tell of the dramatic end of Ensign W.H. Sitwell who 'died on the field of honour 1850. Young, handsome, brave, good, his spirit high and full of hope, life was before him with all its dreams but they vanished at a blow! Gloriously charging the enemy, sword in hand, he fell; and with him Havildar Colaub Ditchet, Naick Mahdoo Singh and Sepoys Meerwan Opedia and Deobund Pandy. These soldiers refused to quit their wounded leader and were all slain together.'

The most handsome building in Kohat is the white-domed bungalow where Sir Louis Cavagnari lived when he was in charge of the district in 1866–7. The son of one of Napoleon's generals, he was sent as British envoy to Kabul in 1879, waved off by army officers who, knowing the mood in the Afghan capital, were certain he would be murdered. He settled into the Residency and telegraphed an 'All well' message to Peshawar. Shortly afterwards, his Residency was attacked and he and his mission of eighty-one men were killed, detonating a war in which the avenging British, led by Sir Frederick Roberts, brought Afghanistan under temporary control.

I went to see the house across the road from Cavagnari's home, a colonial bungalow which is the Officers' Mess of the Punjab Frontier Force, the Piffers. A portrait of Sir Bertrand

War and Champagne

Moberly, who commanded the force from 1939 to 1947, presides over the lobby. A British flag is displayed with the battle honours, trophies, portraits and regimental mementoes. Paintings show Piffers cavalry spearing wild-eyed Pathans. Silver camels haul silver wine coasters across the sideboard, but, of course, the coasters have been empty of cargo for many years.

❉

At first, the British concluded that it was impossible to build a railway through the Khyber Pass. Lord Kitchener judged that the terrain was unconquerable and, in any case, the tribal khans forbade a railway, seeing it as an attack on their independence. After the First World War the British declared a railway a military necessity. Colonel Gordon Hearn's survey of 1919–20 showed how the gorges and water torrents could be mastered. The engineer Victor Bayley was called in to build it. When he arrived to begin his adventure in 1920 he found Peshawar 'a hotch potch of the villainy of all Asia, the wickedest city on earth'. The unruliness of the tribes was reflected in a notice by the telephone at Dean's Hotel: 'In case of Raid ring up No.492'.

Bayley's first task was to win the assent of the tribal leaders. He told them, jokingly he thought, that they would be able to loot the trains. Grinning, they gave him their approval.

The Khyber railway was an epic personal struggle for Bayley, as well as an engineering one. It really was man versus nature. He became obsessed with the battle against geology, flooding, the burning Khyber winds and the extremes of climate. There was also the considerable risk of being murdered, underlined by the shooting of two majors of the Seaforth Highlanders while they took an evening walk at Landi Kotal in 1923. Bayley wore a revolver until a kindly Pathan warned him that tribesmen, with their lust for guns, would kill him simply to possess it. After that he put his trust in the Pathan code of honour and went unarmed; but all the same he ensured that his hut at Landi Kotal was bullet-proofed and guarded by tribal militia.

Theodore Pennell, the missionary, had also reasoned that it was foolish to carry a weapon among heavily armed tribesmen. He entrusted his safety 'to their sense of honour and their traditional treatment of a guest'. On one occasion, visiting a village full of outlaws who would certainly have killed him, he placed himself under the chief's protection and slept soundly. Pathan honour, though, he related ruefully, was sometimes demanding. He came into a village late one evening and was greeted respectfully by the son of the chief who killed a chicken and provided a substantial dinner. After this the exhausted Pennell slept. A little later the village chief himself arrived home and was mortified to learn that his distinguished guest had been given only chicken. His honour was at stake. He ordered a sheep killed and cooked and Pennell was summoned from his bed at one o'clock in the morning to a feast of roast mutton. He knew the form. He ate heartily.

Apart from the difficulties of construction, Victor Bayley was also troubled by the mysterious nature of the Khyber itself. 'I did not like speaking of this to my English friends, as they only laughed at me.' He felt a pervading tension, a hostility. He sensed that his hammering, digging and blasting were disturbing the spirit of the Khyber, rousing some supernatural force within the rock itself. 'I think most people who have served on the Frontier will understand.'

He began to believe in the possibility of demons. 'The longer I lived on the Frontier, the more I became convinced that there was something about this strange country that differentiated it from other lands. I felt very strongly indeed there was something else, something definitely primitive and evil. When you have the luck to be building a great work like the Khyber railway, you cannot help building a great deal of yourself into it. There is an inevitability that drags a man on, yet seems to be taking something out of him all the time . . . In the Khyber, this urge of things yet to come seemed so strong at times as to be almost overpowering. It is at night that the influence is so strong . . . the Silence is over everything. And the Silence is not really silent. There is a deep quiver or vibration somewhere, below all the natural sounds.'

Bayley built twenty-seven miles of line, thirty-four tunnels and ninety-two bridges. Towards the end, 'a fury of energy drove me on, and I grudged every day spent away from my beloved works. Is it possible that so prosaic a person as an engineer can have something of the artist in him and suffer from a frenzy of creative energy?'

The completion of the task broke him. When the last yard of rail was laid he felt no triumph, only an emptiness and regret. He noted that 'the old spacious days of lawlessness were slipping away'. As the train chugged up the railway he had just built he sat morosely over a cup of coffee in the dining-car, a tall, thin, nervous figure. 'Something snapped inside me; this was the end. No more joyous days with the tribesmen striding over the hills in the teeth of the roaring Khyber wind.'

A month later there was a ceremonial inauguration of Bayley's wonder. He did not hear the speeches. He had been ordered to rest. 'I did not go up the Khyber again. Everyone was very kind . . . we travelled by easy stages to Bombay and took ship for Home.'

❋

When I first visited the Frontier in the early 1980s, the Khyber railway was still running one day a week, on Fridays. To make sure of getting a ticket, I called the day before on the stationmaster at the cantonment station in Peshawar.

'No,' he said, 'there is no first class.'

'I am sorry to say he is wrong,' said the ticket office clerk, 'there is first class.'

'Actually,' said the man at the inquiry office, 'they are both wrong, but it is only ordinary first class.'

At Dean's Hotel they told me the train left at eight.

'Nine on the dot,' said the stationmaster.

It left just before one, packed with tribesmen clutching bundles and guns, boys holding squawking hens and women with eyes swivelling above their veils.

This time, since I knew that the trains had stopped running in the mid-1980s, I was surprised to see a poster announcing a revived service, eight times a year, to make money from visitors. It happened that there was a trip the next day and I bought a ticket, costing a hundred times times more than I had paid for my first journey. But it was authentic. The two-carriage train was pulled by one original 1920s locomotive and pushed by another. The whistles shrieked and the chimneys ejected thick black plumes of smoke. The carriages were decrepit and coated with grime. Some of the seats were slatted wooden benches, others were covered with cracked green Rexine. The rusted ceiling fans were furred with dust and had seized up years before.

'There is not much of soft,' grumbled a wealthy Pakistani up from Lahore, giving his family a day out.

The train set off with explosive exhalations, rousing old men dozing on their charpoys beside the track. It clanked past truck repair yards and cricket matches, over dried creeks, past mosques and tailors' shops and eucalyptus groves. Yelling boys gave chase or stuck their fingers in their ears against the piercing whistle.

War and Champagne

At Jamrud Fort the train paused to take on twenty Afridi khassadars. Half a dozen of them sat on the front of the first locomotive, a tableau of fierceness, and others stood in the carriage doorways with their rifles at the ready. This was a matter of honour: we passengers were guests travelling through tribal territory and we were under protection.

The train inched upwards. As we gained height I looked over the walls of fortified compounds and saw houses, fruit trees and neat garden plots. Women pulled up their veils. Children cheered. Almost every small girl stood at an angle, a baby sibling balanced on her hip.

Hot smoke gusted through the windows, gritting every eye and filling every mouth with crunchy specks. In the tunnels the roar of the engines was deafening and the carriages filled with stifling fumes and clouds of hot steam. The guards pulled their shirt tails to their noses and passengers buried their faces in handkerchiefs. After every tunnel, two vain young Pakistani men shared a brush to restore their hairstyles. I saw a young khassadar eyeing my khaki hat which I had parked on the bench beside him. After a while, he took off his beret and picked up my hat and put it on his head. He fished for a mirror in his tunic and spent some minutes admiring himself, turning this way and that, like a girl in a milliner's shop.

The train see-sawed up the Pass, pushed and pulled into the reversing stations to gain height on the steep slopes. It rumbled over bridges, the engines thunderous in the narrow gorges. Here on the mountainsides, in the tunnels and on the ledges, I understood the magnificence of Victor Bayley's anguished struggle, his single combat with the unforgiving Khyber. From a high point I watched lorries far below beetling up the zigzag road from the border with Afghanistan, while beyond, in the dusty haze, stretched the implacable land, the Plain of Jalalabad and the distant lunar fastness of the Hindu Kush.

4

The Point of the Bayonet

THE EARLY MORNING TRAIN from Delhi to Amritsar stopped for a few minutes at Ambala and the Sikh businessman next to me rose and said: 'Please come.' He took me to a stall on the platform, eased through the crowd and bought tea for both of us, the sugar, milk and leaves all boiled up together, served in newly baked red clay cups. After a few minutes, the train gave a preparatory jerk and shudder and we tea drinkers scuttled aboard, first throwing our empty cups on to the tracks where they most satisfyingly smashed.

The farmland was brown and scorched. The monsoon was about three weeks away. Like a benediction it would soothe tempers. It would thicken the sky and take command of heaven and earth and fill everyone's consciousness, swelling the rivers, turning the land muddy and then verdant, making it ripe for lush grass, rice and maize. The mangoes would be in season, India's reward for enduring summer's heat. Mango connoisseurs, like wine experts, judging the fruit by its perfume and flavour, its skin and shape, can identify the district, perhaps even the orchard, where they are grown. India produces seven-tenths of the world's crop, growing more than a hundred varieties. I have only the scantiest mango vocabulary, but devotees know their way around the prized Alfonsos, Avvallas, Langras,

Cobra Road

Himsagars, Payaris, Safedas, Bombay Greens and Collector Sahibs. Jawaharlal Nehru used to send a box of his favourite Dussehris to the Queen. Mangoes are a passion and suggestible poets have always extolled them as the fruit of love, but as much for their association with languor and shady bowers as for their supposed aphrodisiac qualities.

The number of tractors and bullock carts proclaim Punjab's fertility and abundance and the skills of its farmers. Signs by the roadside declare: 'Punjab, Land of Milk'. Punjabis drink five times more milk than the average Indian and consume enormous quantities of curd and butter. In Punjab, buttered toast is not a boarding-house smear, but a generous spread. 'Sir,' an old Sikh tailor used to say to me, 'I will be making your pant waist bigger because in India you will be eating so much of butter.' Punjab is the champion agricultural state. Drought and crop failures bring hardship to some parts of the country, but the defeat of famine, the overall success of its cultivators, is one of the principal achievements of independent India to which Punjab has made a typically robust contribution.

Beyond the fields and temples, I could see the lorries hurtling along the Grand Trunk Road. I was thankful to be on the train. I heard the screaming horns as the hellion drivers careered towards each other, exhausts pumping stinking clouds, each man keeping his position in the centre of the road for as long as his nerve held. You only have to travel a few miles to see that the swerve is frequently left too late.

Dawn on the Grand Trunk Road, and on many other main roads, reveals a spectacle of destruction that makes you think of war. The highway is littered with numerous tableaux of broken-backed wrecks and spilled loads of grain, bricks, apples, pumpkins, steel bars and lentils. They look as if they have been strafed by enemy aircraft. Oil glistens on the road, blood seeps into the dirt and crows flap and peck in the ruins.

The Point of the Bayonet

Lorry drivers often seem monstrous figures, as reckless and cruel as pirates. Even if they can read them, it is hard to imagine such ruffians taking note of the pious wayside-pulpit homilies every few miles:

> If Married, Divorce Speed.
>
> Arrive Home Safe And So Let Others.

But, looked at from their point of view, life for these men is brutal. Drivers have to be tough. Their bosses, more often than not, are unscrupulous men with little regard for safety who cram as much cargo on board a lorry as they can, especially at harvest time, raising the centre of gravity and making the vehicle dangerously unbalanced. That is one reason why there are so many wrecks. Lorries have to creep past each other on narrow roads and when the nearside wheels slip into the soft verge, they often capsize. Even a minor collision will make them roll over. Heavy loads and poor maintenance cause axles to snap and the wheels to fall off.

Among the predators who prey on drivers are bandits and police. Thieves often wait in the branches of trees overhanging the highway and drop down on to likely lorries, cutting open the tarpaulin and throwing the goods to accomplices by the road. In areas where robbers operate, drivers sometimes post a guard on top to repel the boarders with a lathi, a bamboo quarterstaff, or perhaps a machete. As for the police and other officials, they commonly augment their inadequate wages by extracting bribes from the drivers. They, too, have to pay school fees, buy a scooter or bear the cost of a daughter's wedding; and police pay is very low. Lorries stop at state borders to pay octroi, the tax on truck cargoes which is an important source of revenue for state governments, and the clerks usually levy a little extra tax for themselves.

Cobra Road

Up there in their cabs, the drivers have little protection. The roads are lawless and driving skills are often poor and training minimal. The drivers have their prayers, of course, and on the dashboard some colourful pictures of their gods or gurus. To ward off the evil eye they hang a shoe on the front and rear bumpers, or paint a shoe on the tailboard near the 'Horn Please' invitation. Being made of leather a shoe to Hindus is unclean and is commonly used to deter malign spirits. Few drivers travel alone. There is usually a young assistant. This wretch of a driver's mate is there to clean the windscreen, fetch tea, help change the wheels, stop thieves siphoning off fuel and guard the lorry when his master takes half an hour off to visit a roadside brothel. One of his jobs is to jab the driver in the arm when he nods off. Numerous crashes are caused by exhaustion. I once travelled in a bus which carried a co-driver who could not drive and was there to provide company and to ensure the driver did not sleep at the wheel. Sometimes, of course, both the apprentice and the driver fall asleep; and there is little the apprentice can do when his driver drinks too much at the roadside dhabas, those rough-and-ready rest stops, or is dizzied by hashish. And there is not much he can do when his driver plays the warrior and, his knuckles gleaming and eyes staring, heads towards an oncoming truck like a locked-on missile.

Once, while travelling in Punjab in a car with a driver, I made the mistake of setting out after dark on the Grand Trunk Road. A police chief had kept me waiting some hours for an interview. When, at last, I got on my way, the Grand Trunk Road seemed populated with murderous savages. After an hour or so of close shaves, I asked the driver to rest in a dhaba. He and I needed a break from swerving off the road in terrifying moments of dazzling headlights and banshee horns.

As we pulled in, dim lights illuminated a hellish scene. Bare-armed cooks sweated over pans of spluttering oil which was

The Point of the Bayonet

probably adulterated, frying food for tired truck crews who sat on benches and sprawled on charpoys. A smell of diesel floated in from the parked lorries. Perhaps, as sometimes happens, the proprietor's assistants were busily siphoning fuel from the unguarded vehicles. In their oil-streaked vests and greasy bandannas, their eyes white and wild in their blackened faces, the drivers and their men had the look of a gang of desperate mutineers in the engine room of a doomed freighter. As I sipped at a glass of tea, loud talk on the edge of the crowd suddenly erupted in violence. Men sprang to their feet, wielding sticks, and hammered on the windscreens of a couple of lorries, bashing the doors. They struck the heads and shoulders of men who rushed forward to defend the vehicles, swinging their fists and yelling. As plates and tea-glasses and benches tumbled, and uproar spread like a fire, we hurried away and entered the marginally preferable nightmare of the screaming black road.

❂

An Indian once told me that when the British built their railways they made the station platforms very wide in the knowledge that for every person travelling there would be at least twenty to see him off or to greet him.

Perhaps he was right, although my own guess is that the width of the platforms had more to do with the ease of moving troops and the comfort of panjandrums in cocked hats than with the convenience of the Indian traveller. But it is just as well, given the growth of the population and the overcrowding on so many trains, that platforms are, generally, spacious. When we reached Amritsar, I became part of the torrent of struggling people and porters and luggage which swept me from the train in amiable pandemonium along the platform and out of the station, leaving me washed up and blinking in the forecourt. A grey-bearded man appeared at my shoulder like a genie and in a soft and dignified Jeevesian voice offered his services as driver and guide. His Ambassador car bore the dents of battle, but it turned out that Mr Singh was not at all aggressive. He kept his thumb on the horn and firmly nudged his way through the thickets of rickshaws, bullock carts and bikes, but he prudently gave way to a lurching tanker marked 'Highley Inflammbal'.

For a moment I felt I had been sucked into the hot dusty bag of a vacuum cleaner. Fumes and cacophony poured into the car. It takes a while for the senses to comprehend the swirl of an Indian city, to come to terms with the frantically competing colours, movements and noise and the bouquet of stinks. It is like trying to watch a dozen different television programmes at once. The city was roaring in my ears, the shriek of music piercing the din of bells, horns, shouts and hammers on metal. It was hard to focus. Every square foot of hoarding and wall was filled with advertisements for suitings, shirtings, saris, turbans, computers and insurance. Police boxes were painted red by the Thums-Up cola company. Gaudy film posters proclaimed 'Blood and tears splach across massive emotional drama', and voluptuous heroines sprawled on cushions, the better to market their cleavages. Small white signs with red crosses offered relief for sufferers of piles, fistulas and pustules. Grubby laboratories advertised their services – 'Blood Urine Stool Sputum Semen Tested Here' – and I could only imagine the fear and confusion in the minds of those who entered the door marked: 'Men And Women Consult For Secret Diseases'.

In a narrow street I found the small pharmacy where John Wade works. Aged seventy-seven, he is one of the band of former sahibs who, like Tusker and Lucy in Paul Scott's *Staying On*, could not bear to leave when the British pulled out. His humour is dry and his English precise and clear, of the kind spoken and preserved in films of the 1940s and 1950s. He was

The Point of the Bayonet

a child of empire, brought up in Ceylon, and became an officer in the Dogra Regiment. At the time of Partition he was Captain Wade, patrolling with his troops, when he saw Hindu ruffians dragging terrified Muslims through the streets, yelling that they were going to 'feed them pork in the temple and turn them into Hindus'. His men rescued the Muslims who would otherwise undoubtedly have been murdered. In spite of the horrors of 1947 Wade decided in that year to spend the rest of his life in India. Eventually, he became an Indian citizen, a teacher and then a minister in a church in Amritsar. He had last visited Britain more than twenty years ago and did not think he would see it again. There would really be no point: 'After all, here in Amritsar I am home. These are the people with whom I have chosen to spend my life, and I am content.'

It was very hot. In a spirit of egality, cows shared with people the little patches of shade beneath the trees. Mr Singh drove me down The Mall, Old Jail Road and Albert Road and delivered me to a hotel. I was glad of its cool sanctuary. The coffee shop offered 'Snazzy New Tempties Specially Prepared to Satiate Your Taste', but, in search of a more substantial meal, I went into the restaurant. It was dark and crowded, full of talk and laughter. When my eyes adjusted to the gloom, I saw heads nodding in conversation, cheeks full of chicken and mutton, black lentils and unleavened bread. 'God, how these Punjabis eat,' a friend once said; and he was Punjabi himself. Flocks of handsome women chattered through their lunch parties, crimson-lipped, laughing. They all seemed to be called Bunty, Binky, Sweety or Pinky. In their Punjabi plumage, flicking their scarves and shining black hair with their long jewelled fingers, they were as ripe as fruit, vivid and glamorous.

I was pleased to find, when I enquired after lunch, that Mrs Bhandari still ruled at her guest house at No. 10 Cantonment. In its heyday, this was a favourite caravanserai for travellers

Cobra Road

going up and down to Delhi, Kashmir, Lahore or the North West Frontier. I used to stay from time to time. Her house of dark red brick was a pool of peace in the busy city, with lawns and shrubs and fruit trees and rooms full of furniture of the 1920s and 1930s and pictures of faraway places like Bognor. Guests ate their meals around one table and there was a notice saying: 'Please No Tips Allowed'.

An assistant ushered me into Mrs Bhandari's sitting-room and she asked him to bring tea. She was in her habitual long white shirt and baggy shalwar trousers, a chirpy Queen Victoria, with a mischievous twinkle in her eye, primed with gossip and never stuck for a comment. Born in Amritsar, the daughter of a Persian father, she was more than ninety, a witness to most of the city's twentieth-century history. In the years of violence in Amritsar and Punjab, she would talk of the Sikhs like a teacher discussing unruly boys who should have their heads knocked together. 'These Sikhs,' she would say with a tut, 'they get over-excited and then there's bound to be trouble.'

In April 1919, when she was a schoolgirl, she heard the sounds of uproar as General Dyer marched his men into the Jallianwala Bagh and ordered them to shoot into the large crowd gathered there. There have been bloodier and crueller incidents in Punjab, for it is an inherently violent region. But the massacre at the Jallianwala garden is one of those historical events that does not fade. It tolls like a bell down the years. For all that people demand that the past should be buried, Dyer's volleys still reverberate. The emotions they aroused have hardly subsided in eight decades. The bullet holes in the walls are ringed with iron and helpfully labelled 'Bullet Mark'. When the subject is raised, there are still passionate responses in British and Indian newspapers. Sides are still taken. Was Dyer right or wrong?

The Point of the Bayonet

Some of the heat had gone from the afternoon when I left Mrs Bhandari's to walk in Dyer's footsteps through the alley that is still the only entrance into the walled Jallianwala Bagh. Dyer stomped through, at the head of his Gurkhas and Indian troops, utterly determined to kill. There had been disturbances in the city and a British woman had been assaulted. Many in the crowd knew that Dyer had prohibited gatherings, but others had travelled from the countryside to visit a fair and had not heard that meetings were banned. Dyer found an unarmed crowd, not a threatening mob. But its nature and temper did not matter. Dyer's only purpose, as he himself said, was to kill a shockingly large number of people. Without warning, his soldiers fired 1,650 rounds, killing at least 379 men, women and children. Had he been able to get his armoured car through the alley he would have used machine-guns, too, to kill more. Afterwards, compounding it all, he issued orders forcing Indians to crawl along the street where the British woman had been assaulted.

Dyer was an old-fashioned warhorse. He believed shooting was the only language Indians understood. There was the question of pride, too. Having threatened punishment, he felt that if he failed to act his authority as a sahib would be undermined, that he would be jeered at by his Indian inferiors. He was a schoolmaster, punishing disobedience. In private, he bragged about the bloodshed.

The massacre went to the heart of things, to the question of the relationship between the races, of how the country should be governed and of what the British were doing in India. Dyer and his many supporters regarded themselves as morally superior to Indians; and since Indian lives counted for little it did not matter how many were killed. He was hailed by those who, with the shadow of the Mutiny in their minds, saw his savagery as a resolute action that had saved the empire, or at least Punjab.

Some of the shoot-them-all tendency plainly thought that a Dyer-like ruthlessness would be most effective in dealing with the recalcitrant elements in Ireland. Dyer was supported at home by Sir Henry Wilson, the bloodthirsty chief of the British army, who also advocated the severest repression of Irish nationalists.

There was outrage when the official inquiry into the massacre criticized Dyer and he was forced to resign. Winston Churchill, the Secretary of State for War, was one of those who wanted Dyer out. But Dyer was saluted by the House of Lords and presented with a ceremonial sword. The *Morning Post* opened a fund, a kind of opinion poll, which raised a tribute of £26,000, the equivalent of about £700,000 today. Rudyard Kipling donated £10.

A few years before, Dyer's bullets would not have caused such uproar. But Indians fought in their hundreds of thousands for the empire in the First World War. They consequently expected British appreciation of their sacrifice and sympathetic consideration of the case for self-government. Instead the British obstinately brought in oppressive security measures to crush political activities. Some people saw, and many did not, that the tide was on the turn, that it was utterly illusory to believe the empire was a permanent institution. The Victorian epoch was over. Churchill was one of those who believed that Dyer's way was no way for Britain to run India. The man who as Home Secretary sent troops to confront the militant miners at Tonypandy in 1910 was not one to shrink from the use of force; but he did not believe that British power in India could rest upon bayonets.

Jallianwala Bagh was a turning point. Dyer did not 'lose' India but his brutality disclosed a moral bankruptcy in its rulers, a failure to understand that things were changing, the weakness inherent in apparent strength. Considering the times

The Point of the Bayonet

and the circumstances, the British had employed relatively little force in India. Indeed, the marvel was that such a small number of people ruled so many with such ease. The rage at injustice that flowed from Jallianwala Bagh gave impetus and authority to Mahatma Gandhi's independence movement. Those who rushed to send their guineas to the Dyer fund did not consider for a moment how much their action would harden Indian attitudes. India was the grandest of Britain's imperial passions, but ten minutes of firing intended to make its rule more secure sounded a knell. Dyer never slept well after Amritsar. Not long before he died, in 1927, he said he wanted to know from his maker if he had done wrong.

In the years since I had last visited the Jallianwala Bagh, a gallery had been built, telling the story of the shooting. It displayed a copy of the letter the poet Rabindranath Tagore sent to the Viceroy surrendering the knighthood 'which I had the honour to accept from His Majesty the King at the hands of your predecessor for whose nobleness of heart I still entertain great admiration'. The massacre, he said, had 'revealed to our minds the helplessness of our position as British subjects in India'.

It took a few minutes to walk from the garden to the Golden Temple, to my mind one of the enchanting places in the world. I lodged my shoes at the office, washed my feet in a slippery shallow pool and passed through an archway beneath the clock tower, picking my way around a score of dozing men, sprawled or curled foetally on the marble floor. Once I was through the entrance, the turbulence of the city fell away, as if I had been cast by rolling seas on to a peaceful shore. The Golden Temple is not at all a deserted church. It is comfortable and worn, accessible and embraced, loved and crowded, rubbed by feet and hands. Chanted scriptures and the soft melodies of harmonium and sitar float through the air. The cloisters and stairways smell of humanity and the homeliness of simmering food. The Temple serves a free lunch to all comers, for Sikhs hold the sensible belief that a man cannot put his mind to the worship of God if he is hungry.

Hundreds of people sat in the shade, talking, gazing, sleeping, studying small books of psalms in their laps. There are no services and people worship in their own way and in their own time. Meanwhile, unhurried, drifting almost, savouring the sacred air, a couple of hundred pilgrims promenaded the chequered marble quadrangle around the central 'pool of immortality and bliss'. The water is regarded as amrit, the nectar made by gods. Men and boys stripped to their drawers and dunked themselves in the water to rinse away their sins. Fathers dipped their infant sons. Orthodox Sikhs slowly lowered themselves into the water, having tied the daggers from which they must never be separated into the folds of their turbans. They sank into the shimmering reflection of the gilded Harimandir, the temple which rises like an island in the pool and glows like the core of a furnace. I watched the endless line of pilgrims walking along the causeway into this holy heart. Here they made their obeisance to the Granth Sahib, the book of wisdom, more than six thousand verses and hymns, the only object that Sikhs worship. It rests on cloths of gold thread and on one side of it singers serenade the book and their faith.

An elderly man approached me as I strolled. He grasped my hand and asked the usual question: 'Which country?'

'Britain.'

'This is God's house and you are God's son. I am God's son also. Therefore we are brothers.'

He beamed and shook my hand again. 'Congratulations for beating West Indies at cricket.'

Every detail of this sacred place reminds Sikhs of their story. Amritsar itself takes its name from the Golden Temple's pool of amrit. It is with amrit, sugared water, stirred with a dagger, that

The Point of the Bayonet

Sikhs are baptized. Sikh means disciple and the faith was founded in the Punjab in 1499 by the first of ten Gurus whose teachings shaped it. It was a pacifist religion at first, austere, preaching love and disapproving of caste. It became militant to defend itself against the pogroms of Mogul rulers. In 1699, Gobind, the tenth and last Guru, called Sikhs to Anandpur and asked for a volunteer to step from the crowd and give his life in sacrifice. A man rose and entered Gobind's tent. In a few moments the Guru reappeared, clutching a sword running with blood, and called for a second sacrifice. Again a man stepped forward. In all, five men volunteered; and then, in a theatrical moment, all of them reappeared with the Guru. The sword was bloody from the slaughter of goats.

The Guru baptized the five as the nucleus of a new fighting force, the khalsa. He made them drink from the same bowl of amrit, to symbolize a rejection of caste, and gave them the name of Singh, meaning lion, the name that all Sikh men bear. It has a martial ring to it, but the Guru also meant it to replace the surnames which indicated caste. Caste, however, so fundamental in Indian tradition, has not been defeated and remains a fact of Sikh life.

Gobind ordered his Sikhs to be ever ready for battle, to wear shorts and to carry swords or daggers. The Sikh right to carry a dagger is enshrined in the Constitution of India. He also ordered them to wear an iron bangle as a symbol of humbleness, to leave their beards and hair unshorn and to secure their hair tidily with a comb. Many men in India wear a turban of some kind, but the Sikhs have made it their particular emblem, tying it carefully and evolving various styles. A Sikh considers himself improperly dressed without a turban. It is a gross offence to knock it off and it is not, generally, something to be joked about.

The tenth Guru's injunction against tobacco is widely respected. 'Kissing A Smoker Is Like Licking An Ashtray', said an American-style sign in my hotel in Amritsar. The Guru's ban on alcohol, however, is widely ignored. Many Sikhs celebrate liquor and adore whisky: it is part of their Punjabi vigour. Once when I had dinner at a house in Amritsar, my Sikh host went to his bookcase and pulled open a false front of books to reveal a cache of Scotch. Many Sikhs believe that a proper measure is a Patiala peg, a measure of two fingers of whisky, the fingers being the first and the fourth.

A Sikh who shaves, cuts his hair and gives up the turban is seen as having abandoned his faith, often a matter of disappointment to his family. I met a man in Amritsar who told me that his great-grandfather had been a Sikh, 'but boils grew on his head and a doctor told him to cut his hair. Thus he ceased to be a Sikh and his sons cut their hair, too. But for the boils on my ancestor's head, I might have been a Sikh.'

In the 1980s the question of beards had a curious place in the vortex of plotting, terrorism and madness that culminated in the storming of the Golden Temple and the assassination of Indira Gandhi, the Prime Minister. These events left India badly wounded. The chief, though not the only, cause of them was Mrs Gandhi's misrule. She was neither wise nor perceptive. She was not wicked and had no wish to be a dictator, but she allowed herself to become despotic. She broke the framework of the Congress Party, the dominant force in politics, and rebuilt it around her own personality. Crucially, Congress ceased to be a federal party in which relatively independent leaderships in the states managed local issues. India's myriad minorities found they no longer had the means through which they could express grievances. Every local question had to come to Mrs Gandhi's office, but regional grievances were then defined by Delhi as just that: irritating minority matters, a threat to national integrity, to India itself. There was no venting of the gases of discontent. At a time when there was a need for political modernization, Mrs Gandhi and her younger son Sanjay ran an old-fashioned centralized court.

Mrs Gandhi and Sanjay wanted Congress, not the Sikh party, to rule Punjab. The way to do this was to exploit the notorious differences of the Sikhs. To this end Mrs Gandhi set the fanatical preacher Jarnail Singh Bhindranwale to undermine the Sikh leadership and deliver Punjab to her. He did. Unfortunately, she thereby created a monster she could not control. Punjab was, in any case, a turbulent land with a history of property feuds and vendettas; and Bhindranwale was a flame in the tinder. He dwelt on Sikh grievances and revived old calls for an independent Sikh state, something the large majority of Sikhs did not, and do not, want. Because of his rule of terror and murder, the most prosperous state in the country, the home of some of its most talented and energetic people, fell into anarchy.

Bhindranwale was obsessed with beards. He encouraged and reflected the belief among his followers that the Sikh faith was waning. They feared oblivion, absorption into the Hindu mass whence Sikhism had sprung less than five centuries before. They were dismayed to see large numbers of young Sikhs taking up with gusto the pleasures of modern life – Western clothes, cars and real Scotch – drifting out of the faith and eschewing the external differentia by shaving and discarding the turban. For orthodox Sikhs, beards are one of the distinguishing marks of the real man and devout believer. Bhindranwale created a politics of beards. His wild-eyed disciples went shaggy-bearded: more Sikh than thou. 'My responsibility is to see that your beards remain intact, that your hair is uncut . . .' he told his followers. He jeered at Sikhs who trimmed or dyed their whiskers or used nets to make them neat.

It had been common for Sikhs and Hindus to intermarry, for one son of a Hindu family to be raised as a Sikh, for both peoples to worship in each other's temples. Bhindranwale saw danger in this easy relationship and sought to accentuate the differences and end the traditional harmony. He began a campaign of murder to terrorize Hindus. In Hindu villages razors rusted as men stopped shaving. They also tied on turbans, hoping to save their lives if Bhindranwale's gunmen called.

Mrs Gandhi lost control. Bhindranwale fortified the Golden Temple and became a minotaur in its labyrinth. He and his followers were killed when the army assaulted it in 1984. In the fury that followed this desecration, Mrs Gandhi was murdered by her Sikh bodyguards. This in turn triggered a massacre of more than two thousand Sikhs in Delhi, partly directed by Congress members. As if this were not blood enough, the authorities in Punjab decided that only the extermination of Sikh militants would bring peace. There was no question of taking men to court. Many hundreds of militants were killed in 'encounters' with the police. The institutions had failed. Brutality worked. 'Ruthlessness', the Punjab police chief K. P. S. Gill said to me at the time, 'is an important part of my policy. The fact that I am a Sikh is vital, too. I know the culture. It takes a Sikh to fight Sikhs.'

Leaving aside Mrs Gandhi's disservice, the Punjab crisis turned on the question of how India should be governed and what sort of country it should be. Sikhs form less than two per cent of India's population, but they are distinctive and stand out in a way that belies their numbers. They are champion farmers, big in transport, engineering and the armed forces. Like all minorities they have to cope with the indifference of the majority, asserting their identity without being so strident and hermetic that they fall into extremism. It is India's problem too, because the country is so phenomenally diverse in its faiths, cultures and aspirations. Its democracy depends on a civilized elasticity in the management of minorities.

In the Golden Temple's museum hangs a horror-show of

paintings of Sikhs being done to death in various ways. Some of the Mogul rulers persecuted the Sikhs: the paintings depict Sikhs being beheaded, sawn in half or skewered in showers of blood. In the eighteenth century assassins were paid fifty rupees for a Sikh scalp. In 1716 hundreds of Sikhs who defied the Mogul empire were paraded in chains through the streets of Delhi. They walked behind 700 bullock carts, each piled with Sikh heads, and were escorted by 2,000 soldiers, each bearing a pike with a Sikh head on it. The prisoners were beheaded at the rate of a hundred a day. In photographs of recent victims of violence their blood has been made more vivid with paint. Children gaped at the gory scenes. A man touched my arm and said happily: 'See how the children look. This is their history. It is good for them to learn how we have been persecuted.'

❁

The fading light cast a coppery glow over the people ranged along the road at the border station at Wagah, on the Grand Trunk Road between Amritsar and Lahore. A few hundred spectators stood on each side, quiet and expectant. The spectacle that unfolded was astonishing.

It began with a dramatic and percussive overture. Soldiers with rigidly set faces marched to the centre of the road stamping their boots with tremendous force. With a clang that startled the birds in the dark trees, they threw open the steel gates marked, in large brass letters, INDIA and PAKISTAN. The Indian gates were striped in the national colours, saffron, white and green, and the white gate pillars were surmounted by the Indian leoglyph emblem, four lions seated back to back, one of the symbols of power of the Emperor Ashoka who ruled in the third century BC. The Pakistani gates were embossed with the Islamic symbol of the crescent moon and star, originally the emblem of Christian Constantinople retained by Turkish sultans after they conquered the city in 1453.

There was something in this opening of the gates that was like the lowering of a drawbridge. The spectators inched forward on the pavements and craned to get a better view, Indians looking at Pakistanis, Pakistanis at Indians, each side staring into a mirror.

On the strip of swept and tidy road, about eighty paces apart, two soldiers faced each other, one Indian, one Pakistani. They bristled with masculinity. Their uniforms could hardly have been crisper and cleaner, their creases sharper, their buckles and boots shinier, their moustaches neater. They were tall and well-made, holding themselves stiffly, heads tilted well back, rifles slung on the shoulder. The men of India's Border Security Force – 'Duty Unto Death' – wore khaki with pale blue gaiters and ornate pugris, or turbans, of dark blue tied with a thick band of scarlet and gold, a gold-tasselled sash over one side, covering the ear, the whole splendid concoction finished with a starched and pleated cockscomb fan of red and white stripes; and even this had perky little starched spikes of cotton. Each man's belt was fastened over a striped blue and scarlet cummerbund that matched his cravat. The Pakistan Rangers wore dark blue long shirts and trousers, striped red cravats, their belts over red cummerbunds. Their pugris had a long tail falling to the waist, a red badged band around the brow and a jaunty blue cockscomb.

Suddenly, the two men started marching rapidly towards each other, so quickly and purposefully, so mechanically, I thought they could burst through a brick wall. The knees rose very high and the boots crashed down hard. They hammered the road as if their bones would crack. And then, a few feet from each other, they stopped abruptly. They threw out their chests, stuck out their elbows and thrust their knuckles on to their hips.

The Point of the Bayonet

Their jaws jutted. They fixed each other in a wide-eyed glowering gaze and exhaled through their flared nostrils, chests heaving, snorting at each other like bulls. I was reminded of the *haka*, the Maori dance of challenge.

Then they turned on their heels and marched away, and two more soldiers performed the same drill, then two more. In the ember-light of the day, the soldiers hauled down India's tricolour and Pakistan's crescent moon, each man's hand movements matching the other's. Buglers sounded the Last Post. The flags were respectfully folded and carried away on a soldier's outstretched arms. Officers shook hands in the thin strip of no man's land and the gates were shut with another clang and the birds squawked again.

There was a brief and poignant aftermath. The spectators, who had been applauding the performance, were allowed to gather at the closed gates to contemplate each other. Mostly, they were silent. Some looked wistful. After a few minutes, the soldiers shooed them all away. The ceremony provides the only official aperture through which these divided cousins can peep at one another over the chasm of their estrangement. As often happens in broken families the mutual curiosity is intense and enduring. Anyone who travels in both countries is questioned about life and attitudes on the other side. It is as if, rather than being neighbours thigh by thigh, they are separated by an ocean.

This stretch of road on the Punjab plain crosses the incision where, most bloodily and agonizingly, the old India was sundered. In the fields and towns and villages around here, in 1947, the slaughter that followed Partition was maddest and the streams ran reddest. There are many men, now old, who have lived for half a century with the memory of how, when they were young, crazed and murderous, they took up guns, knives and spears, and, making no distinction between grandfathers and baby boys, women and girls, turned on their neighbours and added them to the heaps of corpses. Around here the ambushed trains leaked blood. Loving fathers cut their daughters' throats to save them from rape as the killing squads roamed. It has been called a frenzy, but there was a lot more to it than hot temper and rage. In this mutual genocide, gangs of men felt licensed to kill cold-bloodedly. Methodically, bureaucratically, they worked from lists, concentrating on the weak and defenceless. There was, as a subtext, much score-settling and looting. About a million people were murdered and around seventeen million fled their homes in a fearful stampede. The sheer scale of the depravity has meant that in the half-century since most people have been unable to address or even begin to understand what happened. Partition is a seeping well of poison. Its horrors have not been exorcised and it is unlikely that they ever will be.

Although the gutters around here ran with blood, this border is in another sense an artery that was clamped off. No other place symbolizes so starkly the pity of Punjab. This is 'the land of the five rivers', the Sutlej, Beas, Ravi, Chenab and Jhelum. For many centuries the Punjab plain was a marchland between the immense territories of Hindustan and Islam. It was an historical entity and for forty years in the nineteenth century was a kingdom ruled by the one-eyed Ranjit Singh, the Sikhs' greatest warrior. He built the Harimandir in the Golden Temple and clothed its dome with leaf of gold. He created the most formidable army in India, brought the North West Frontier and Kashmir under his control, stopped the Afghan and Pathan conquerors of India and took the Koh-i-noor diamond from the ruler of Afghanistan. His common touch and his evident weakness for wine, women and horses endeared him to Punjabis. His kingdom did not long survive his death in 1839. The British annexed it in 1849 and, as booty, took the Koh-i-noor and gave

The Point of the Bayonet

it to Queen Victoria who passed it to Prince Albert who sent it to a diamond cutter who butchered and considerably reduced it. Queen Victoria later showed it to Ranjit Singh's son, by then living in London. In a comment on the means by which she came by it, he, being well-educated, referred to her in private as Mrs Fagin.

Partition cut in two a proud and self-conscious land, a cultural whole with its definitive Punjabi language and literature and its well-watered myths. Its people were families who shared the same house and had much in common. Lahore, Ranjit Singh's capital and the most lovely and beloved city of Punjab, was suddenly fenced off. Like Amritsar it became a frontier town. Many of those who fled across the new frontier in 1947 did not imagine that they would never return. Indeed, they thought they might be back in a few weeks when the situation grew calmer and so they did not take with them even their most treasured possessions. The writer Kuldip Nayar, then a student, told me he left his books, half-read, in his home in Sialkot, believing he would retrieve them later. 'People thought there would be a soft border, like Canada's with the United States, so that they would move easily to and fro.' They did not think that there would be such a defining and enduring hostility.

In the sunset ceremony at Wagah lies a distillation of that hostility. Here the burnished tips of the spears touch. Two rivals, two ideas, two powerful faiths stand toe to toe. After three wars, 1948, 1965 and 1971, the bulk of the armies of Pakistan and India are based along the frontier that runs through Punjab and Kashmir. The costs of mutual mistrust are crippling. Both countries make their defence assessments principally in relation to each other.

Yet the ceremony is also a manifestation of that love of soldierly panache that grew especially in the years of the Raj: all that show and glitter, the parade-ground strut, the excellence that arises from discipline and love of military custom. Here are two proud armies which were once one. Their officers had soaked up the values of Sandhurst. Regiments had been marinaded in British tradition. The senior men had been classmates and messmates. In their wars, they still thought each other fine fellows. Although India and Pakistan glare across the frontier, the soldiers have decided that here in martial Punjab the sunset lowering of national flags at Wagah should be a spectacle of military dignity and precision. In smartness and drill both sides are absolutely equal, the choreography and the flourishes machined and polished in joint rehearsals, so that each thud of boot and spring-loaded salute is exactly mirrored. Neither side should be seen to have any advantage.

In the morning the border would open for a few hours. Travellers would have to negotiate four check points on each side of the zero line. Usually, it is not too difficult for foreigners with patience and the right paperwork to pass through. It is much harder for Indians and Pakistanis. Few get permission to make the journey and, when they do, this crossing is often mined with obstructions, pretexts and vindictiveness, the hallmarks of the relationship. But that is the point. If entry and exit across the border were easy, if people could travel freely to see each other, the purpose of Partition might be questioned.

5

The Palace Theatre

IT WAS NOT THE first wreck of the day, but the slogan painted on the side of the green bus lying crumpled in the rubble of a wall made it one to remember: 'A Healthy And Positive Way Of Life In Haryana'.

A sign down the road said:

>Always Be Mr Late, Not The Late Mr.

The driver of my car had tied a bundle of green chillies to the broken stump that had once held a wing mirror.

'Against evil eye,' he explained.

The speedometer was obscured by a picture of a Sikh guru, his hand raised in blessing.

Rajasthan was tawny in the early light, the distant hills blue islands in a misty sea. Strings of swaying camels picked their patient way through the scrub. By the time I reached the fort at Neemrana it was hot. A steep, curving cobbled lane led through heavy timber gates into the main courtyard. At a small table in the shade, writing on sheets of foolscap, sat Amitabh Bachchan, India's greatest film star, a kind of god. He was freshly bathed and shaved, his wavy hair combed to perfection, and he wore a crisp long shirt the colour of a buttercup. He was quite alone.

I had no appointment and if he minded being disturbed when I approached him he did not show it. Smiling graciously he called a waiter and asked for tea, softly and courteously, not in the peremptory finger-snapping fashion of some political and business rajas I have met. I should not have been surprised. I had read that in an industry notorious for arrogant and sulky stars he stood out as a gentleman who always arrived for work punctually and was never temperamental.

He finished the sentence he was writing, capped his fountain pen and sat back. The fort rose in haughty grandeur on a bluff among the outriders of the Aravalli mountains. For five centuries it had commanded the district that spread beneath it. From its ramparts one could look into the life of the village below and listen to its sounds, the conversation of women, the chatter of children, the bleat of goats, all stitched together by music. The flat roofs of the houses were coloured with drying saris. Beyond, to the west, as far as the eye could see, stretched the flat brown-green plain.

'As you can see, it is perfect for the film we're making,' Bachchan said. 'You will be familiar with the sort of plot we have. There is a damsel in distress. She is pretty. She is held prisoner in this fort by the wicked villain.' He smiled. 'I play the hero, of course, and, after a lot of exciting action, I defeat the villain and rescue the damsel. The basic structure and texture of films have not changed very much over the years. Good always triumphs over evil and the boy gets the girl. Some purists say there is a greater Western influence in our films now, and too much of it. But I think we are a people who like our traditions, our embedded culture thousands of years old. That applies to everything, our customs, our eating habits and our style of making film stories. And in the cinema escapism is all.'

Critics have been wringing their hands for years over the

quality of Indian films. They have run out of synonyms for rubbish. But the millions who flock to them want reliable entertainment. They see enough wretchedness in their own lives and do not want ambiguity and sad endings on the screen. They like long films, beautiful heroines, wickedly sexy bad girls, extremely loud music and explosive action.

When I first wrote a story about Amitabh Bachchan he was almost dead. He had been seriously injured in a film stunt and all India was gripped by his struggle for survival. The daily hospital bulletin was headline news and many thousands of people flocked to rallies to pray for his life. They were joined by producers aware that his stardom was one of the rocks on which the world's largest film industry depended. The prime minister flew to his bedside. It was no wonder that when he recovered, advertising hoardings shouted: 'Amitabh Lives'; and financiers joined the crowds in prayers of gratitude.

Before they start work on a new film, the director, actors and crew gather round a ritual fire, at a time chosen by an astrologer, and decorate the camera with flowers. With the gods saluted and good fortune requested, shooting begins. Bachchan was hoping that his latest film would more than make up for the losses of his previous production which had been a rare failure. He became an actor in 1969 and made his name as an angry young man who challenged the mute acceptance of oppression. His films suggested people could fight back, so that when he punched a scowling ruffian the men in the stalls were punching with him, landing metaphorical blows on all their tormentors – rapacious landlords, brutal cops and crooked politicians.

At times it is difficult to distinguish the real Bombay film world from some of its films, for it has its own petty tyrants and violent parasites. Gangsters extort money from producers and directors, demanding cash and a share of the royalties, and those who refuse to pay risk being murdered. The business has for many years been a laundry for black money, untaxed income, and it has not been easy to raise straight finance. 'Money comes from the market at exorbitant rates of interest,' Bachchan said carefully. 'It's a haphazard industry.'

On this trip across Rajasthan, I stayed mostly in small forts and mansions owned by the remnants and descendants of the minor aristocracy. The splendid palace hotels of Rajasthan have commanded the tourist business in this region for forty years and more. They represent wealth, the romance of the desert, the swank of the Rajputs and feudal rule. But after a while, I develop an aversion to chandeliers, top prices and heaped-up splendour. The minor princelings have spied a niche in the market and have started augmenting their incomes by opening their castles to visitors. These are more modest places but they are still strong on fantasy and, usually, the prince is in residence to guide, chat and provide a touch of style.

Sure enough, Maharaj Dalip Singh, a striking figure with a rakish Rajput moustache who had restored his home, Fort Chanwa, presided over dinner on his veranda. He was knowledgeable about warriors and explained to me the importance of opium to the fighting man. 'The ritual use of opium was always widespread in western Rajasthan and eastern Gujarat. It was most popular among the warrior classes for four important reasons. One, it was a relaxant that diminished fear before battle. Two, it was a stimulant that worked against fatigue. Three, it was a blood coagulant that helped to heal wounds. Four, it also promoted constipation. A most useful benefit to a warrior riding off to fight, don't you think?'

The seventeenth-century fort at Deogarh, raised on a hill above a lake, had recently been renovated by the sons of its owner, Rawat Nahar Singh. 'During the work we found gunpowder and cannon balls,' one of them said, 'although, to be honest, we had hoped to find gold. A number of these old

The Palace Theatre

palaces are bought by speculators who tear them apart in the belief that gold is hidden in them. Sometimes they are right.'

As we looked out over the town spreading beneath the ramparts, the Rawat, who had been a schoolmaster for many years, told me he had been placed on the throne as soon as his father died. He was proclaimed Rawat at once and, in an echo of an age of intrigue and drama, the palace gates were locked to prevent any pretender entering to claim the kingdom. When I remarked on the magnificence of the rooms and the bathrooms, he said: 'Actually, the hardest part of restoration was the installation of bathrooms. In my youth, there was no plumbing. When it was needed, a pot was brought and taken away by a servant. When you wanted a bath, well, you called on the servants and just asked them to bring pitchers of water. The household was full of servants, you see, scores of them, paid five rupees a month.'

After 1947, when the princes extinguished themselves as a ruling class, some of the royal families fell into obscurity and even poverty. But most have not vanished. They still have their palaces. Some still use their titles and some hold to a sense of duty, of *noblesse oblige*, and believe they can serve the people their forebears once ruled. Many are in business or politics. Since all aristocracies exist partly to entertain the crowd, they remain a source of pageantry; and the newspapers like to report their activities, their weddings, their family quarrels over property and money, and their scandals.

The Rawat's wife, the Rana, said that her family remained a focal point for the inhabitants of the town and its hinterland. 'Local people like to know that we are here, in residence, a part of their lives, of continuity. They want a certain formality from us, too. For example, they like to see me wearing a sari and would be disappointed to see me in Western dress. And they would feel uncomfortable if I went to shop in the town, as if

I were patronizing them, just as people would in England if the Queen were to do her shopping in the High Street.'

I thought she had a point; and many former rulers say the same thing. But a man I met a couple of days later in Udaipur shook his head emphatically. 'You see, these old princes live in their dreams of the past. They are not looking to the future. With all that show, their palaces and jewels and people bowing, you would think they were kings who were still ruling. That is what they would have you believe. Of course, some of the common people have a sentiment in favour of the old royalty and they bend down and touch the maharaja's feet. But really, it is like a superstition. The truth is that most ordinary people are democratically minded and do not have a deep respect for these former rulers. How could they? What did these princes do? They squandered their wealth. They fought wars among themselves and made the ordinary men and women suffer and did not do much for them.'

Britain ruled India with the co-operation of 565 native princes whose territories covered more than three-fifths of the country and a quarter of the population. There were maharajas, rajas, ranas, rawats, raos, maharaos, khans, mirs, jams, chiefs, thakurs, nizams, gaekwars and nawabs. The grandest of them ruled kingdoms as large as France and the smallest commanded just a few acres. The co-operation of these princes enabled a cadre of just over a thousand officials of the Indian Civil Service to rule more than three hundred million people. In return for their loyalty to the British Crown, the princes were allowed to do much as they liked. A few were decent and responsible and improved the existence of their subjects; but most did very little.

Princely consent was oiled by flattery. The British had a keen instinct for deference and, as governments have today, a cynical appreciation of the usefulness of honours. The baubles and coats of arms they dispensed to their Indian feudatories were prized by most of the recipients. The rulers grew proudly sensitive about their place in the princely pecking order and about such matters as titles, gun salutes and the small print of protocol. Gun salutes were awarded on a scale ranging from nine to twenty-one. The Viceroy was far ahead with thirty-one. Kipling reported that the first bribe he was ever offered was an attempt to get him to put in a good word for a prince who wanted to add more guns to his salute.

For many years only the most important princes, those who rated an eleven-gun salute and over, could be addressed as His Highness; but later the nine-gun princes were awarded this honorific, too. The mightily rich Nizam of Hyderabad longed to be addressed as His Majesty, but the British forbade it, just as they refused to allow any ruler to be styled His Royal Highness or His Illustrious Highness or His Imperial Highness. The Nizam was, however, permitted to use the honorific His Exalted Highness. No ruling family was allowed to call itself a Royal Family. No tent or pavilion, no matter how splendid, could be termed a Royal Pavilion. No coronet or crown could be worn if it were similar to a diadem worn by a British royal or other aristocrat. Moreover, princes were strictly forbidden to call a throne a throne. If the ruler were Hindu, the term gaddi had to be used for the regal chair. If he were Muslim the word was masnud.

Nowhere is the awareness of old princely power stronger than in Rajasthan, the domain of the Rajputs. The origins of these rulers remain much disputed, but it seems that they sprang from thirty-six clans of warriors who appeared in the desert country of northern India about two thousand years ago. According to one theory they derived from Central Asian tribes, among them the Huns. Whatever their roots, the Rajputs themselves held to the modest and simple explanation that they were descended from the sun. They were famously averse to tilling the land and, through conquest, made themselves the ruling class, creating more than twenty kingdoms in Rajputana, 'the land of the kings', which is today the state of Rajasthan.

Few men in India swaggered more. With vivid turbans, curved swords and upturned moustaches they cut a mighty dash. The chivalric code of the Rajputs mirrored that of medieval Europe. They stood for arms and honour and magnanimity towards their enemies. Pictures in the museum in the City Palace in Udaipur depict in brilliant detail the exotic savagery and chivalry of Rajput collisions. Even the elephants are warriors, wielding swords with their trunks. Sliced-off heads bounce about the battlefield like so many footballs. And here in his pomp is an elephant-borne Maharana of Mewar accoutred with two swords. One is for himself and the other is for his enemy should the enemy lose his own: the level playing field of honour. Rajput rulers garrisoned their lands with fortresses that enclosed the towns. Their excursions were awesome demonstrations of power. Billows of dust rose from immense wagon trains in which the rulers packed their wives, dancing girls, servants, bankers, moneylenders and other necessities. The bullocks drawing the carts were fed by regiments of grass cutters. The tapestry of Rajput history is as bloody as it is gorgeous, punctuated by great sieges and marked by acts of courage still lauded in song. On three occasions, in 1303, 1535 and 1567, the Rajput women in Chittor Fort burnt themselves to death rather than surrender to attackers.

The largest of the princely states of Rajasthan was the kingdom of Mewar, of which Udaipur was the chief city. Its maharanas have ruled since the sixth century and the present one is the seventy-sixth of the line in the world's oldest princely dynasty. Perhaps the greatest was Kumbha, who ruled for thirty years in the fifteenth century and towered over the age of chivalry. He was a poet, scholar, playwright, patron of artists and

The Palace Theatre

the architect of more than thirty fortresses, the most magnificent of which bears his name: Kumbhalgarh. I was promised that if I explored it I would be drawn into the spirit of the man and his times. Climbing out of the valley of a boisterous river, we ascended through forests and gorges until Kumbhalgarh rose theatrically into view. Kumbha intended this first sighting to be awe-inspiring and, to his enemies, forbidding. A Martian fortress, comprising twenty miles of high red walls and pot-shaped towers, it snakes over the ridges, encircling the hill on whose pinnacle rears the keep and palace. The walls are wide enough for eight horsemen to ride abreast on them, the massive gates bristle with iron spikes to stop war elephants breaking them down. The rocky ground felt like warm cinders as I walked to the small temple where Kumbha died a death that Shakespeare might have fashioned. Kneeling at his prayers in 1486, he was murdered by his son. As far as is possible the name of that reviled killer has been expunged from the records.

For a couple of days I lived in preposterous splendour at the Shivniwas Palace in Udaipur. Two sets of baronial doors, secured with brass bolts, opened into a marble-floored suite and spacious bedchamber. I felt like a mouse in a jewel-box. Gilt mirrors and portraits of stern nobles surrounded the seigneurial and fantasy-evoking bed which I thought might sleep six. Above it hung a gigantic blood-red chandelier dripping with glass pendants. The frames of foliate arches encompassed a view of blue-green hills and of Pichola Lake. The creamy-yellow palace in the centre of the lake, served by small boats, seemed at sunset a pleasure-ship anchored in wine.

If only it were. Over the past few years the lake has become choked with water hyacinth and badly polluted by sewage. It is little better than a drain, and it is shrinking, too. From the fourteenth century onwards, the far-sighted maharanas of Mewar created seven lakes to make their Udaipur an oasis in the desert, a place of beauty, but their legacy has been badly damaged by unscrupulous modern developers building on the shores of the lakes. In the usual way of things, politicians and bureaucrats have worked with the builders to circumvent the planning laws. One by one the seven lakes have become silted and poisoned dumps for sewage and industrial effluent. It hardly matters to the developers that some of the lakes are the main source of drinking water for many of the people.

The Shivniwas Palace was built largely by Maharana Sir Fateh Singh who ruled Udaipur from 1884 to 1921. I went to see the portrait of him in the museum. He wore his beard, as does the present Maharana, parted distinctively in the centre and swept up at each side. He posed for his portrait with his right hand resting on the curved sword which testified to his rank and his Rajput warrior tradition. I thought I detected the vein of dignified pride and stubbornness which conditioned his life and so irritated the stiff-trousered British. He was the seventy-third ruler in the line and keenly aware of the House of Mewar's nobility and seniority. No ruler of Udaipur had ever bent the knee to the Mogul emperors who ruled India for four centuries; and none had offered a daughter in marriage to a Mogul, either. Fateh Singh had no reputation for arrogance and was widely regarded as a humble man; but he did not think that the British Emperors of India were more august than he. Lineage for lineage, he was surely right. His cousin, who had preceeded him as Maharana, had hesitated when Queen Victoria offered him the Star of India, on the ground that a descendant of the sun should not accept a mere star; but he took it in the end as a mark of respect from one monarch to another.

Fateh Singh was a very difficult old man. I rather warmed to him. His refusal to offer the expected obeisance either to the King-Emperor or to the Viceroy caused consternation among British officials who lived their lives by protocol. But Fateh Singh

The Palace Theatre

never saw himself as subordinate to the British and certainly did not think he ruled by their favour. He regarded himself as the chief of all the Rajputs, a leader among Hindus and, quite simply, the top prince of all India. The fact was, however, that the British had awarded him a salute of nineteen guns, while five other rulers were twenty-one gunners.

The Maharana was, of course, invited to Lord Curzon's great viceregal durbar in 1903 and travelled to Delhi by rail with a retinue of a thousand. But on arrival he discovered that he had been placed fifth, not first, in the princely procession. He made no protest. That was not his way. But he did not disembark from his train. He and his retinue went back to Udaipur in dignified silence.

The crisis of precedence arose again when the durbar of 1911 was planned. This was even grander, for it was the coronation durbar presided over by King George V and symbolic of British imperial power. The British diplomatic enforcers put pressure on the Maharana to attend. They warned him they would reduce his gun salute if he failed to do so. He, in response, made it clear he was prepared to kill himself if he were slighted, a threat that made the British shiver. To get around the problem of precedence and obeisance, the British made him a member of the King's staff, Ruling Chief In Waiting, so that he would not have to join the jewelled regiment of princes bowing before the King. The Maharana travelled to Delhi but complained of illness. Doctors, it is said, found boils upon his buttocks. In exquisite compromise, the King met the Maharana at the railway station and here, king to king, equal to equal, the Maharana congratulated him; but he did not attend the durbar itself and returned to his Rajput fastness. He had not bent the knee. However, the British deposed him in 1921. They thought him out of touch with his people who, in the political excitement of the time, were growing increasingly restless. His son took over. But the old man retained the title of Maharana until he died in 1930.

❂

Maharaja Sir Jai Singh of Alwar, Rajasthan, who ruled his state for forty years, was a Rajput and a contemporary of Fateh Singh, He, too, was deposed by the British (in 1933) although he had annoyed them in a different way. He was a highly intelligent, elegant and charming man and a gifted talker. Many, however, found him strange, sinister and cruel. Some of the stories about him sound apocryphal. Few accounts of his life omit the tale of his using village children as tiger bait and the story of his setting fire to a polo pony that displeased him.

His great-grandson, Jitendra, told me that one of the true stories about him was of his visit to a Rolls-Royce showroom in London. He wanted to buy a Rolls but the salesman sniffily doubted whether he could afford one. Thereupon the Maharaja bought seven and used them as dustcarts for collecting rubbish in Alwar. Jitendra prized the two Hispano-Suizas and the custom-built Lanchester his great-grandfather bought in the 1920s. When the Maharaja died in 1937 the Lanchester did duty as his hearse. Like a Rajput El Cid, he was propped in the back of it, his sunglasses on his face, and driven through the streets of Alwar while his subjects wept.

Jitendra's father had died in extraordinary circumstances in 1976 during the Emergency declared by Mrs Gandhi. In response to growing dissent, she suspended the democratic process and assumed authoritarian power for nineteen months. Many people were summarily jailed. Inevitably, some officials felt licensed to act roughly and settle scores. Jitendra's father was hounded and humiliated. His water and electricity were cut

The Palace Theatre

off. Nobody was allowed in or out of his house, not even a doctor. In a state of acute depression, he instructed his household's veterinary surgeon to shoot him. The vet did so, and then turned the gun on himself.

I met Jitendra at the time of his marriage in Delhi. He was tall with striking Rajput features. His bride, Ambika Singh, had been marked out as a wife for him when she was a month and he a year old. 'She will make a lovely bride,' Jitendra's mother had said, looking into the pram, 'and you won't have to search far for a groom.' It was not exactly a traditional arranged marriage. Ambika's father, Brijendra Singh, said he would not tell his daughter, his only child, what to do. But Ambika and Jitendra were introduced in their teens and liked each other, as their families had hoped. Brijendra is a scion of the Punjabi princely family of Kapurthala and has made himself a name as a tiger expert and wildlife photographer. His wife, Dawn, is the daughter of Dutch missionaries. She and her sister were orphaned when they were little girls and were brought up in India in the family of L.K. Jha, a distinguished civil servant.

After a date for the marriage was arranged, Jitendra's grandfather became uneasy. He thought a winter date was inauspicious. Astrologers were set to their charts again and the wedding was rearranged to coincide with the first sparkle of spring. Brijendra planned a sumptuous pageant, a union of two princely houses, entering into his computer the details of priests, feasts, turban-makers, musicians, transport, tent-builders, garlands, singers, hand-painters and bangle-sellers. On the grass square in front of his house in Delhi, which usually rang to the shouts of boys playing cricket, an army of two hundred nimble Bengalis raised shamianas, huge yellow tents, for the wedding reception; and another tent for the ceremony itself.

Cobra Road

A thousand people were summoned to witness the spectacle and three days of ceremonies began on Sunday morning. A coconut was placed on each side of the front door. A wedding demands sunny colours and the house and garden, hung with marigold strands, teemed with aunts and and female friends wearing saris of gold, red, orange and peach. Servants bustled in saffron turbans.

I recognized one of them. Some time before, still in his bandages, Subedar Ali had told me about his amazing escape. He was a mahout, cutting fodder for his elephant in Corbett Park, in the Himalayan foothills, when he was seized by a tiger. Usually a tiger kills with its first blow, but Subedar Ali went down alive and fighting as the tiger straddled him, slashed at his back and ripped off his left ear. He saw his torn-off scalp in the tiger's mouth. Flailing desperately, he punched the tiger's head and bit its nose. At this moment, a fellow mahout, riding an elephant, rushed in and drove the tiger off. Subedar Ali was scooped up by his elephant's trunk and he clambered on to its back. In a forest office his wounds were crudely stitched with cotton thread and a rusty needle. His second stroke of luck was that Brijendra was informed immediately and had the mahout brought to Delhi to be repaired by surgeons.

In the golden light of the marriage tent, priests chanted mantras and began the process of separating the bride from her family. Ambika, in a scarlet-bordered saffron sari, sat with her parents behind a small altar strewn with rose petals. A conch was blown, incense drifted in the air and a priest sang a haunting song. Ambika's mother, grandmother and female friends ritually smeared her arms and face with a paste of sandalwood and turmeric which made her eyes smart.

The male guests of the bride's family, crowned with red turbans and carrying trays of fruit and sweets, drove from the house in white cars to see the bridegroom. He was installed in a

The Palace Theatre

spacious pavilion in the garden of a house a mile away. Seated on a red carpet, his hand on a curved sword, he wore a long coat of pale green brocade, gold slippers, a pearl collar and a red and green turban, surmounted by a jewel. Four men in yellow turbans and white tunics attended him, two of them waving whisks to move the air. Those who approached Jitendra made a circle with their fingers around his head, to ward off the evil eye. In accepting the gifts brought from the bride's house, he became irrevocably engaged. Five khaki-clad policemen were on hand, clutching sub-machine guns. They were there to guard Jitendra's mother who was a Member of Parliament. 'Actually,' she said to me, 'I don't like being an MP, but these days it is the only way to get things done. As Maharaja, Jitendra will have no power, but local people will expect things of him; so I hope he will go into parliament one day.'

We had lunch and departed. At Brijendra's house that evening, there was a reception and dinner. Men sipped Scotch and women sat on sofas and cushions, talking or dancing to the rhythm of drums. They chose bracelets from a tray and offered the palms of their hands to artists who painted them with henna in intricate curling designs. Next day, at dusk, the trees around Brijendra's house glowed with lights. Guests flowed into the yellow shamiana. The floor was laid with green carpets and set with white sofas. Soft lights shone on silk and satin saris, on hair of gleaming jet, on necklaces of gold, pearls and rubies. A shimmer of maharajas in silk and brocade coats formed a court-card pageant. Straight-backed military gents with crisp moustaches and regimental ties gossiped with men in dark jackets and jodhpur breeches. A band played. Servants bore trays of drinks and hot iron griddles of kebabs. The crowd pressed forward to see Brijendra symbolically wash Jitendra's feet. As priests chanted, Ambika appeared, heavily veiled, in a shower of rice and rose petals. She garlanded Jitendra with flowers, and he her. As she withdrew, cooks and servants opened shining dishes of rice, meat and vegetables, the wedding feast.

A little after three in the morning, the auspicious time for the marriage service fixed by the astrologers, the families and priests gathered in the marriage tent. A low altar was set with grapes, pomegranates and petals. Bells tinkled and a conch sounded. Four friends helped Jitendra into his golden coat and turban and fastened his sword. Ambika, her face concealed, wore a magenta sari, sixty years old, rich with jewels and silver, the gift of Jitendra's family. Priests lit a fire and began a ritual of chanting and blessing. The couple circled the fire seven times and fed rice into the flames. Smoke billowed into the air. Three hours later the ceremony ended with drumbeats and songs.

There was a breakfast of coffee and hot, spicy potato cakes. Cheeks shone with the tears of farewell. Brijendra's wedding present to Jitendra was a white car. The couple climbed into it, and, preceded by a police jeep with armed men aboard, and followed by a van full of wedding gifts, the convoy sped down the road to Alwar, a hundred miles away. In the days when princes ruled, Alwar was a state of more than three thousand square miles. As soon as the convoy crossed the border of the former state, a crowd greeted and garlanded Jitendra with marigolds and fired shotguns into the air. There were shouts of 'Long live the heir to the throne!'

Jitendra said that when he inherited from his grandfather he would not use the title of maharaja. 'I think it would be showing off. But people consult me over their difficulties, things like roads, schools and the water supply, and I want to help.' A brass band was playing as the couple entered the gates of the Phool Bagh Palace and there were more cheers and a dozen shotgun blasts. The people had their first sight of Ambika as she got out of the car and slowly took in the palace and its gardens, the new

The Palace Theatre

home of which she was now mistress. In keeping with custom, she had never seen it before.

❋

Perhaps more than any other people in India, Rajputs see the descendants of the old princely rulers as a link with their fading traditions, with the beginnings of history. The warriors have gone, the swords have rusted and the armour lies in museums. The code of chivalry lives in songs and history books, in the cenotaphs of kings and queens and in Rajput paintings famous for their depictions of romantic love.

It is not surprising that traditionalists among the Rajputs were dismayed by the marriage in 1997 of Princess Diya Singh, the only child of the Maharaja of Jaipur. Not only did she go against the convention of an arranged marriage and follow her heart, she also broke one of the old codes of Rajput life. This rule insists that men and women should not marry within their own gotra, or clan, because they are considered to be like brothers and sisters. But Princess Diya and the man she loved belonged to the same clan. Conservative Rajputs were outraged. They declared the families of both the bride and the groom to be beyond the social pale, saying that such a marriage was 'unheard of and unacceptable – there has never been such a thing in Rajput history'.

The Maharaja, a former army officer, made no comment at the time of the wedding. A week later, however, in a letter to a newspaper, he said that because of 'the gotra factor' he and his wife had not at first approved of the alliance, adding that the long delay in their accepting the marriage caused the couple unnecessary anxiety and mental stress. He accused 'misguided Rajput fundamentalists' of stirring up trouble, adding: 'I am constantly receiving threats to me and my family and my estate.

Cobra Road

I would like to ask these people: are laws for Rajputs any different from laws for other Hindu citizens of free India?' It was a collision between old and new, between an educated and modern-minded young Indian woman and the traditionalists who saw her independence as a wedge driven into a hallowed custom that was part of their identity. The angry roar sprang from the pain of men whose old certainties had been struck by modernity.

❋

You go to Jaisalmer, above all, for the unchanging look of the place, the view of an enchanted sandcastle across the duney distance, especially evocative at sunrise and sunset. In the great pan of the desert in the far west of Rajasthan the eye falls on no other feature. The city appears as magical now as it did to medieval merchants working the trade routes in one of the remoter parts of India. The streets and buildings inside its Jerusalem-coloured walls have the patina of centuries of wear by feet and hands; and buttocks have scoured out comfortable hollows in stone seats. The streets are crooked and narrow and the upper storeys almost kiss, as in Tudor London, permitting only thin oblongs of sky to show through. As I wandered, women sat in their scrubbed doorways talking to their neighbours a few feet across the street, and through open doors I noted cool and spotless rooms, the walls bright with whitewash and ochre paint, the kitchen pots stacked as neatly as soldiers' kit.

The city had changed, though, in the fifteen years since I had seen it last. It was crumbling. Some of its ninety-nine barrel-bellied towers had fractured, houses and walls had split and fallen, sandstone rubble lay in the streets. One of the palaces was a ruin, and a tower was breaking away from another palace like a slice from a cake. Some of the balconies and roofs of the

The Palace Theatre

old merchants' houses had crashed down as if touched by an earthquake.

For eight centuries, the inhabitants of Jaisalmer collected their water by hand, and open drains coped with the waste. Then a piped water supply was installed. Until the 1980s Jaisalmer's remoteness kept down the number of visitors. But a new air service and a boom in tourism led to the development of more hotels, restaurants, shops and desert tour agencies. More water was used, the drains could not cope and the underlying rock softened. In heavy monsoon rains a fifth of the historic buildings collapsed. Repairs were poor. Cement meant to hold sandstone blocks together was not only hideous; it made them less stable.

Conservationists and state and local authorities have sought to prevent more devastation. New drains have been installed. As I sat watching boys playing cricket in a cramped temple square I got talking to a young man who was sceptical about attempts to stop the crumbling. 'People want only to make money. Some owners of houses are bloody rich, but they do not have the idea of maintaining and repairing. They do not invest in the future because tomorrow is not in their thinking. These businessmen want profit today only.'

6

The Duty Baby

A BOTTLE OF MAHARASHTRIAN red wine stood on the table in the hotel room in Bombay, a greeting from the management. The word Welcome was piped in white icing on a wedge of dark chocolate cake. A cockroach emerged tentatively beneath the rim of the plate.

I went down to the bar where businessmen were drinking Indian whisky and beer. A pianist, wearing a green bow tie, a tuxedo and a wig like black plastic, crooned 'Tie a Yellow Ribbon Round the Old Oak Tree' in an American accent. A pretty and perky girl in a black dress joined him to sing 'Ma, He's Making Eyes at Me' with the forced jauntiness that often deepens melancholy.

At breakfast next morning the mingled smells of printing ink and omelette wafted from my table as I beachcombed the columns of the newspapers. The first item I read set the tone. A senior politician was quoted as saying: 'As far as the state of the nation is concerned, things are falling apart and chaos prevails.' A man and his wife had been beaten to death in a village in Bengal for practising witchcraft. The evidence, as usual, was flimsy: the unfortunate couple 'was suggested to be responsible for widespread cases of cough and cold'. A building contractor reported that a mahua tree he was about to cut down spoke to him, telling him to desist because it was holy. As his story spread, more than a hundred thousand people flocked to the tree, assuming that it had been possessed by a god with healing powers.

Elsewhere, I read, twenty tons of bark from jackfruit trees, and two tons each of clarified butter and honey, were being assembled to make a bonfire intended to propitiate the gods and ward off a perceived threat to the Prime Minister's rule. Police reported that a man they arrested had 'shouted unprintables'. An accident victim 'had been amputated'. It was noted, briefly, that three hundred fishermen were missing after a cyclone had passed by the west coast.

I went walking through the old Fort area. It was a Sunday and there was not much traffic among the tenements and offices. The side streets had been colonized by cricket-mad boys and the games overlapped each other like Olympic rings. Stumps were fitted to wooden bases and the boundaries were defined by rickshaw stands, food stalls and the railings on which trousers hung to dry. These boys, batting and bowling, fashioning their square cuts and googlies, were utterly absorbed in the subcontinental passion. The air was hot and heavy and, dodging a cover drive, I retreated to St Thomas's Cathedral, the oldest British building in Bombay, to read the marble memorials to those who 'fell a sacrifice to the climate', or, like one unfortunate, were 'sunk, at the age of thirty-three, under the hardships experienced in the discharge of his duty'. I heard the sound of a pillow fluffer, twanging his bow. For a fee, he opens up pillows and mattresses in which the cotton stuffing has become hard and matted and, with the aid of his bow, separates the lumps and makes the cotton fluffy again.

Near the Gateway of India, the grey imperial paperweight on the edge of Bombay harbour, I bought a ticket for Elephanta Island. It was a family day out, and the blue and white boat was crowded with parents and children sitting in rows on grey plastic chairs and eating spicy fried snacks. In the aftermath of the cyclone, the sky was steely and the sea had the ugly look of cold and greasy gravy. The boat lumbered away, biffing into the choppy water, and the city fell astern, a steeple on the skyline offering the merest suggestion of Sussex. The boat rolled on its way under the lofty bows and sterns of dozens of anchored freighters, container vessels and tankers, from Africa, China, Japan and Indonesia, black, green and red, as rust-streaked and battered as buckets. Sailors in singlets and shorts leaned on the rails and smoked, looking down on us.

At Elephanta, a shoal of fishing boats lay on the mudbanks, about eighty of them crowded together as if dumped there by a gigantic wave. They were stout wooden craft, the thick planks roughly sawn, flying the Indian tricolour and little pennants, and around them was a swarming activity. Teams of half-naked men and boys, a dozen to each boat, made a tremendous din scraping and bashing off barnacles with chisels and hammers, and slapping on anti-fouling paint with coarse brushes. They grinned up at us like mudlarks, while pot-bellied owners shouted instructions from the jetty. This long construction was only a few years old, but the concrete was prematurely aged, already crumbling like biscuit. It displayed the friability of things in India noted by Babur, the first emperor of the Mogul dynasty, in the 1520s – 'the air becomes very soft and damp. A bow after going through the Rains in Hindustan may not be drawn even; it is ruined; not only the bow, everything is affected, armour, books, cloth, and utensils all; a house even does not last long'.

I fell into company with an Australian water engineer. A guide attached himself to us and led the way to the cave temples, past the hard-eyed criminal monkeys which leapt like muggers at visitors and snatched food. The temples hewn from the grey rock were unlit and gloomy, but evocatively moody. The

Portuguese, with Christian disrespect for the magnificent eighth-century sculptures within, had hacked off their limbs and shot off their noses.

A limping scarecrow approached us, begging for rupees. The Australian said: 'I'll give you food instead.' Perhaps he had read somewhere that this was a proper and positive thing to do. He rummaged in his bag and found a few biscuits.

A scowl formed on the beggar's face and the guide laughed. 'He doesn't want food – he wants five rupees to buy a little bottle of whisky.'

The guide showed us the large tank which fills in the monsoon and provides water for the island's two thousand people living in a settlement three-quarters of a mile down the hill. The Australian cast his professional eye over the arrangement and told the guide that it would be easy and cheap to run a pipe to the village and set up a tap so that the women would not have to climb the hill to fetch water twice a day.

The guide stared at him. 'You see, there is no problem. The women carry the water because it is their custom.'

No doubt the tank was polluted. To a greater or lesser extent, seven-tenths of the water in India's rivers, tanks and lakes is poisoned, the main reason why dysentery and diarrhoea are so widespread and why so many children die in infancy. A quarter of all the people in the world who die of water-borne diseases are Indian. Two-fifths of the houses in Bombay lack safe drinking water. Most rivers are dumps for sewage and industrial effluent. Of more than three thousand cities and towns in the country only eight have full sewage treatment plants. Industries get away with polluting the water by bribing their way around the regulations or by ignoring them. India is one of the wettest parts of the world with more than enough rainfall for its present and future needs, yet drought is a serious and growing problem in many regions largely because of the mismanagement of water

The Duty Baby

development schemes, corruption and wholesale tree-cutting for fuel. There is no serious inclination to look ahead.

The ferry back to Bombay had a rough wooden privy projecting over the stern; but someone had supplied the captain with the wrong word and instead of Toilet it was labelled Kitchen.

The boat plunged heavily in the red sunset swell and the spray flew and soon the children started vomiting. At last, the skipper brought the lurching vessel alongside the grey stone steps beneath the Gateway of India. Before the crew could secure it, before they could get a rope ashore, passengers jostled impatiently to leave. Heedless of danger, young and old alike recklessly leapt the gap between the deck and the slippery steps as the boat rose and fell; just as airline passengers in India often spring to their feet as the plane touches down, anxious to grab their bags and flee. The young Winston Churchill, landing from a troop ship at Bombay, grasped at an iron ring as the boat suddenly dropped in the swell and dislocated his shoulder – 'an injury which was to last me my life, which was to cripple me at polo, and prevent me from ever playing tennis'.

But this scrambling haste was all of a piece with the urgency and energy of Bombay, the push and shove for opportunity, the frantic and impatient surge of a city whose favourite god is the elephant-headed Ganesh. He is the Remover of Obstacles, the god of business prosperity, jovial, chubby and baby-limbed. He has luscious twin wives and only one tusk, the other, depending on the story, lost in a fight or worn down like a pen in the writing of an epic. Ganesh rides upon a rat and, for protection, has a cobra for a belt. He is a brave sentry, posted at the doors of homes and temples, and, as the Lord of Beginnings, is always invoked at the start of journeys, projects and weddings.

So often I have been happy to depart Bombay, only to enter it again through the seething doorway of its airport with feelings of excitement, wonder and trepidation. In a way, I envy those who come under its sensual assault for the first time and experience its deluge of astonishments.

Everything ever written about this city is true. Newcomers gape, sniff, shudder, admire and unfailingly jot down in their notebooks the essential words of any Bombay portrait: filth, stink, mob, poor, rob, slum, shack, hope, star, film, rich, loot, luck, Scotch. Every year or so, someone chronicles the death throes of Bombay. Meanwhile, the skyscrapers of wealth shoot up like rhubarb in a midden.

There is no doubt about Bombay's edge of madness, or its optimistic spirit. It is glamorous and horrible and also absurd: the greatest city of India squashed into this inadequate pendant of land on the Arabian Sea. It has no Statue of Liberty but it gets the huddled masses anyway. The commuter trains carry more than twice their designed capacity, passengers clinging to the outsides, and falling to their deaths from time to time, yet there is always room for more. At busy junctions policemen hold ropes which they jerk to waist height to keep the crowds on the pavement; and when the lights turn green, the ropes are dropped and the people pour over the road.

Every day another thousand people squeeze in to swell the millions, like desperate survivors from a ship scrabbling on to a life-raft. By the year 2015 the population will be heading towards twenty-eight million. Slumlords exact monstrous sums for a space barely the size of a grave. Half the population lives in shanty towns and the rules are simple: work or starve. A man in a shack of sticks and plastic sheeting once told me of his hatred for Bombay and his life of grinding labour. 'So why not go back to your village?' I asked. 'Because I earn much more here,' he said. 'Bombay is terrible, but home is worse.' An executive said: 'I have lived, loved and hope to die in Bombay. In Delhi you are who you know. In Calcutta you are known by the books you have read. Here, what you do is who you are.'

The Duty Baby

To be on the streets of Bombay is to feel pressed and beset; though no mere visitor, no foreigner, can experience or even imagine the pressures and fears under which so many live. Perhaps it was inevitable that the political mastery of the city was secured in the 1980s by men whose movement harnessed resentments and anger and was the political manifestation of a snarl. Bal Thackeray, a former newspaper cartoonist, founded the Shiv Sena party in the 1960s to stand up for Maharashtrian people, the Marathi-speakers. He named it after Shivaji, a renowned Maratha warrior of the seventeenth century who waged war against the Moguls. In a familiar big-city story, with parallels in the immigrant heyday of New York and Chicago, Thackeray stood against the swirl of immigrants who were taking jobs. First, he articulated a Maharashtrian prejudice against people from the south. He founded a news-sheet in which he simply printed the distinctive south Indian names of people on Bombay payrolls. He moved Maharashtrians into jobs in textile mills and big hotels. With its control of some of the unions, Shiv Sena forged a good relationship with the businesses that financed it. Institutionalizing bigotry, it set itself against the old cosmopolitan style and flavour that were part of Bombay's greatness. It changed the city's name to Mumbai, which did not have the same ring to it (though most citizens continued to use Bombay). Later, the Shiv Sena orchestrated violence and turned its networks of tough young men against the Muslims who form a sixth of the city's population. The party worked and profited through riot, pogrom, threat and extortion. On the eve of an election, the *Indian Express* reported from a Muslim slum where people raised families in hovels five feet by six and where police had taken part in arson and looting. People would vote as they were told, for the Shiv Sena and the Bharatiya Janata Party, the Hindu nationalists, and they would be voting for protection. Elections here, the paper reported, were about choosing someone who would keep your killers away.

Still, Bombay's good intentions shine through. Walking in the streets one day, my ears filled with the city's roar, I found myself laughing in wonder at the signs on the roads saying: 'Avoid Noise Pollution'. I could not imagine that anyone in this jungle would take any notice of the pious appeal pasted on hoardings by a wildlife conservation group: 'Boys Grow Up To Be Men – Tiger Cubs Grow Up To Be Rugs – Help Stop Tiger Being Skinned Alive'.

An indefatigable civic mindedness, people setting their faces against all the odds, was demonstrated in the tiled toilet blocks built by Rotary clubs and others. I noted the plaque on one of these lavatories which charted its genesis:

Courtesy Dawood Shoes Under Auspices of Mumbai Citizens Committee Municipal Corporation of Greater Mumbai (Solid Waste Management Department) Beautification Sponsored by Inner Wheel Club of Bombay West 1996-97 Co-ordinated by Inner Wheel Public Services Committee.

I walked across the city, moving from pools of cool respite into the hot clamour and out again. The massive Victorian buildings are the stanchions of Bombay. They are grandfatherly now but still assert the confidence of the men who built them. The University, the old Town Hall, the Victoria Terminus station, the buildings in the aldermanic Gothic style, speak of Bombay's power. The Prince of Wales Museum is of 1920s vintage and the grandiose Reserve Bank is 1930s, but both are all of a piece with their Victorian brothers. In the forecourt of one of these immense old architectural lions I saw a notice which encapsulated an appropriate pomposity: 'Photography Of The High

The Duty Baby

Court Complex Is Forbidden Without The Permission Of The Hon'ble The Chief Justice, By Order Of The Prothonotary And Senior Master'.

I had been invited to lunch at the Bombay Gymkhana Club and afterwards, looking into the darkened room marked 'Siesta – gentlemen only' and seeing snoozers whiffling in comfortable chairs, was mightily tempted to ask if I could join them. But I took to the streets and within five seconds felt as flaccid as warm dough. At the pavement bookstalls, among the mass of paperbacks, I saw that the proprietors had trawled the Bombay deep and had brought up the libraries of long-dead sahibs and Indian scholars. Here for a few rupees were *The Pride and Love of England*, volumes of sepia photographs of the Lake District, pictures of oast houses in Kent, bulky tomes of anatomy and psychiatry. There were also remnants of the age of educational imperialism, a remarkable number of very old copies of Spenser's *Faerie Queen*, *Tom Brown's Schooldays* and complete sets of Sir Walter Scott's novels. They had sun-dried burgundy covers and the spines cracked softly when I opened them, releasing the faint suggestive smell of learning long ago. Such books were in the vanguard of the English culture that Thomas Macaulay, the historian, writing in the 1830s, advocated for the improvement of certain young Indians. His purpose was to create an élite of Indian gentlemen who would be 'a class of interpreters between us and the natives we govern, Indian in blood, but English in tastes, in opinions, in morals and in intellect'.

Walking on, I became pleasantly lost in streets smelling of sewers, fried sweets and pastries. Signs warned that 'Spitting Spreads Disease' and the pavements were plentifully spattered with gobbets of red juice projected by the chewers of betel quids. I came to a fishing colony of little wickiups built of scrap wood and sacking where boats were drawn up on the foreshore and lay tilted at an angle in the mud. Men squatted in the sand and dust playing cards on a cloth while boys untangled nets of blue and white nylon and women cooked on little fires. Half a dozen cricket games were on the go, the splintered bats tied with string and tape. I came upon a crowd of policemen shouting at people, ordering them to pull down their illegally built pavement shacks while women wailed and beseeched them to leave them alone.

I felt the usual relief at leaving and, looking forward to my return, resigned myself to the hellish chariot race to the airport. There are more than 800,000 vehicles in Bombay and it often seems that they are all bound for the airport. Every week, 1,400 more cars and scooters join the struggle, adding their molecules of carbon monoxide to the smog of 4,500 tonnes of poisons released daily into the Bombay air.

At the traffic lights the beggars waited for us to stop and then came hopping and crawling, bundles of grimy rags suddenly animated, displaying their sores. Their eyes sought mine. Once the gaze is captured the entreaties are hard to resist. Most of the pitches are organized by beggar leaders and some beggar families pay protection money to mafia gangs. Skinny fingers reached into the car like tentacles, tugging at my sleeve, tweezering the hairs on my forearms. There had been a complaint in *The Times of India* about the growing aggression of eunuchs, the way they spat and clawed and pestered for money at traffic junctions. The advice of the police was to shoo them away.

The driver growled at the ragged corvine shapes hopping around the car. I was aware that he was watching me in his mirror as they groped and wheedled. He did not want me to give any money. But I knew that in the end I would, because I always do; although I know the arguments that say you should not, that giving only spreads the plague, that beggars maim their children to make them more pathetic and, therefore, more efficient earners.

At last I fumbled for some money and gave it to an anguished woman with a lolling baby. The driver leaned over, flicking his fingers to drive the woman away, and he clucked his tongue at me in contempt.

'Sir,' he cried, 'that baby does not belong to that lady.'

'No?'

'Sir, it is the same baby as before, but it is passed around to make the ladies look more sad.'

It was the duty baby, a dirty, dribbling, sore, half-conscious pupa with mucous in its luminous velvet eyes. A child, all the same.

As the lights turned green, the driver flung us back into the maelstrom, back into the race. I glimpsed a slogan on a huge sign over the highway, but I could not tell whether it belonged to an advertisement or whether it represented in some crazy way the hope, spirit and energy of Bombay. There were just three words:

PROLONG SEXUAL PEAK

7

Where the Coconut Goes

LURED BY THE PROMISE of a different India, of a world apart, I flew to Kutch, the north-western peninsula of Gujarat. The plane landed at the Indian Air Force base at Bhuj, the chief town of the region, and as I descended the steps the heat struck its familiar stunning blow and perspiration prickled on my brow.

'The more you sweat in peace the less you bleed in war,' said a little Christmas-cracker sermon on a notice I passed on the way out. There must be a sub-caste of pencil-suckers turning out these beloved maxims.

A car was waiting for me, the ubiquitous 1950s Morris Oxford, endlessly reborn as the Hindustan Ambassador. The driver, Prakash, was an alert and amiable young man with a broad smile. I was relieved. He was going to drive me for a fortnight. Since there were travel restrictions in this area, which is close to the Pakistan border, I went first to register at Bhuj police station. A sign on the police officer's desk asked: 'Do You Believe In God?' But this required no response. After registering, I went to the Collector's office where the solemn clerks were benign and efficient and gave me a permit to travel in the villages.

Kutch is virtually an island, bordered in the north by the Great Rann of Kutch. Rann means wasteland and the Great Rann is a forbidding immensity of desolate black tidal mudflats, dried creeks and veins of salt merging seamlessly into the desert of Thar.

Little rain had fallen in the district in the past two years and the land we travelled was a cracked crust on which withered trees struggled and rocks lay like clinker newly raked from a furnace. Mongooses scuttled over dusty roads. Goats worried at the meagre wiry scrub, watched by boys wearing turbans piled up like laundry. Although parched and tormented, the landscape was also dramatic and entrancing, with a jingling traffic of sheep, donkeys and nomads; and punctuated here and there by convocations of cranes and flamingoes. Floating camels fastidiously trod the distant haze. The land is not entirely dry: monsoon waters are trapped by hard rock to form pools, and the low hills support a little farming. Nevertheless, life in Kutch has always depended on hardiness and ingenuity. A local guide book told me that for all the storm and drought of this region its people 'are not despaired . . . they have not yet cultivated the sense of absconderness'.

The people of Kutch alleviate harshness with their art and the celebration of their religion. A simple beauty characterizes their settlements. The pleasing round houses are tiled or thatched and the mud walls are whitewashed or painted pale green and decorated with entertaining geometric and floral designs of lilac, yellow and blue. It was a relief to duck through the decorated porticos of these houses. They were neat and spotless, sparsely furnished, with columns of gleaming brass pots. And they were cool, their small windows cunningly sited to catch and channel faint breezes. I passed a night in one and felt well-protected. The brilliant white walls were studded with glittering mirrors, the size of an old-fashioned half-crown, to ward off the evil eye. I was awake before dawn and saw the sun snuff out the stars.

Women wear the startling and welcome colours of desert

Where the Coconut Goes

flowers, their blouses brilliant with beads and mirrors, their cloaks scarlet. They tattoo their hands and arms. As they glide, their bangles, anklets and elaborate rings in their ears and noses tinkle like wind bells. Each village has its different skill. There are lacquer workers, weavers, dyers, block-printers, potters and cobblers. Others paint cloth with coloured pastes piped out like cake icing. Some fashion the bells which dangle on the necks of cattle and camels and compose the gentle carillon of the countryside.

From time to time in India my heart sinks when I see that another royal palace straddles my route. To see it or to pass it by? Surely not another seat of some priapic and self-indulgent raja, with his slopping bucketful of diamonds, his slurry of topaz, his golden bathtub, his silver nostril-clipper, his inevitable secret staircase giving access to his musky concubines? From gilded portraits the tubby forebears in silk and brocade, chests shining with imperial stars, gaze out at glass-eyed tigers from the golden age of taxidermy, at pearly palanquins, ivory chairs, jewelled howdahs, silver toy trains, golden umbrellas and racks of tarnished swords. I find myself nodding with precious metal fatigue and the gems begin to look like so much broken glass. But I like the solemn faces in the sepia photographs and the bookshelves with their encyclopaedias, their tiger-hunting manuals, the *India Year Book* for the 1930s, *The Wonder Book for Young Folks of India*, *The Golden Book of Ruling Princes, Chiefs and Nobles* and – 'Oh, thank you, just what I wanted' – the *Speeches of Lord Hardinge*. Some of the kremlins of India played their commanding roles in history and their appearance is striking: they are great feats of architecture and will. A few were occupied by principled men, innovators and improvers; but you need not look hard to find tyrants and grotesques, off their heads with gold and petty power. Many palaces are theatres without actors, empty stages, ghostly and decayed, their balding red plush membraned with cobwebs. Musty chambers, long fallen into desuetude, speak of jaded appetites, indolence and the banality of wealth.

Anyway, I thought I should not miss the Mirror Palace at Bhuj. Apart from the familiar stuffed beasts and portraits adorned with precious stones, there were English foxhunting scenes, studies of English beauties, rose-cheeked and *décolletées*, and a painting of Dame Adelina Patti, whose voice had enchanted a potentate of Bhuj. A framed letter to the Maharaja from Lord Mountbatten began 'My dear Friend . . .' The palace masterpiece was the hall of mirrors built by Ramsingh Malam, an eighteenth-century craftsman who had been shipwrecked in the Arabian Sea, rescued by a Dutch ship and taken to Holland. There he studied architecture and also glass-making and enamelling; and when he returned he passed his new skills on to artists in Kutch and the crafts flourish to this day. His hall of mirrors was a kaleidoscope, a pleasure chamber of white marble where the ruler lounged upon an island in a pool while fountains and musicians played and bards sang and dancing girls swayed. It looked exactly the sort of room that Hollywood in the 1930s would have dreamed up and I suddenly saw it in grainy black and white, with harem houris popping betel concoctions into their master's mouth to make him dizzy.

I went south over the long causeway that crosses the salty marshland of the Little Rann of Kutch. The skimpy shacks that stood far out on the mudflats were the homes of salt workers. Thousands of them were toiling out there, ground-down men and women pumping seawater into salt pans and harvesting the crystals after evaporation. They work from October to May, before they are driven away by the monsoon. It is a horrible life. Most of the workers are trapped by debt and interest payments and have sold themselves to salt merchants. They spend a life-

Where the Coconut Goes

time in bondage, as virtual slaves. It is a common story among the poor in many parts of India. There is a dash of bitter irony in the poverty and oppression of the salt workers of Kutch, for Mahatma Gandhi declared the salt tax imposed by the British as the iniquitous example of the oppression of the Raj. Indians were forbidden to make their own salt and Gandhi chose this as the issue for the greatest of his non-violent campaigns. His salt march from Ahmadabad to Dandi in 1930 was seen by his followers as a version of Christ's journey to Jerusalem. It was a powerful emblem of his long struggle, celebrated in statue, picture and film.

Many of the salt workers go barefoot because they cannot afford rubber boots. Certainly their bosses do not supply them. Over the years their feet are marinaded in the brine. They have noted, to their distress, that these pickled extremities are not reduced to ashes on cremation pyres, and what remains resembles charred boots, like the trunkless legs of Ozymandias. They feel doubly cursed: by the misery of their lives and by the failure of the final flames to dispose of them completely.

❊

At dusk I sat out at a table with some Gujaratis. The moon rose, the colour of apricot, and the stars swarmed. We drank bottles of beer, a breach of the law. In deference to the memory of Gandhi, its most famous son, who preached often against the evils of alcohol, Gujarat maintains prohibition.

'This rule is in Gandhiji's honour,' one of my companions said, running his finger down the condensation on his glass. 'You may also like to know that towns and cities in Gujarat are safe for women. That is in Gandhiji's honour also.'

Prohibition has made the smuggling of liquor a large and richly profitable business, carried on with the connivance of many police officers and state officials. Liquor consumption here is as high as in any other state in India.

'You see,' one of the men said, 'the sentiment that attaches to the name of Gandhi in Gujarat makes it impossible to repeal the law. The outcry would be tremendous. There would certainly be demonstrations, protest marches and strikes, and perhaps bloodshed. It is very easy in India to whip up crowds and passions.'

I had no doubt that he was right. Some politicians only have to snap their fingers to summon up a crowd to scream and face the whirling staves of the police. It says something about the enigma of Gandhi that, more than half a century after his death, at a time when the principles he stood for are largely forgotten, his name is still invoked as a moral force. On the other hand, I could not imagine any serious attempt to have prohibition overturned in Gujarat. Too many people are making money in the smuggling racket.

'With prohibition plus smuggling', my companion said, 'you have equilibrium.'

Hindu sacred laws condemned the drinking of alcohol, particularly among brahmins, the highest caste, who are meant to be pure and closer to God than others. Branding on the forehead and banishment to the mines were prescribed for brahmin transgressors. But Hindu epics and history are replete with tales in which brahmins, warriors, kings and gods drink freely; and classical poets wrote suggestively about the wine-flamed cheeks of women. Some state governments have banned alcohol for high-minded reasons, often in response to the demands of women who complain, with some justification, that many men drink the family money away. Some states operate a partial ban by declaring public holidays as 'dry days'. But prohibition is undoubtedly a serious cause of crime. Moreover, high taxes put legally manufactured liquor beyond the pocket of the poor.

Where the Coconut Goes

Millions of ordinary people therefore turn to illegally distilled hooch which is often poisonous and kills drinkers in their scores.

Towards the end of the evening, one of my acquaintances opened more bottles.

'One for the road?'

'One for the family planning,' another man said; and everyone laughed.

❂

The crown prince of Wankaner had asked me to have lunch with him next day in his palace on top of a hill. 'As far as tourism is concerned, alcohol is a difficulty,' he said, as we ate an exquisite bread-and-butter pudding at his long table. 'I cannot open a bar. Perhaps foreigners could get a special stamp with their visas, perhaps some way could be found to give concessions to people who do not belong to Gujarat. The problem is that because of the Gandhi tradition no political party has the courage to change things.'

After lunch he showed me the large trophy room filled with the mounted heads of animals, scores of them. He indicated an important-looking desk. 'From this', he said, with a wistful note in his voice, 'my grandfather ruled.'

❂

Each morning, Prakash made a temple of the car. He lit incense sticks stuck on the dashboard beside the picture of his protecting goddess and bowed his head to pray before turning round to me with a smile and driving off. At least we did better than the driver of a truck we saw one morning soon after Prakash's prayers: he had skidded off the road, spilling his load of dozens of lavatory units whose shattered bowls and s-bends lay across the highway in sparkling shards of blue, white and tasteful eau-de-Nil.

We drove fairly fast because roads in Gujarat are better than in the rest of India. The state government spends more money on them. Our horn trumpeted as we dashed past work gangs resurfacing the highway. Many of the labourers were barefoot women and girls, sweating their bodices black, moving in an endless chain, their faces made stony by fatigue. On their heads they bore wok-like metal dishes, brimming with tar and gravel, which they emptied on to the road to be raked and flattened by a steamroller. They worked under the eyes of a foreman, enduring a life sentence of unremitting hard labour, though the labour would make their lives quite short. Their tar-baby children, the futureless future slaves, played among the leaves on the road's dusty edges.

But in a few seconds the car was past them and the women's tattered saris fluttered in its wake. The tapestry of the landscape filled my gaze once again. Sitting there, it was easy to be beguiled. I rolled along on an endless ribbon, through the timeless India of villages and temples, past the snapshots of wells attended by women drawing water, in and out of the panoramas of cotton fields, cactus and acacias and the dark avenues of banyan trees, their long tresses reaching to the ground.

Beneath the veneer of picturesqueness and rural rhythms, many of the people I saw working the fields were landless and desperately poor, oppressed by feudal tradition and vindictiveness. The women who formed such charming vignettes at the wells were not always free to draw water when they wished. They were allowed to do so only at times dictated by their caste superiors, who did not want to be polluted by their presence. The land appeared to be fertile enough to my inexpert gaze, but I had just read newspaper reports that food production in many parts

Where the Coconut Goes

of Gujarat was well below the national average. I had read, too, that doctors at Wankaner hospital employed needles that were not sterilized, using them over and over, insisting that there was no money for disposable syringes. Health workers took vaccines with them on their tours of villages but were not equipped or qualified to perform any medical function other than to stick a needle into an arm. They also carried contraceptives on their tours, but were too shy to explain the use of them. A survey of schooling in Gujarat concluded that many teachers hated their work and, in any case, lacked the text books they needed. Politicians on their election rounds had promised to give schoolchildren a midday meal, but this pledge remained unfulfilled. The evidence of broken promises can be seen in many places. Small brick pillars standing in open spaces have a plaque on them recording that this or that honourable pooh-bah had laid the foundation of a factory or depot or irrigation project. Nothing has happened since. They are the pillars of deceit.

❁

Those flags I could see, like pennons on tall, thin sticks, marked temples, alcoves and simple painted stones in the corners of fields and beside lanes. These were the abodes of village deities called upon in prayers to guard the crops, animals and labourers in the fields against malevolent spirits. Hinduism is complete in its encompassing of the natural, the supernatural, the material and the spiritual. Wherever you go you are on a pilgrim road or close to a sacred hill or stream or homage-worthy stone or cave. To the hundreds of millions of village Hindus, living within the circle of their local beliefs, almost everything has religious significance and may be worshipped: rivers, of course, and springs, rocks, trees, pools, animals, heroes, the earth, sexual organs, the rain, the sun and moon and sky. The skies are constantly scanned for omens. The goddess of smallpox is feared and must be propitiated and, similarly, the deities of cholera, fever, plague, dropsy and the itch. In villages, dozens of local gods exist in the orbit of the central mother goddess. She is the symbol of life and death and fertility, the deity to whom the people make sacrifices and to whom they pray for rain, pregnancy and abundant crops. One calculation counts 333,000,003 deities in the Hindu pantheon, an extrapolation of the thirty-three gods numbered in the Rig-veda, the ten ancient books of hymns, scriptures and legends.

When I first visited India I thought that the true motif of the country was not the Taj Mahal or the elephant or the patient peasant behind his plough, but the crowd, the ocean of multitudes, teeming like spermatozoa. But another motif, an aspect of the unity of India, is the gigantic skein of pilgrimages, the interconnected threads of journeys of religious duty and spiritual longing made to places that are often very far from the pilgrims' homes. Far from declining, the numbers of pilgrims are increasing. No doubt this springs partly from the general increase in population; but sociologists and others say that religious belief among young people is growing, and speculate that this may be a reaction to insecurity and turbulent times.

Many millions of people travel for days or weeks to touch a significant stone, toil up a hill, shiver in a cave, scoop up water, immerse themselves in a river or amble clockwise around an idol or a temple: always clockwise, keeping the superior right side of the body closer to the object of worship. These are journeys of the body and of the imagination to the sources of spiritual energy and the grand junctions of sacredness.

Pilgrims count seven sacred cities, seven sacred rivers, seven sacred mountains and nine sacred pools. There are twelve major sacred sites of the lingam, the source of life, of the god Shiva. But in truth the places of pilgrimage are numberless. The legend of

Where the Coconut Goes

the goddess Sati, the wife of Shiva, tells that she was sliced up by a discus and that the pieces were scattered over India. Each place where a fragment of her body fell is a sacred destination of pilgrimage. But there is confusion and not much agreement about where the pieces fell. Some stories say five, some a hundred and eight. But more than a thousand towns and villages claim a piece of Sati, most of them asserting that theirs is the true site of the breasts and sexual organs. Mount Abu, in Rajasthan, claims the right breast, so does a town in Punjab. Ujjain claims an elbow. Other places say they are the resting place of the left breast, the left knee-cap, the right big toe, the ears, lips, teeth, hair, feet, hands and anus. A town in Assam claims the buttocks, so does a place near Poona. Another, in south India, insists it has three pubic hairs. Patna, chief city of Bihar, is said to be where the pat, Sati's loincloth, fluttered to earth. Kamakhya, in the blue Kamagiri hills of Assam, is the place where Sati made passionate love to Shiva and also where her vagina descended to earth. A cleft rock in a cave at Kamakhya, moistened by a stream which sometimes runs red with iron oxide, is one of the most venerated of Sati sites. In 1565, the heads of one hundred and forty men were brought on dishes to the temple here as an offering to Sati; and for many years her adherents gladly offered their lives in worship. The British stopped this human sacrifice in 1832 and goats were substituted for men.

Some pilgrimages take a few days to complete. Some take years. A pilgrim earns more merit if he travels in pain or discomfort, hopping or crawling. People who die during pilgrimages are considered to have earned an immediate ticket to heaven.

On the road to Rajkot, I glimpsed a man in a loincloth prone on the roadside.

'Please stop the car,' I said.

The man glistened with sweat. His body rocked in the hot slipstream of passing lorries.

Cobra Road

He was a pilgrim, travelling the hard way, moving a coconut, painstakingly, a few feet at a time. He placed a thin cushion on the edge of the road and prostrated himself with his middle on the cushion. The coconut was beside his thigh. With his right hand he reached for it and stretched his arm in an arc to put the coconut at arm's length in front of him, so that for a moment it was held by his fingertips in the way that a rugby player steadies the ball for the goal kicker. He rose, moved the cushion to the coconut and repeated the action.

After fifty yards, he got up, left the coconut, walked back and retrieved his mobile temple. This was a four-wheeled cart, like an ice-cream vendor's, painted orange and decorated with pictures of gods. A red pennant flew from a bamboo pole. The vehicle carried a cassette-player and a battered red conical loudspeaker, a paraffin lamp and stove, a torch and an umbrella, metal dishes and containers of sugar, milk and tea.

The pilgrim pulled his temple cart up to the coconut and recommenced his punishing progress. After another fifty yards, he stopped to talk. He had a ragged beard, grey hair secured in a topknot, a sacred red thread across a chest stained by tar and studded with pieces of grit.

Two trucks drew up in a swirl of stinging dust and their drivers climbed down. They approached the pilgrim respectfully, pressed their palms together in the namaste greeting, and bent down to touch his feet. He gave each one a blessing and then took down his stove and utensils and made tea for us all, boiling up milk and sugar and stirring in a handful of tea leaves.

He said he was fulfilling a vow. He prayed that a new temple would be built at Dwarka, on the Gujarat coast. This is one of the seven sacred cities and one of the four Holy Abodes of Vishnu, the preserver of order and, like Shiva, one of the major gods. In order that his prayers for the new temple would have greater merit he had vowed to move a coconut, in this laboured manner,

Where the Coconut Goes

from Dwarka to Bhuj, and back again. In Bhuj he would break the coconut at a temple, as an offering, and after two days' rest would set off with a fresh coconut back to Dwarka. The round trip took him eighteen months, he said cheerfully. He had been travelling like this for six years, backwards and forwards to Dwarka, and had vowed to do so for twelve. He would be sixty-six when he finished. 'I am a familiar sight on the road and, as you can see, lorry drivers stop for tea and a blessing if they have time. Otherwise they sound their horns in salute as they pass by. People respect my pilgrimage and give me food and shelter because what I do is holy work.'

He cleaned the tea glasses with water, put them back on his cart and smilingly bade farewell. He set out his cushion, lay on the hot road and, resuming his holy task, swung his arm to move the coconut another four feet towards the distant city.

❀

The best school in Rajkot is the Raj Kumar College, built in 1870 for the education of the numerous princes of Gujarat, so that they could assist in managing the empire. It is now a leading co-educational public school. It is a perfect piece of Victorian England, as if transported from Berkshire, with its quadrangle and cricket field and large parasols of trees. In the shade of a gulmohar tree rises the white statue of J.W. Coryton Mayne, principal from 1903 to 1923. The pose and expression suggested to me a man who believed in such cardinal principles as duty, punctuality, good grammar, fair play and a straight bat; a man who awoke every morning knowing he was doing right in India.

The second-best school is the Alfred High School. A marble plaque salutes its most distinguished old boy as 'Mahatma in the Making'. A painting in the lobby depicts Gandhi with Buddha and Christ. Gandhi was born in Porbandar on the Gujarat coast and moved to Rajkot at the age of seven when his father was appointed finance minister to the ruler of Rajkot, one of the numerous small princely states of Gujarat. In 1880, when Gandhi was eleven, he went to the Alfred High School. Two years later, he married Kasturba. The schoolboy-husband was an indifferent pupil, finishing thirty-ninth in his class in one year, and in his final year scoring four out of ten in reading, twelve out of thirty in parsing. The school's gloomy brown hall is a half-hearted museum with photographs of Gandhi's teachers and a dog-eared display of reports and attendance registers, with Gandhi listed as Mohandas K.

A helpful man told me there was more Gandhiana in the museum nearby and offered to take me there. But when we arrived we found it was closed because of a holiday. My guide fizzed with anger.

'You must be knowing in India', he said, spitting out the words, 'that every person wants a job in government because it is a life of holidays and idle chat and going for tea and not caring about the wants of the ordinary people and if ever a person comes before their desks wanting something they are going for tea and making them wait.'

In 1915, when Gandhi returned from his years in South Africa, a public figure, if a puzzling one, the British awarded him a Kaiser-i-Hind Gold Medal in the New Year's honours. That January he travelled to Gondal to be honoured with the title of Mahatma, or great soul, in recognition of his growing status as a religious figure. I was shown the cement plinth on which the ceremony took place. It stood in the yard of an ayurvedic medicine factory where more than two hundred men were pounding and mixing herbs and spices into tablets and potions. The air was prickly with the herby dust and smell. As a guest, I was taken to the temple in the compound and stood before the brilliantly painted image of a goddess while two priests chanted prayers for my health and wealth and one of them, with his thumb, pressed vermilion powder on to my forehead.

Gandhi arrived for his investiture as Mahatma in a coach drawn by four horses, but the crowd unyoked the horses and started pulling the vehicle themselves. Gandhi drew the line at this. People, he said, were not beasts; so he jumped down and walked.

The scholar who bestowed the honorific on Gandhi gave a gloriously ornamented address. 'Your fame, fresh as a jasmine flower in bloom, is being acclaimed by learned men. Your light of repute has eclipsed the enemies in your path. It is a matter of wonder how your widespread glory, sweet as nectar, fragrant as lotus, clear as a ray of moonlight, variegated like pearl, can pass through the holes of a man's ears. Scholars hearing of your fame wonder whether it is a nectar falling from the heaven upon earth as a remnant after the gods have drunk it. Or is it the juice of a flower dripping from the mouth of a bee tasting it in heaven?'

I stayed in the Maharaja's palace hotel in Gondal and the Maharani invited me for coffee in another palace nearby which I reached through a grove of lemon and lime trees. The Maharani was elegant, in a blue-green sari, and charming. Her room was guarded by a stuffed leopard and a mounted cheetah. The Maharani wondered whether, in these days of increasing Western sensitivity to the treatment of animals and the spread of 'political correctness', tourists would be dismayed by the trophies which adorn Indian palaces so abundantly. I said that stuffed leopards were part of the character and history of such places and should remain on show; that people knew that tigers were no longer shot for sporting fun; and that, in any case, tiger skins and snarling heads coincided with visitors' ideas of palaces and that they would expect to see them, just as they would expect to see swords, paintings, jewels and a good ration of splendour. She nodded, a little relieved I thought. I asked if people visited Gujarat for its Gandhi connections. No, she said, most did not know that he was a Gujarati. She told me she went to England for three months every summer, to a flat overlooking Hyde Park: it was too hot in Gujarat, and the hill resorts of India were too crowded. At her suggestion, I visited her husband's museum of classic cars. His favourite was stored in a plastic tent to stop rats eating its electrical wiring.

In the palace hotel that evening I sat at the head of a long table built for twenty and had a dinner of spinach soup and macaroni cheese and curry. I dined alone, although there was a uniformed waiter on my left, who stood throughout the meal to serve me, and another on my right to clear the dishes. A third sat in front of me, not eating but watching, making sure, I supposed, that I was properly attended.

Just before five o'clock next morning, as I lay in my princely brass bedstead, I heard film music and the piercing aria of an enraptured heroine. Somewhat closer, a repetitive temple chant began and bells and tambourines jingled an accompaniment. These sounds awakened the lion, or what I assumed was a lion, in his cage in the travelling circus encampment across the road. He emitted, not a roar, but a groan which seemed to sound deep in his gut, like a tuba in a cavern. This, in turn, alarmed the foolish peacocks in the palace grounds and they uttered sharp 'Miaow, miaow' cries, like children imitating cats. The dawn muezzin joined the swelling symphony, switching on the loudspeakers in the mosque, clearing his throat productively and launching his high-pitched call to prayer. Through all of this, cracking the wax in my ears, cut the whistle of a train. India was awake.

❊

Where the Coconut Goes

The lion I heard was obviously an African one and I had no doubt it was pathetic and moth-eaten. The last of the Asiatic lions are now in their final redoubt, in the Gir forest of Gujarat. This, in the end, is what might become of the tiger. Asiatic lions once roamed from central Europe through Persia and northern India as far as Bengal. In the last century British and Indian sportsmen shot them to the edge of extinction. They were wiped out in the Delhi area by 1834, one hunter killing around three hundred of them. By 1880 their population was down to about two hundred, but today, because they are not hunted, there are more than three hundred. The males lack the kingly manes of African lions and one theory suggests that hunters pursued those with the most handsome manes and thereby steadily reduced the quality.

Gir is a forest oasis in an arid region and, although it is the lions' last and rather small refuge, the encroachment of people and livestock threatens their survival. Forest dwellers poison lions because they eat their cattle. Pilgrims demand access to old temples in the forest, insisting on the right to worship in them and ignoring the authorities' attempts to limit their numbers. The respect accorded to pilgrims gives them considerable leverage.

I went for a drive in the jungle. A sign said 'Lions Have Right Of Way Here', but I entertained no hope of seeing one. It was the wrong time of the year and the grass cover was too high. The forest jeeps were noisy diesels and the guides, although enthusiastic, plainly knew little about the jungle. But the drive was enjoyable and the air was good and there were plenty of birds to see. At dinner that night I talked to the manager of the forest lodge about the people of the district. He himself was not a Gujarati. 'Many people in this region do not want to make much money,' he said. 'Like many Indian men I will work hard, economize and save to educate my son and see that my daughter is properly married. But here the shopkeeper will close at half past twelve and will not re-open until four. If I ask him the price of something at twelve-thirty he will ask me to come back at four. These people, you see, want to spend time with their families. They say that if they worked all day they would never see their wives and children. If a young man has a Walkman he is happy and he does not want for more. Boys around here do not want higher education. They learn the basics and leave school and get a job with the forestry department. It is modest, and for most of them enough.'

Next morning, while waiting in the forest office for my permit for the day, I watched a young blond Australian pit himself against the might of India. He was at the counter paying the admission and camera fees for himself and a group of companions.

'You've overcharged me.'

'No, sir,' said the forest official, pushing forward a chit, 'this is to pay.'

'Look, nine cameras at seven-fifty. That's sixty-seven fifty. So where's this extra fifteen rupees coming from?'

'Sir, this is to pay.'

The Australian pointed heatedly at the tariff board. 'Look, it says seven-fifty.' He was right. 'That's sixty-seven fifty. You've charged fifteen extra.'

He made a desperate and hopeless throw. 'I'm fighting for a principle here.'

The forester was unmoved. He had a winning card to play. 'There is new charge.'

The Australian faltered. He sensed the shadow of the elephant's foot over his head. 'Yeah? So when did that come in?'

'Some time back,' the forester said. He put the chit into the Australian's hand. 'This is to pay.'

When I returned from my morning drive in the forest, Mr

Where the Coconut Goes

Singh, the chef at the forest lodge, asked me if I had spotted any lion. When I shook my head he said: 'Not spotted? I shall take you. I adore the jungle.'

Sure enough, in the late afternoon, he presented himself as my guide and driver. He cut a dashing figure in his chef's uniform of white coat, check trousers and black-and-white check neckerchief. He jumped into the jeep and drove off in high spirits. He was utterly determined that I should spot a lion. It was his personal mission.

We drove this way and that, criss-crossing the jungle. 'This is good place,' Mr Singh said. 'Lion was seen here three days back.' Later, with less conviction, he paused at a ford and said: 'Lion is often here also.' The shadows lengthened, the sun sank and, with it, Mr Singh's spirits. It was quite dark before he admitted he was beaten.

'Today,' he concluded, 'there is not good spotting.'

At the hotel reception desk there were expectant faces.

'Did you spot?'

'No, I did not spot.'

'Sir, come back when there is better spotting.'

'Yes,' said Mr Singh, brightening, 'I will take you and then you will spot.'

❀

The astonishing stink of the fishing port near Somnath scoured out my nasal passages and made me gasp and blink. If it could be bottled it would be more efficient and safer than a British policeman's CS gas. It made me think of Dom Moraes's description of his distinguished father, Frank, going to edit *The Times of India* at an office near a fish-dock in Bombay, holding to his face a handkerchief soaked in eau-de-Cologne.

Small fish, in the process of becoming delicious Bombay

duck, were drying in the sun on lines strung bow to stern over the fishing boats. Motor tricycles dumped boulders of ice on the quayside and boat crews wielding heavy axes cut them into chunks and fed these into grinders which poured the ice into the holds. Those boys who were not squatting and mending nets played cricket on the foreshore. I watched the shipwrights building new dhow-like vessels on the beach, their graceful lines fashioned by eye and the distilled experience of centuries.

At noon in the temple at Somnath I found myself squeezed in a warm, moist crowd of people, their palms pressed together in prayer. Priests chanted and a youth beat a large drum with two sticks, the sound growing steadily louder, while younger boys struck bells with metal bars.

Through an archway I saw waves breaking on the yellow curve of the shore. The temple air was rich with the smell of the sea, of seaweed, drying fish and incense. The drummer was replaced by another who beat the drum harder and faster and chewed rapidly in time with his beat; and when he tired he was replaced by yet another who beat harder and faster still. It seemed to me that my bones were resonating to the beating.

The chanting, bell-ringing and drum-banging spiralled to an intense and prolonged storm and then, when it seemed to have reached an almost unbearable frenzy, an undeniable tension, it suddenly subsided. There was a moment of profound stillness, but my head was still full of the noise. Now the crowd pressed forward and offered coconuts to the priests gathered around the black knob of the Shiva lingam, one of the most sacred lingams in India. The nuts were smashed and the priests anointed the lingam with the fluid and scattered blossoms over it. Towards the back of the temple, student priests chanted prayers.

The worshippers began to disperse. On their way out, they passed their hands over the flame of a lamp and briefly touched their foreheads, cheeks and lips and smoothed their hair. Many

Where the Coconut Goes

of them paused to pray at alcoves containing images of Hanuman, the monkey god, and of Ganesh, the elephant-headed god of prosperity. Men knelt to offer a short final prayer and ducked their foreheads, and then each ear, to the marble floor.

Outside, close to the temple entrance, half a dozen policemen sat on chairs, Lee-Enfield rifles in their hands. The police have mounted guard here since 1992. In May of that year a mob of Hindu extremists and thugs, encouraged by members of the Bharatiya Janata Party, sacked the old mosque at Ayodhya, in northern India. It was a violent assertion of Hindu nationalism. More than a thousand people were killed in the ensuing riots. The armed police at Somnath were there to deter any Muslims who might wish to avenge Ayodhya; but their presence also symbolized those atavistic hatreds that cynical politicians so easily exploit.

Somnath has been a sacred city for thousands of years. In the eleventh century the fabulous wealth of its temple inevitably attracted Mahmud of Ghazni, the Afghan ruler who led seventeen looting raids into India, almost an annual excursion. Temples were treasure houses, filled with gold, silver and jewels, and Mahmud robbed many of them. The ferocity of his assault on Somnath in 1024 was etched into Hindu consciousness and to this day his memory is despised. Thousands of men were slaughtered and thousands more drowned when they ran into the Arabian Sea to escape the swords. Mahmud, an enthusiastic iconoclast as well as a looter, shattered the temple's celebrated Shiva lingam with a mace. The temple was destroyed three times and finally, in 1706, the Emperor Aurangzeb had it pulled down.

Some of the carvings from the ruins were incorporated into a new temple of honey-coloured stone completed in 1951. One of those who contributed to the reconstruction was Nathuram

Godse, the fanatic who murdered Gandhi in Delhi in 1948. In his will, written the day before he was hanged at Ambala jail, Punjab, the following year, he left a donation to the temple's dome of 101 rupees: such gifts are never in round figures. Godse had been the editor of two extremist Hindu publications, had come under the influence of the Hindu revolutionary Vinayak Savarkar and was among those incensed by the creation of Pakistan and by Gandhi's attempts to conciliate between Hindus and Muslims. The plotters were determined that Gandhi should die violently and they killed him ten days after bungling their first attempt. At his trial Godse praised Gandhi's service to India, adding 'before I fired I actually bowed to him in reverence. But even this servant of the country had no right to vivisect [it] ... So strong was the impulse of my mind that I felt this man could not be allowed to meet a natural death, so that the world may know that he had to pay the penalty of his life for his unjust, anti-national and dangerous favouritism.'

On the day of his execution, Godse chatted with prison officers and, when coffee was brought, said to the jail superintendent: 'Do you remember I told you once: "I don't mind the gallows, but I must have a cup of coffee before the swing"? That cup is here! Thank you very much.'

Godse, and his fellow conspirator Narayan Apte, took to the gallows a map of undivided India. Then, as Godse's brother, Gopal, described it: 'Nature embraced the two in gravitation and gave their souls a lift in her invisible chariot.'

Gopal was found guilty of conspiracy and imprisoned until 1965. He remained unrepentant. Nearly fifty years after the assassination he said to a journalist: 'It's not as if we went to Delhi to steal Gandhi's watch. That would have been truly sinful.'

8

Walking on Stilts

I crossed to Diu on the long causeway from the Gujarat mainland. The place is a curiosity, a dot of an island seven miles long, defined by the shining white towers of its Catholic churches and the grey and yellow sandstone ramparts of its fort above the Arabian Sea.

Like Goa and the little enclave of Daman, north of Bombay, Diu was a Portuguese colony for more than four centuries until 1961. In December of that year more than thirty thousand Indian troops poured into Goa, Daman and Diu, preceded by what the Indian press called 'a mighty thunder of artillery fire'. Apart from a naval skirmish in Goa they encountered virtually no resistance, took more than three thousand prisoners and restored the territories to India.

As liberations go, it was hardly glorious. But these enclaves were unendurable excrescences on the face of a country itself not long liberated from colonial rule and sensitive about its territorial integrity. The French had already seen that the game was up and in 1954 had ceded with dignity their once-profitable little baguette of a colony at Pondicherry. Antonio Salazar, the Portuguese dictator, was intransigent and would not return Goa, Daman and Diu. India's patience expired. The Soviet Union said the oppressed had been liberated, but otherwise world opinion was bitter. India had adopted a self-created posture as an advocate of world peace, and its sanctimony grated. In annexing the colonies, Jawaharlal Nehru, the Prime Minister, had acted against the principles of non-violence of which he was an apostle. Consequently, he was reviled as a humbug, a bandit and a Hindu Hitler; and cartoonists put a bloody dagger into his hand. India had explained its action, said *The Spectator*, 'with all the usual excuses that aggressors have used'. *The Economist* recorded: 'A sad day for the friends of world peace who had grown used to India as a neutral ally and Mr Nehru as their spokesman.' But there could hardly be any sympathy for Salazar.

As a colony, Diu was mostly useless, turning in very little profit. But in Portugal's sixteenth-century colonial heyday, when the monsoon drove spice-seeking ships to India, it had a position of command on the Arabian Sea. Indeed its viceroy was so convinced of its value that in 1545, when money was needed to rebuild its fort after a siege, he pawned his beloved beard as security for the loan.

Bronze cannon still point out to sea from the fortress walls and iron spikes bristle in the heavy door of the old magazine. Heraldic carvings and eroded inscriptions in Portuguese speak, or perhaps squeak, of a small colonial importance. The Portuguese influence survives in carnival, costume and cuisine, in guitar music and the Iberian feel of charming narrow streets and red-tiled houses of ochre, pink, primrose and green. Diu is a Union Territory, out of reach of Gujarat's prohibition laws, and its bars serve rum and beer.

I called on Mr Om Prakash Mishra, the Collector of Diu, who reigned from a large and well-ordered desk. Stacks of letters, anchored by glass paperweights, fluttered in the downdraught of a fan. A messenger padded in and out. Mr Mishra had only to raise his eyes to read on the wall opposite the Collector's creed:

Walking on Stilts

'A Collector should be learned, eloquent, dispassionate and impartial. His judgement should be only after due deliberation and application of mind. He should be a guardian to the weak and a terror to the wicked. His heart should covet nothing, his mind be intent on nothing but equity and truth.'

I had seen few men so contented in their work. As Collector, Mr Mishra was king in his realm, in charge of taxation, education, transport, development and tourism. 'Because Diu is so small I can supervise everything. Therefore, there is much less of red tape. I am also Chief Magistrate and I am happy to tell you my crime rate is virtually zero. Honesty and respect are strong here. I will give you an example. Suppose you mislay your sunglasses: I can assure you that someone will hand them in to the police station. I have never known such a peaceful place. The people have a strong sense of fair play. They are educated and clear about their rights under the law. Their view of me is that I am their servant.'

He presided over an administration in which local communities, organized on caste lines among Diu's forty thousand inhabitants, managed their own affairs and enforced standards of social behaviour. A man who got drunk and beat his wife, for example, was punished by the elected community elders with a fine; or he could suffer a form of banishment, his local shopkeepers refusing to serve him. A boy who dallied with a girl without intending to marry her, thus bringing her honour into question, faced a heavy fine. 'This system', the Collector said, 'is not recognized in law, but I accept it because it works.'

❁

To avoid the heat I set off before sunrise to climb more than three thousand stone steps to the summit of Satrunjaya, a hill in southern Gujarat. Many of my fellow pilgrims were of the elderly but game variety, like the doughty pensioners who take part in marathons. Some leant on staves and had the look of Gandhi setting forth on a protest march. The first half of the climb was very steep. White-haired women, as frail as sparrows, wheezing and arthritic, hauled themselves up by will-power, for they had no muscle that I could see. A cool breeze blew and the sound of the waking town of Palitana drifted upwards, strains of music, hawking, barking, bleating and crying. The disc of the sun emerged and slowly pushed away the counterpane of darkness to uncover the panorama of the valley. The top of the hill came into view and I saw some of the pale yellow pinnacles of the 863 temples rising from the summit ridges, the largest Jain temple city in India, like a fortress in a fantasy.

As the air grew warmer the pilgrims sought shade under the trees beside the steps, pausing for breath and sipping water before hauling themselves forward again. A cow toiled upwards, too, its scarred brown skin, stretched over its ribs, creaking like an old leather chair, the smell of its dung sharp in my nostrils. I reached the top in just over an hour and claimed my extraordinary reward. Here spread the spectacle of a city of the gods and, beyond, a prospect of mountains, of blue-green land stretching to the Gulf of Cambay and a silvery river threading across the plain. A man cracked a coconut and gave me the milk to drink.

I left my shoes at the gate and entered the temple city. A notice requested menstruating women to keep out. This is one of the holiest places of the Jain faith, a congregation of domes, cones and spires, fine carved columns and courtyards, temple after marble temple, some large, some very small, connected by mazy passages. The temples date from the eleventh century and are enclosed in massive defensive walls, a reminder that this place was sacked by the Moguls four centuries ago. Everything was pale and clean, the courtyards swept and dustless. There were thousands of images of seated gods, almost identical, bone-

Walking on Stilts

white, their hands folded in their laps, their faces set with glittering eyes, crimson lips and black eyebrows. Above the head of a snake god, seven hooded cobras reared to form a protective shell. Pilgrims prayed and sang softly. Outside, yet in a place of honour near the front gate, was the tomb of a Muslim saint who had defended the Jain temples. It was covered with a turquoise cloth and surrounded by dozens of small wooden cradles lacquered yellow, green and red, left there by women who had come to pray for pregnancy. On the cloth itself there were metal models of legs, ears and hands, the injured or diseased parts of the body for which pilgrims had asked for a cure.

Walking down the hill, I met half a dozen pilgrims squatting in doolis, cushioned trays swinging beneath poles and borne along by two sweating men. The task was evidently hard labour. Some of the bearers were resting, drawing breath before the next stage, while their cargoes, a couple of them rather plump, sat cross-legged and fanned themselves. To a pilgrim, reaching the temple city here is as meritorious as visiting all of the other Jain sacred places combined, even if others perform the grinding work of carrying them there. It was the first time I had seen people transported in such a fashion, but there was a time when the man-powered litter was common: Captain Seymour Burt was carried in a palanquin for 1,200 miles from Bombay to Simla in 1838. It was powered by a team of sixteen bearers, working in relays, at a rate of thirty miles a day. The captain complained, of course, that the bearers exacted a 'rascally charge'.

Returning pilgrims descended into a street busy with horse taxis, fruit and drink vendors, mooching black pigs with bristly backs, inquisitive cows and pestering children. A man resting under a tree with his wife and two children dabbed his brow and smiled at me. 'It's a lovely religion, isn't it? We are not Jains, but we come up from Bombay every two years to make this pilgrimage.'

Because Jain ascetics swear not to kill any creature, a number of devotees resting in a canteen wore face masks that prevented them from inhaling insects and gave them the look of conferring surgeons. Some Jain monks do not go out after dark in case they should step on insects. Strict adherents of the religion used to walk on stilts to reduce the chance of squashing beetles underfoot. Members of the purist 'sky clad' sect go naked, believing that clothing traps insects and increases the desire for possessions. They never touch money. Most Jains have avoided farming because ploughing kills insects. Many have prospered in banking and the cotton trade, and their wealth has paid for some of the most beautiful temples in India.

There are only three million Jains but their influence is far greater than their numbers would suggest. Jainism began as an austere reform movement about twenty-five centuries ago. Its traditions are particularly strong in Gujarat and were imbibed by the young Gandhi. He counted a Jain poet, Rajchandra Mehta, as one of the three most powerful influences on his thinking: the others were Leo Tolstoy and John Ruskin. Gandhi accepted the Jain teaching of ahimsa, non-injury, non-violence, and always insisted that its political application, passive resistance, was a matter, not of weakness, but of discipline and toughness. He accepted, too, the tolerant Jain doctrine that truth cannot be narrowly and dogmatically defined, that it is multi-faceted and that no religion by itself offers the sole road to salvation. He put the Jain emphasis on self-reliance at the forefront of his teaching. He never adopted the extreme measure of wearing a mask, but he was drawn to the asceticism, prolonged fasting and meditation of Jain monks. He embraced austerity. Later, one of his disciples, looking wryly at the amount of money needed to support his social and political organization, joked about the expense of keeping Gandhi in poverty. In 1921 the man who had once ventured at being an English dandy, and

Walking on Stilts

worn white flannel suits and top hats, took to the homespun simplicity of the dhoti and never wore anything else.

❋

In the florid light of the late afternoon, heading north along the Gulf of Cambay, I left the main road and came to Alang. I had not heard of it before, and it was not on the map. A chance remark at lunchtime that day – 'Oh, it's the largest ship-breaking yard in the world' – led me there. I changed my route, sensing a spectacle.

The road into Alang was narrow and broken and busy with lurching trucks. On each side of it, and along its tributary lanes, sprawled scores of yards and depots crammed with great stacks of furnishings and equipment taken from ships. Some of these enclosures were filled with sofas, doors, chairs, tables and bunks. Others were covered with ranks of refrigerators, water closets and baths, and kaleidoscopic banks of mirrors. There were hundreds of eccentric towers of dinner plates, soup bowls and pots and pans, mottes of lifejackets, yards full of capstans, lifeboats, pumps, engines, cranes, winches, instruments, anchors, hawsers and chains with links the size of a man.

All of this was the prelude to one of the extraordinary sights of the world. Along a four-mile crescent of sandy beach, more than a hundred and fifty ships had been driven ashore. Among them lay the behemoths of world shipping, gigantic brown-red supertankers, enormous container vessels, cruise liners and vast freighters. I was looking at a slaughtering yard. Armies of men were tearing the ships to pieces, eviscerating them, felling the funnels and derricks, hauling out the engines and machines, stripping out the woodwork, instruments and cables, peeling off the hull plates, slicing up the decks, sectioning keels and frames.

Cobra Road

The towering hulls made insects of the thousands of helots swarming in and out of them. Illuminated in showers of sparks, the bodies ran with sweat, the whites of the eyes were stark and the faces seemed seared and half-mad. The spectacle suggested something primeval, hunters hacking at the carcass of a dinosaur or slicing into the body of a monstrous whale. There was a tremendous racket of hammers and chisels banging on steel, the hiss and crackle of oxyacetylene cutters, the throb of crane engines. In front of the ships' bows rose hills of steel sheets and beams, brass fittings, copper pipes, chains and cylinders, into which cranes dipped like vultures. The work was ceaseless. Thousands of men laboured around the clock and as one ship was reduced to its last rivet another was driven ashore at high tide.

A dozen years ago, Alang was a hamlet on a quiet beach. Then a young man set himself up as a breaker, with one ship, and the business developed. Shipowners turned to Alang as labour costs increased in established ship-breaking yards in Taiwan, China and elsewhere. Alang expanded rapidly and very profitably, meeting India's huge appetite for steel. As we watched a crowd of men attacking steel beams, a marine engineer said to me: 'If you could somehow put the air here into a box, it would be worth money: it is full of metal dust. This business has made men rich, and no breaker has let down his bank. When it started the breakers did not know much. They just went for the steel. Then they became wiser and separated out the copper and other metals.' He forecast that Alang would continue working as long as there were ships on the ocean. 'At any one time there are hundreds of ships in the world that are worn out and have to be broken up. When a ship reaches a certain age, say about twenty years, the insurance costs go up and it becomes less economical to run. About four hundred ships are broken up along this beach every year. There is no real competition between the breakers because they know that there are

Walking on Stilts

plenty of ships waiting for a space.' All of this is highly satisfactory for the central and state governments which draw revenues from the business, and for the officials and politicians bribed by the breakers.

Alang is a frontier town, populated by young men who have flocked here from all parts of northern India in the hope of earning twice the money they could get anywhere else. The top men, who use the gas cutters, receive two or three pounds a day. The working conditions are hazardous. I was told that on average every month four men are killed, ten are injured so badly that they never work again and a hundred suffer burns, broken limbs and small wounds such as the loss of a finger. Many of the deaths and injuries are caused by explosions of gas cylinders and of gas pockets left in the hulks. Thousands of workers suffer not only from malaria but also from respiratory illnesses caused by the polluted air. Because of the complexity of safety laws in the West, it suits many shipping companies to send their worn-out ships, laden with poisonous materials like asbestos, to ship-breakers in India and Pakistan where safety rules are lax.

The worker-ants of Alang have no voice. Exhausted after their shifts they flop into huts in the shanty towns that have sprung up to house them. They lack clean drinking water, a regular electricity supply and proper latrines. Sewage flows directly into the sea. Some time after I left Alang I read a news item about the working and living conditions there. 'Compared with their lives back home,' said a spokesman for the ship-breakers, 'this is heaven.'

❀

The word palace conjures up the idea of magnificence, but the Utelia Palace south of Ahmadabad, where I spent a couple of

Cobra Road

days, is a working country mansion, about a century old, and comfortable rather than luxurious. It is the commanding building of a fortified village of about three thousand people. From my room above the courtyard and stables there was a view over brown roofs and temple-studded fields to a distant river. I saw the cattle driven out in the morning and dawdling back in the late afternoon. In the days when this landscape was the domain of the Thakors of Utelia, it was a district of fifty-one villages.

'My family ruled here for three hundred and fifty years,' said Thakor Takht Sinh. 'We used to take half the crops and in return we looked after the people. We protected them and provided doctors when they were ill and took action in times of calamity, like a drought. We sorted out disputes. We were judge and jury.'

I had already seen the two jail cells built into the gatehouse: the ruler had the power to lock up a man for a year and impose a fine of up to a thousand rupees.

'The important part of it all', the Thakor continued, 'was that we had responsibility. Now we are farmers with five hundred acres and although we have no power, and our relationship with the people has changed, I think we are respected. An affection persists, and so does a sentiment. This palace remains a central point, a focus of the community. As you can see, it is in the heart of the village, not at a remote distance. Today, in our place, there are bureaucrats, and people complain that there are difficulties in getting these people to act. They say: "You used to own us, but now nobody is our owner." By that they mean they could knock at our door, that someone would listen to their troubles and take action. Overall, there is disappointment at the way politics have turned out.'

The Thakor was courteous and humorous. He had been educated at the Raj Kumar College in Rajkot and at Mayo College in Rajasthan. 'They were schools for princes which instilled into us the idea of ruling and serving the people. The British were good

Walking on Stilts

at certain things, like strictness and punctuality. They also taught respect and that, I am sad to say, has all gone now.' He took me to the room where portraits of his ancestors hung, proud men wearing cockaded turbans and fine brocade coats, strings of pearls around their necks, their feet in embroidered slippers. Here was a full-length portrait of his grandfather, the last thakor to rule Utelia, wearing the two medals he received at the Delhi Durbar in 1911.

Next morning, a villager showed me the local sights, a small workshop where young men cut and polished diamonds, a primary school, a gushing hot sulphur spring and several temples. He also took me to a samadhi, a small stone memorial, and told me its story. 'Ten years ago, when he reached the age of sixty, this man announced that he had had a dream in which a god had called him. He told his family: "I will be here today, but not tomorrow." He dug a hole in the earth, about four feet deep, and sat in it and, quite soon, he died. This samadhi honours him as a holy figure.'

Around midday, nine of the village elders arrived at the palace and were greeted on the veranda by the Thakor. They were fairly prosperous men, cotton and wheat farmers, wearing loose white shirts and trousers and turbans of crimson, white and powder blue. They rolled out a blue-striped cloth in the veranda's shade and sat on it, side by side, facing the Thakor's chair. They chatted and joked and puffed bidis, small cheap cigarettes. After some minutes of lively talk, one of them produced a thumb-sized black pellet of opium. He put it into a small steel saucer, poured on some water from a jug and rubbed it with his forefinger to dissolve it, as you might an Oxo cube. The opium, I was told, had come from Madhya Pradesh, delivered in a pouch like a jockstrap. The elder took out a wad of raw cotton, dipped it in the brown liquid and moulded it with his fingers into a cone. He dripped more water into it so that the opium solution soaked through, like filtered coffee, into a bowl. Over the next twenty minutes, and watched carefully by the other men, he repeated this process several times until the bowl was half-filled with a clear coffee-brown filtrate. Then he rinsed his right palm with water, poured a small puddle of opium into it, and offered it to the first man in the line. The man bent forward, dipped in his tongue and licked it up, then washed it down with water. The server washed his palm again, charged it with opium and moved to the next man. The last in line washed his own right palm and offered a puddle of opium to the server. It is an old ceremony: the Emperor Jahangir took opium from the hand of his own mother and grew to love it.

The elders gathered on the veranda to take opium twice a month. 'It is better for a man than wine or whisky,' one of them said. They explained that it was a social ritual, a matter of fellowship, something that men mature into. 'As you can see,' said the Thakor, 'they are all respected and respectable men.' I asked them what Gandhi meant to people today and they discussed the question for a few minutes before coming up with a consensus answer. 'Gandhi gained us our freedom and will always be remembered for that. But after the British left we were saddled with politicians who were interested only in filling their bellies and their wallets. So the legacy of Gandhi has been squandered.'

The following day, as I was packing to leave, there was a knock at my door. There stood the Thakor, smiling, every inch a gentleman, my laundered shirts over his arm.

❂

Some of Gandhi's ashes were immersed in the Sabarmati River at Ahmadabad, near the ashram he founded on his return from South Africa. When he was not travelling or serving a prison

Walking on Stilts

sentence, this was where he lived for twelve years. In those days the ashram was on the rural and peaceful edge of the old industrial city but it has long since been overrun by the modern sprawl. Outside the gates of the ashram, the fumes and thunder of traffic promise nothing but a headache. Nearby are a petrol station, a car showroom and a large motorcycle emporium full of the new scooters that exemplify the burgeoning of the middle classes. Although it is small, unstable and vulnerable, the scooter is, nevertheless, family transport. The father drives, and between his knees stands his son. Behind him perches his wife, elegantly side-saddle, her sari or dupatta scarf fluttering in the slipstream. She cradles her new baby, and behind her sits her brave little daughter. In and out of the anarchic traffic they weave, and my heart is in my mouth just to see them go by, a cork in India's rushing tide.

'Sir,' cried the rickshaw driver, dropping me off at the ashram, 'you must be giving me extra money. Please be giving a hundred rupees.'

'Why?'

'Sir, because I am a Christian.'

Gandhi would have laughed.

For all the noise outside, the ashram retained the atmosphere of a sanctuary. When I walked in, quite early in the morning, sunlight filtered through the cover of neem and mango trees on to pale red buildings. A few elderly people in white clothing dozed on the veranda of the old guest house. Pigs foraged at the back of it. One old man, wearing wire spectacles on his hazelnut skull, and bearing more than a passing resemblance to Gandhi, nibbled a frugal breakfast. Women swabbed stone steps and floors and bent at right angles like gleaners to sweep the sandy ground with brooms. There was a prayer space beneath a tree overlooking the river, and a notice said that here 'the hallowed voice of many a sermon of Gandhijee still lingers'. To my left along the river I could see the bridge into Ahmadabad and the silhouetted traffic of buses, high-sided trucks and undulating camels.

A picture on the veranda of Gandhi's red-tiled house showed him wrapped in a shawl, meditating, his head haloed by the moon. His room was Spartan: pale blue walls, straw mats on the flagstones, a spinning wheel, a low writing desk and a paperweight of the three monkeys who are blind, deaf and dumb to evil. Most of the artefacts are replicas.

Gandhi's ashram was financed by Ahmadabad mill owners and was based on the experience of communities he had set up in South Africa. Under his direction, the regime was simple. The disciples ate sparely, meditated and turned their spinning wheels every day to fashion the threads that kept them in touch with village life and showed their commitment to ending caste distinctions in clothing. Gandhi, meanwhile, wrote and debated his theories of non-violent resistance, self-denial, the power of truth and spinning-wheel economics. But the supposedly simple life was also challenging. Gandhi's insistence on bringing a family of untouchables into the ashram almost shattered the experiment. Most of the disciples felt defiled by them and were angry with the Mahatma for offending deeply seated beliefs and prejudices. Kasturba, his long-suffering wife, was one of the protesting rebels.

Mr Desai, one of the ashram's part-time guides, remembered that 'everything was in Gandhiji's eyes, big eyes with a steady gaze. His body was thin, yet he could walk very fast; and he had a quiet voice which he never raised. You know, I was behind him in Delhi when he was shot. He was walking quickly because he was late. I saw Godse bow to him. One of the girls with Gandhiji said: "We are in a hurry." Then Gandhiji was shot. Everyone knew something was going to happen.'

I asked him if Gandhi were half-forgotten. 'Jesus Christ hasn't

Walking on Stilts

been forgotten, has he? No. Gandhiji set ideals exceedingly hard to live up to. He offered a new and enlightened way to India, but the nation has become corrupt from top to bottom and the leaders have forgotten the people. My faith is that God will send another Gandhiji.'

The ashram, which is partly a museum and library, has more than thirty-four thousand of Gandhi's letters in its archives. A photograph of him in the library is captioned: 'My life has been so public that there is hardly anything about it that people do not know.'

Gandhi himself laid bare his life and thoughts in his discourses and confessions, his copious correspondence and autobiography. One of the most famous passages of his autobiography relates that in 1885, when he was sixteen, he was making love at the moment his father died. The anguish endured. He was troubled by guilt and by his sexual desires for most of his life. He forswore love-making when he was thirty-six, by which time he had been married for nearly twenty-four years. With this renunciation he intended to find a transcending spiritual strength in keeping with the Hindu teaching that the conservation of semen, the vital force, is essential for mental strength. He began to believe that his diet stimulated the desires that troubled him for years and he experimented constantly with different foods. Many of his followers were deeply shaken when he confessed that he slept with naked young women. Two of them were his great-nieces and another was his personal physician. The practice, he said, was intended as the extreme test of his resolve and purity as a celibate. He admitted to it because he felt concealment was dishonest.

Nothing was ever easy with Gandhi. He was sometimes severe with his wife and demanded painful sacrifices from her. He himself admitted that he could be cruel. He posed difficult questions and even to those devoted to him he often seemed quirky, harsh and radical. It remains something to marvel at that in its struggle for independence, India channelled its hopes and ambitions, its mass of contradictions, splintered loyalties and prejudices not into a drum-beating warrior, a thundering orator or nascent dictator, but into a man Churchill derided as a 'naked fakir', an ascetic stick-insect in a dhoti, a cranky and difficult man who travelled third class, believed himself to be God's instrument and, as a social and religious reformer, took on not only the British Empire but India and its traditions as well. He seems a distant and almost mythical figure now, hardly the parent of modern India. Many of his ideas have blown away in the wind and were discredited even while he lived. India would certainly have achieved freedom without his efforts. The forces of history would have ensured that. But Gandhi transmitted to the mass of people gifts of immeasurable value: an inspiration, an identity, dignity, an idea of India, a part in the great play.

9

Shouting at India

BACK IN DELHI, I ducked out of the tumult into the Imperial, one of the city's colonial hotels, whitewashed and stately on the outside, polished wood and brass on the inside. The garden was a tranquil dell and I sat on the veranda by the lawn. A waiter in a white tunic and a turban crowned with a starched fan brought me a beer. It was brewed by Inertia Industries, a name that perfectly matched my afternoon mood. Indian beer contains glycerine to give it body and a better appearance. I had heard that in large enough quantities this can make you unwell or a little crazy.

After I had eaten my lunch of chicken tikka the scraps were swiftly cleared by one of the brown kites which hang around the rooftops of the hotel and swoop like Stukas on unattended plates. A sudden shadow, a startling rush of air and the raider soared in a thrilling parabola beyond the rank of tall royal palms. Circling slowly in the thermals, kites are the constant witnesses in the Indian sky. Those stationed at the Imperial have learnt to wait for that final clink of cutlery and the leaning back in the chair that indicate that the luncher is content.

The newspaper I read as I sipped my Inertia carried a tribute to a cricketer under the headline: 'A True Master of the Willow'. Indian sports writers still enjoy the terms and phrases which have vanished from British writing. Here and there you can see the cricket ball called the red cherry; and it was in Indian newspapers that I first saw snooker players described as cuists. In the political news, I read that the Uttar Pradesh government had seventy-two members of whom sixteen had criminal records. A dozen members of another state government had criminal histories and the police, who had formerly been out chasing them, had been reassigned to act as their protectors.

I was touched by the story of poor Lizie, only twenty-five years old, who became seriously ill on the train from Delhi to Kerala. A doctor examined her but there was little he could do. Lizie died in her seat and her friend Biju was distraught. When the train reached the next station the doctor told the stationmaster who told the Government Railway Police Force who sent a posse of men to remove the body. This is where the Indian public stepped in. Biju did not want his dead friend unloaded and taken to a morgue far from home. He preferred to travel with her to their destination. His sympathetic fellow passengers surrounded the police on the platform and stopped them getting their hands on Lizie. The police tried to push through the crowd. But passengers from every carriage joined the throng and barred their way. They shouted at the police that 'rules are man-made' and if they, the passengers, did not mind travelling with Lizie why should the police and the railway officials object? The argument continued for two hours and the authorities finally relented. Compassion and democracy triumphed. Perhaps there was a flicker of Gandhi's flame, too. Biju, the loyal friend, was allowed to take poor Lizie home.

I walked the pavements for a while. A serpent-wallah's reedy pipe would squeak half-heartedly and a cobra would be nudged into action in its basket, only to flop, in sleepy detumescence, as I passed. To the rapid clickety beat of a drum, dancing monkeys were poked into life and made to perform like tiny tired strippers. Thin women flicked spindly brooms at little mounds of spittle-stained leaves, fragments of bread that even the gutter dogs spurned, shreds of cow dung, coconut whiskers and fruit peel. The sweepers seemed like links in an eternal relay, moving the litter heaps and acrid dust from one end of India to the other.

Some shouting caught my attention. A couple of Western men, wearing the multi-coloured circus pantaloons favoured by many tourists in India, and with beaded pouches on strings around their necks, were arguing with a taxi driver. India has a way of magnifying, intensifying and distorting emotions and incidents, and you have to watch for the signs that you are becoming unhinged. One of the early symptoms is shouting.

V.S. Naipaul recalled that, during his first exploration of India in the 1960s, 'I was shouting almost as soon as I entered government offices'. His patience nearly exhausted by a fiddling bureaucracy, he found that the mere sight of clerks engaged in the futile work of sorting bundles of paper was more than he could bear. He wondered if the heat was indeed making him unhinged. Paul Scott, travelling in India to gather material for his Raj Quartet novels, stayed in a village where he had to come to terms with excreting in a field like everyone else. 'It was a severe strain on my civilized liberal instincts. Towards the end of my stay I found myself shouting.'

I have seen many shouting tantrums. Young tourists shout with the best of them. 'You can't treat me like this,' they cry. 'I don't need this.' Overcharged by taxi and rickshaw drivers, they dispute pennies with poor men, shouting like the blimpish sahibs of old. Anything to do with money, flying or official documents shortens tempers, so that banks, government offices and airports are prime shouting sites. I remember a usually affable Englishman who, while talking to an unhelpful official at Delhi airport, suddenly exploded.

'Bloody hell!' he roared. 'I shall report you. Give me your name.'

'My name', the official shouted back, 'is bloody hell!'

A friend admitted that after a long spell in India he found himself raising his voice to an airline clerk in Ottawa, until his wife soothed him, saying: 'Darling, it's all right. It's Canada, not India.'

India has its ways of breaking strong men. Its bureaucracy is a game of long snakes and short ladders. A British guide to doing business in India strongly advises: 'NEVER lose your temper'. Officials and clerks who guard the bureaucratic labyrinths are the descendants in spirit of the torturers of the royal courts who would sew their victims into the slippery skins of newly slaughtered animals and watch them being squeezed to death as the skin shrank in the sun. Slowly down the Ganges is exactly right. There is no other way.

No doubt the enervating heat undermines tempers. Nerves become overwound like the elastic of a model airplane propeller. The irritation count soars with the approach of the monsoon. In the days of the Raj many British people felt that one more monsoon would finish them off. It is not just the climate. There are also the extremes, the paradoxes, the immensity, the assaults on the senses, the way that India so often seems inside-out, its raw side to the front.

Just as alcohol shrinks inhibitions, so India dismantles the armour of restraint and reveals the shouter beneath. It can be humbling and humiliating. Naipaul remembered that his shouting was often received with a cold courtesy that reduced him to shame and exhaustion. But Indians shout, too. Nehru once tutted that a shouting MP had lowered parliament to the level of the bazaar. Now screaming and bellowing are the regular currency of political exchange. Some politicians roar like toddlers in a supermarket. A Cabinet minister famously stormed into the Delhi telephone exchange in 1986 brandishing a gun because he could not get a call through to Bombay. The retaliatory angry protest by telephone operators cut off Delhi from the outside world for three days. But there was a certain sympathy for the minister in his fit of madness.

There is something in the nature of India, too, that profoundly exasperates. It encourages people to believe that if only the country were grasped by its lapels, or its throat, and thoroughly shaken, it would improve. It brings out the latent Peter the Great: he would not leave old Russia alone and dragged it for its own good towards the better world he envisioned. His belief that beards symbolized backwardness led him to station barbers at city gates to cut them off. Recently, the authorities in Delhi sent teams of barbers into the slums to cut the inhabitants' nails to prevent the spread of disease. An official agreed that manicures would not actually limit infection but thought they would instil a sense of hygiene. Meanwhile the people await the clean water and drainage that would make a real difference. Similarly, some lawyers would like to throw off their Gray's Inn gowns, black coats and neck bands, which they think are symbols of colonial rule, as if new clothes would improve a legal system notorious for delays and injustice.

It was a version of the Peter the Great impulse, evangelical out of exasperation, that drove Sanjay, Mrs Gandhi's bullying younger son, to rush into slum-clearance, enforced vasectomies among the poor and a hopeless tree-planting programme. Some people still think he had a point, that what he did was necessary. 'The bloody country needs discipline,' they growl, seeing anarchy all around them. But population control, the state of the poor and the disastrous destruction of forests are matters too serious and complex for sporadic fervour. The fear that Sanjay spread made birth control a political taboo for several years. When health authorities began to take it up again, I went to see the work of a rural birth control centre. At the decorated gateway was a large colour portrait of Rajiv Gandhi, by then Prime Minister, framed by foil packets of condoms, each neatly fixed with a pin.

As saintly as he was, Mahatma Gandhi was also mightily exasperated by his countrymen. He was appalled by the dirt he saw everywhere and was obsessive in his lifelong campaign to get rural India to improve its excretory habits and build latrines. There was something evangelical, too, in the films I saw when I first went to cinemas in India. These were short official films depicting anti-social behaviour and urging people, when in public, not to spit, urinate, pick their noses or vigorously scratch their groins. From time to time, Indian newspapers and magazines publish anguished articles on the theme of the ugly Indian, of a society corroded by cynicism, corruption, dishonesty, dirt, a lack of civic sense, self-righteousness, the obstructions of clerks, the failure of education; and much else.

The evangelical imperative, the belief that somehow India could be shaken and changed, drove many of the administrators of the Raj. While some loved India for itself and did not want to change it much, others believed in a divine mission to reform, in an aggressive civilizing, in making benighted Indians see, like it or not, that only discipline could lift them from their poverty and moral squalor. These district officers and other lapel-graspers were fundamentalists and patriarchs and absolutely certain of their superiority. They flung themselves into the struggle. Recently the Bharatiya Janata Party, the Hindu nationalist party, which has prospered as the Congress Party has declined, has reached for the lapels in pursuit of an illusion, an attempt to redefine Indian identity by fitting a majestic and intrinsic diversity, all the defining plurality and paradox, into the rigid template of a Hindu state.

Among hopeless crusades, I have seen people make it their

Shouting at India

personal mission to teach India to drive properly or to form an orderly queue or to use the car horn more sparingly. My own useless battle, perhaps a sign that I am becoming unhinged, is to ask in restaurants and hotels for the thunderous music to be turned down.

'Sir, I am the manager. What is the problem?'

'The music. We cannot hear each other speak.'

'Sir, I will see what I can do, but it is hotel entertainment system.'

Once, in a hotel in Bhopal, I tried to turn off the music which appeared to be blaring from the radio beside the bed. The off-knob did not work, so I removed the front of the set with a screwdriver in order to disconnect a terminal. Kneeling, I found myself looking through the wiry intestines of the radio at a pair of hairy naked legs in the next room.

Disconnecting the switch made no difference. The noise still filled the room. I went down to the front desk to see what could be done.

'Sir,' said the receptionist, 'music is playing in entire hotel and all guests are liking.'

❂

Early on crisp winter mornings, in the first sparkle of the sun, I used to drive across Delhi to play squash. The city lay between dreams and wakefulness. There was little traffic: some camel drays up from the country, a few trucks and rickshaws, a bus listing like a drunk. Chowkidars, the night watchmen, nodded in gateways, sunk in their khaki greatcoats. Taxi drivers slumbered on the back seats of their vehicles in the taxi encampments beneath the trees. Men struggled stiffly out of sleep, perched on charpoys and prodded smoky little fires of sticks and leaves. They puffed at bidis and hugged themselves inside their shawls. The way they tied their headscarves around the chin put me in mind of the Queen at Sandringham.

One chilly morning in January I greeted the marker, the man who looked after the squash courts.

'Good morning.'

'Good morning, sir. May I warm your balls?'

'I beg your pardon?'

'Sir, may I warm your balls?'

'Ah. Oh. Yes. Certainly.'

I gave him a couple of squash balls and he held them in front of the glowing bar of his electric fire. A cold ball has the bounce of a dried prune and a game cannot begin in earnest until it is warm, a state usually achieved by thrashing it around the court.

The morning drive is no longer the pleasure it was. Delhi's growth has been explosive. In a few years it has become the fourth most-polluted city in the world. Clear light and blue skies are rare and the leaves of the trees are coated with grime.

'It is you Westerners who worry about pollution,' an Indian businessman said, 'but our lungs are used to it.' Still, one of the characteristic sounds of modern Delhi is a persistent coughing and throat-clearing. Almost a third of the people who visit a doctor do so because they have difficulties with their breathing. The incidence of lung cancer is twelve times the national average. For much of the time a smoky haze lies over the city. India Gate and the dome of the Presidential Palace, the landmarks of the New Delhi designed by Edwin Lutyens and Herbert Baker, are visible only through a thick muslin of smoggy mist. The Jumna River has become a poisonous stream. I walked over one of the bridges and down the embankment to the home of an elephant keeper who hired out his beast for ceremonies and festivals. He said he no longer took his elephants to the river to bathe because it was too polluted. 'Now we have to fetch water from a well,' he said, 'but the elephants would prefer to splash in the river.'

Little is done anywhere to reduce pollution. Khushwant Singh, the writer who has lived in Delhi for much of his life and is one of its distinguished chroniclers, said that 'pollution is now beyond control'.

Khushwant's life has been a mirror of the modern history of India and of Delhi. He was born in a small village in Punjab, in 1915, a few weeks after Gandhi returned from his twenty-two-year stint in South Africa to begin his campaign for Indian independence. New Delhi did not exist at that time except in the minds of its architects who envisaged it as an Anglo-Indian Rome that would endure for a thousand years. The city was rooted in the older Delhis – seven, eight, twelve: historians argue over the number – built under the protecting wall of the western ridge and close to the Jumna. Every conqueror knew that Delhi was the heart of things, that there was no holding India without control of this fulcrum city of the northern plains.

Four years before Khushwant was born, George V, as King-Emperor, presided over the Delhi durbar of 1911, the Indian celebration of his coronation, a never-to-be-repeated spectacle of imperial pomp. Ninety thousand rats were killed to make the site more salubrious, and on it rose a silken city of luxurious pavilions and marquees, of lawns and avenues, covering twenty-five square miles. The King wore a suit of white satin, a purple-lined ermine mantle and a diamond crown. A 101-gun salute boomed. Bands brayed and sunlight blazed on the cuirasses of wheeling cavalcades. Twenty thousand British and Indian troops paraded in gorgeous patterns of khaki, yellow, blue and crimson. Clinking and coruscating, jewelled princes paid homage to the enthroned King and Queen as attendants flicked yak-tail whisks at imaginary insects. Keeping a policeman's watchful eye was Eric Handyside, the future hero of the Frontier.

Cobra Road

The King spoke. He revealed the secret that he had kept even from his Queen: Delhi would henceforth be the capital, displacing Calcutta where adventurers had cut their first rich slice of India. He laid the foundation stone of a new city intended to assert Britain's imperial permanence. In celebratory mood, he went on to Nepal and shot twenty-one tigers.

The field of vanities where the King and the princes postured survives like the temple of an extinct cult, reclaimed by the relentless jungle. The King-Emperor presides. His nine-foot marble statue looks out over tamarind trees and the rusty gates of a park, over tangles of bushes and unkempt grass. In a semicircle behind him are twenty-three crumbling red sandstone plinths, twelve feet high, on which once stood the statues of viceroys and governors. Only four statues remained when I was there: of Lords Chelmsford, Reading, Irwin and Hardinge, in robes and knee breeches; all, like the King, slightly chipped.

After the durbar, surveyors declared the site utterly unsuitable for the new Rome, exhumed the foundation stone and took it by bullock cart to the new location. Khushwant Singh's father, Sir Sobha Singh, and his grandfather, Sujan Singh, were builders and transporters who had helped to recruit Indian soldiers to fight for the British in the First World War. Their reward was to be included in the group of Punjabi contractors who profited handsomely from the building of New Delhi. They shrewdly bought land very cheaply. It was then on the outskirts, a wilderness where jackals and leopards still roamed; and it was long ago overtaken as Delhi spread across the plain.

British clubs excluded Indians, but Sir Sobha Singh joined the Gymkhana in Delhi after Lord Willingdon, the Viceroy, said Indians should be admitted as members. 'But it was an ordeal for my father,' Khushwant said. 'The Englishmen at the club were always pleased to accept the drinks he bought them, but no one bought him a drink in return.'

Shouting at India

When Khushwant was a schoolboy he met Gandhi. The Mahatma fingered the material of his blazer and asked him if he would not prefer a garment made of Indian, rather than British, cloth. Khushwant was educated in Delhi and Lahore and left for London to train as a barrister, seen off by hundreds of friends and relatives. In England he courted a fellow Sikh, Kaval Malik, and married her in Lahore in 1939. A river of champagne flowed at the reception and one of the fifteen hundred guests was Mohammed Ali Jinnah, founder of Pakistan. At Partition, Khushwant saw Lahore burn. He and his family fled to Delhi.

He was a diplomat in London before turning to writing. His novel *Train to Pakistan*, published in 1956, is one of the very few by an Indian to describe the savagery of Partition. The subject is too raw to attract many writers. The book was not filmed until fifty years after the events it described. 'So much blood and sorrow,' Khushwant said. 'Fifty monsoons can't wash them away.'

His prolific output as novelist, historian of the Sikhs, magazine and newspaper editor, popular and acerbic columnist, has made India more accessible. He is also a humorist in a country where it is not easy to be one because so many subjects, religious and social, are dangerous tinder. He thinks Indians have a sense of fun but not of humour. He is a true reporter, always curious. Descriptions of birds, flowers and trees adorn his writing. He taught himself botany and bird recognition because he was ashamed as a young man to realize he lacked the vocabulary of nature. Into his writing life he once fitted a six-year stint as an MP.

He has cultivated the persona of a Scotch-drinking ladies' man, summed up in the title of one of his numerous books: *Sex, Scotch and Scholarship*. He certainly likes women and they like him. He loves Scotch, too. But the regimen he has followed for many years is strict. He gets up before five o'clock, listens to the

Cobra Road

BBC news and starts writing, always in longhand. He drives to the Gymkhana to play tennis, then returns to his writing. Every evening he drinks three whiskies and holds court for a few friends. He has rejected the Delhi way of entertaining, the very late dinner, ravenously consumed after hours of drinking. When Khushwant invites someone for a drink at seven he means seven and scolds late arrivals. But he is a merry man, a life-enhancer, who sits in a chair in the corner, his saffron turban untidy, his feet on a stool, enjoying the words. After drinks and talk, dinner is served, three or four simple dishes. Everyone leaves by nine and Delhi's most sober playboy is soon in bed, with a book of ribald stories to ease him into sleep.

He is proud to be a Sikh, although he calls himself agnostic. During the 1980s he strongly criticized the Sikh terrorists fighting for a separate state. They put him on a death list and he has been guarded ever since. He protested furiously when Mrs Gandhi ordered the storming of the Golden Temple in 1984. When she was murdered that same year, and Hindu mobs launched a pogrom against Sikhs, Khushwant and his wife fled to the safety of the Swedish embassy.

❋

Khushwant Singh's father and grandfather built part of the railway line to Simla that hoisted the lords of the Raj and their camp followers to a pastiche of Surrey high above the roasted plain.

For the best part of a century Simla was the most powerful small town in the world, summer capital of the Raj, a place known in ancient Hindu texts as the Land of the Gods. Here in their private Olympus, for seven months of the year, the imperial administrators ordered the lives of a sixth of humanity. Lord Dufferin, when Viceroy, thought it absurd – 'a place a child might dream of after seeing a pantomime'. He himself lived in Viceregal Lodge, a stranded Scottish baronial pile. I noted the inscription on the sundial in the garden stating that 'Madras or Railway Time is 12 Minutes Fast of Simla Mean Time'. Railway Time, used in drawing up railway timetables for all of India, was an alternative name for Indian Standard Time. Until national synchronization, cities also kept their local times, and Bombay was thirty-nine minutes behind IST. Nepal, incidentally, still runs ten minutes ahead of Delhi time, a horological assertion of identity.

Simla has the appearance of a town created from a mail-order catalogue, as if people chose houses from pictures, picking out 'The Dorking' or 'The Stoke Poges Tudor'. Viceregal Lodge, I fancied, was 'The Speyside' and Christ Church, the colour of clotted cream, was from 'The Taunton' range of country churches. Complete with Town Hall, clock tower and Mall, Simla was a fantasy among the Himalayan cedars and yellow roses, scenery painted for a stage.

Indeed, the Amateur Dramatics Club was the social heart of things and the whole place was a theatre of English middle-class manners and pretensions on the edge of Tibet, an alpine setting for riding, racing, picnics, dances, flirtation, seduction, bitchiness, sycophancy and cliquery. Lockwood Kipling, Rudyard's father, noted Simla's 'strong light-brigade of sportive matrons'. Kipling, the studious young reporter in a white ink-spotted suit, scribbled 'Simla people frivol' and was branded 'bumptious' and 'a subversive pamphleteer' for his caricatures. Simla was rigid with protocol, and Indians, of course, were kept at a distance. Princes were admitted but things sometimes went too far: the Viceroy had to 'have a word' with a prince who dressed his dogs in dinner jackets and had servants wheel them about in rickshaws, like sahibs.

One look reveals the preposterous reality of Simla, that it

required prodigious human and equine muscle power to get the people up the hill, to move them around in rickshaws, to ferry up their gin, cigars, snooker balls and theatrical wigs, to lift their tons of state documents and rubber stamps, to keep their inkwells brimming. The Raj moved up to Simla in March and returned to the plains in October or November. Before the railway was built in 1903, the sheer scale of the baggage columns, all the elephants and horses, would have been envied by a Mogul invader. Here at 7,000 feet the rulers kept the people and the country at a distance, isolated and insulated from the India which lay far below their noses.

At first glance, when I arrived, there seemed to be a heap of rusted corrugated iron on the hillside, as if a landslide had carried buildings away. But as the mist cleared and the town took shape, I saw how houses, shops, offices and winding lanes clung to the hill. With streets this steep there are few fat men in Simla. The parallel population of monkeys swarmed and scrabbled over the buildings, drumming and scratching on the corrugated roofs, swinging over the doorway of a building which bore the most dreadful sign in town: 'Office of the Government Examiner of Questioned Documents'.

Now, spelt Shimla, it is the capital of Himachal Pradesh, crushingly overcrowded, polluted, scarred by ugly buildings, a pint pot with a quart of traffic. 'When the Raj ended,' said Raja Bhasin, a Simla writer, 'people could not leave the town fast enough. The old way of life just drained away. Then Simla was rediscovered. It became a government town and people moved into the old British houses. For Indians the architecture is exotic and we have plenty of brown sahibs now, enjoying a touch of the old lifestyle, interested in preserving the old buildings. And Simla, after all, is part of Indian culture.'

A conference of government officials was going on. Cars dashed to and fro, red lights flashing. Leather-jacketed bodyguards lounged against walls, fondling Stens. It was doubtful whether the officials were really at risk or whether their gunmen were much more than status symbols. The sound of a siren or the flashing of a red light usually has little to do with helping the injured or tackling crime. It is part of the theatricality of power and status in a country whose hierarchy has VIPs, VVIPs and VVVIPs.

A friend of mine, feeling in need of comfort, once went to a VIP lounge. The receptionist said politely: 'Sir, this is for VIPs only.'

'But I am a VIP.'

'Sir, may I ask who you are?'

'I am His Excellency.'

'I am sorry, Your Excellency. Please come in and would you sign the book?'

'Certainly,' he said, and wrote: 'His Excellency.'

From Simla station – 'Ticketless Travel Is A Social Evil', said a sign – I took the little train down to Kalka to get a connection to Delhi. Monkeys scattered and grumbled as we wound through the tapestry of forests, villages, streams and temples, through scores of tunnels and over hundreds of bridges. I looked down on blue and yellow houses, their red roofs speckled with the yellow of ripening corn cobs. The train stopped at neat, brightly painted toy stations, gay with flowers, where notices informed me that 'The Allah Of Islam Is The Same As The God Of Christians And The Ishwar Of Hindus'.

❦

In Delhi's Lodi Gardens I heard the sound of organized laughter, a regimented Ha, Ha, Ha, Ho, Ho, Ho. Paths wind through groves and circle the domed tombs and mosques of the Lodi dynasty which ruled Delhi from 1434 to 1526. The gardens are

Cobra Road

in the heart of the Delhi-of-the-avenues, the district of trees and spacious bungalows laid out by Lutyens and Baker. Couples come here to court and hold hands. Once, I found some letters and envelopes scattered on the dewy grass and, curious, saw that they were the smudged and rejected replies to a newspaper advertisement for a bride.

Schoolchildren sit in circles for open-air history lessons. A few young men and women run around the paths, but mostly people walk for their morning exercise. Retired military officers stride as if crossing the parade ground, striped cravats at their throats, swagger sticks in their hands. Government secretaries and politicians are keen Lodi walkers. I often see a political figure accompanied by three or four Black Cats, soldiers in black uniforms, armed with sub-machine guns. They are, indeed, rather feline, tall, skinny and long-legged with small heads and moustaches and cat-like faces, so that they have the look of Korky in *The Dandy*; and they are the antithesis of security, for they only draw attention to their charge. Compared with the ownerless street mutts of India, the pedigree dogs that walk around these paths are canine maharajas. At a dog show, I saw an owner wave his hands furiously in front of a television cameraman. 'Do not film that judge,' he shouted, 'he is a liar and a cheat.' In the mornings men and women come to exercise and to sit, eyes closed, in meditation. In an interview, a foreign journalist asked Mrs Gandhi, when she was Prime Minister, whether she meditated. 'Oh, yes,' she said, 'I find I can meditate during this interview.' Groups of forty or fifty men and women squat on mats by the tombs obeying the commands of their yoga instructor. On his command, because it is a healthy thing to do, they shout with laughter. Ha, Ha, Ha, Ho, Ho, Ho: the Lodi laughing club.

The taxi driver did not know the way to Gandhi's deathplace. He had not heard of Birla House. Gandhi spent the last five

Shouting at India

months of his life in this colonnaded white mansion with its lovely garden. Ghanshyam Das Birla, a banker and industrialist, had been an admirer for more than thirty years and was one of the wealthy benefactors who saw greatness in him. In the turmoil that followed Partition Birla House was an oasis. Gandhi prayed and talked. Such was his moral grandeur that he had extinguished violence by threatening to starve himself to death unless the machetes and clubs were laid down. But he was a fragile dam against the torrent of hatred. His preaching of communal reconciliation and visits to Muslim refugees enraged Hindu extremists.

Just after five o'clock on the afternoon of 30 January 1948 he left his room for his usual prayer meeting, resting his arms as always on the shoulders of his two great-nieces, whom he called his walking sticks. The room is as he left it: a carpet, a spinning wheel, a low white table, a mattress and cushion.

The few dozen steps he took are marked as red stone footprints on a path beside the lawn. He was anguished, torn by the fact and the violence of Partition. A photograph in Birla House shows him talking to Jinnah in 1939. Jinnah is elegant in a three-piece suit, a cigarette in his left hand, his right held out in argument. Gandhi faces him, in shawl and dhoti, his peasant's willow staff in his left hand, his right hand, too, outstretched. The picture speaks of the distance between them.

The red footprints turn to the left and ascend five steps to the lawn. The last footprint is a left one. Gandhi knew his life was in danger, but refused protection. 'If I am to die by the bullet of a madman, I must do so smiling. There must be no anger within me.' As the crowd pressed in to seek his blessing, Nathuram Godse emerged. Gandhi's palms closed in the namaskar greeting which means: 'I acknowledge the divine in you.' Godse shot him three times. The photograph of the dead Gandhi in Birla House is captioned: 'The assassin of the ages came with unholy design and lodged hot lead in the flesh of the man who had known no enemy.' Gandhi's followers saved Godse from attack and later sought to keep him from the gallows.

I tagged along with a party of schoolchildren as Gandhi's story was related to them. Every child learns that Gandhi was the father of the nation. The primary school books about his life are like illustrated Bible stories. Kuldip Nayar, the writer and former High Commissioner in London, was a young reporter when Gandhi was murdered. He hurried to Birla House. A picture of Gandhi hangs in his home. 'Gandhi lived to be disappointed,' he said. 'Today the India that follows him is very small. He was so extraordinary, though, that people in the future will not believe that such a man ever trod the earth.' Khushwant Singh reflected and said: 'Some things he did were asinine, but were part of his humanity. When it came to the great issues, what was morally right and wrong, he never deviated. He has become a national mascot. But he remains a point of reference. People still ask: What would Gandhi have done?'

❃

Approaching the border between Haryana and Uttar Pradesh we passed a line of more than a hundred stationary lorries. The drivers were queueing to pay freight taxes. It was a slow business. Truck crews squatted in circles, playing cards to while away the time, and others worked on their engines or changed wheels.

As we moved slowly by, three men were touting for rupees in the road. 'Dancing bear,' they called into the windows of passing cars, 'video, photo, dancing bear.' They tugged at the strings that passed through the nostrils and palates of a trio of sad, shaggy brown bears. The holes had been made with red-hot needles. The animals' necks were rubbed raw by collars attached to chains.

Shouting at India

Vrindavan, our destination, sixty miles south of Delhi, is the goal of one of the popular pilgrimages of India. It is the legendary birthplace of Krishna, one of the most adored of the gods, famously charming, a slayer of demons, his dark skin rendered blue by painters. In a popular story, related in erotic detail, a forest here was where Krishna had his fun with the gopis, the village women who looked after the cattle. The magical sound of his flute made them frantic with desire and soon he was making love to one of them, the bewitching Radha, the very sight of whom had made him tear off his clothes. Afterwards, ever mannerly, he set out to pleasure the remaining gopis. Since there were 900,000 of them he divided himself into 900,000 men and the forest rang to the jingling of the gopis' bangles and ankle bells.

For many years Vrindavan has been a refuge for widows escaping not only the emptiness but also the oppression that often follows the death of a husband. In the white saris that proclaim their widowhood they are a familiar sight on the streets and in the temples. They find solace in the worship of Krishna and many enter a spiritual marriage with him in the way that Christian nuns commit themselves as brides of Christ.

Widowhood has made many of them virtual outcasts. Among orthodox Hindus, widows are expected to relinquish colourful clothing, jewellery and the bindi, the small dot married women place on their forehead, its colour often matching the sari they are wearing. High castes have traditionally forbidden remarriage, but others allow a levirate union, the widow marrying her husband's brother. Remarriage, however, is usually an unattractive option because prospective second husbands are so often old and poor. A widow may be regarded as unlucky, an inauspicious presence at a wedding and not wanted by her in-laws. A young widow may be considered sexually threatening, with the potential to pollute the family lineage.

Several thousand widows live in Vrindavan. They have travelled from many parts of northern India but mostly from Bengal because there is a tradition of Bengali widows settling here. Many decide to come because they are frozen out by their families. Some are brought on the pretext of a pilgrimage and are abandoned. Younger women are sometimes lured here and encouraged to become prostitutes. I met a dozen of them at a welfare centre run by Dr Kamla Ghosh, a school head teacher. They sat on the floor beneath a portrait of Krishna playing his flute and uttered the name of Krishna's bride – 'Radha, Radha' – as a greeting.

'Widows here', Dr Ghosh said, 'may be aged from ten to a hundred. Their widowhood is a stigma, as if it were a sin to be a widow. Many live in pathetic conditions, often neglected by their families and receiving little or no support. They feel they have no future. Worshipping Krishna gives them something to live for, a sense that they belong. They don't beg. They sing hymns in the temples and for eight hours of singing receive two rupees and half a pound of rice. The temples like to have them because they make the places look busy. They work as servants, too, though they are sometimes exploited by their employers, and sexually exploited. And they are harassed by rickshaw pullers, shopkeepers and ashram staff.'

Govind, aged thirty, told me that when her husband died of tuberculosis she was fourteen and childless. 'His family tried to marry me off to men who were sick or old, to anybody, just to get me off their hands. I came here about fifteen years ago, to get away from them. When I pray to Krishna I see him as my son, because he was very young when he was here.'

Umilla, who was aged about thirty-five, said she was married at eleven and widowed at fourteen. 'I stayed with my father and eight brothers and sisters, but it was hard for the family to live. There were too many of us, so I came here. I wasn't allowed to find another husband. The family said: if you try to marry again the honour of the family will be lost. That is how life is. One life, one husband, that is all. It is well known that you may get into trouble if you remarry. There is a film in which a woman remarries and her new husband takes her property and kills her. Men can marry two or three times, but not a woman. Now I am married to Lord Krishna and all I want is to live in Vrindavan and pray to him for the rest of my life.'

The increasing popularity of the Krishna cult makes life harder for the widows. Vrindavan is growing in response to the pilgrim traffic and enormous crowds arrive for the Krishna and Radha birthday festivals. As new buildings replace old and rents rise, widows are squeezed into ever meaner accommodation. Landlords often insist that widows pay them a sum in advance to meet the cost of a funeral. Some of these women have lived in the city, in strange internal exile, for fifty or sixty years and I met a number of them living out their last years in charity homes. One of them said: 'I was married at seven and widowed at twelve. I have been here for many years, though I do not know how many, or how old I am.' I was told she was more than ninety.

10

The Poisoned Garden

I USED TO TRAVEL to Kashmir for the right reasons, to walk in the alpine woods and meadows, to ride ponies and stay in small hotels with mountain views. I watched craftsmen shape cricket bats in the willow groves of Sangam and rented a shikara, the local version of a gondola, to drift down the centuries in the watery medieval labyrinths of Srinagar.

All the kings and poets who saw Kashmir were dizzied by its spectacle, and all their lyrics were true. Fields blazed purple with crocus, orchards dazzled, boats perched like insects on the mirrors of the lakes; and the poplars and Himalayan cedars were noble. For an enthusiastic drinking man like the seventeenth-century Emperor Jahangir, beauty was heightened by Kashmiri wines. Daring to enhance paradise, he created the exquisite gardens above the lakes, while his son, Shah Jehan, who shared his interest in nature, planted Persian chenars, lovely dappled plane trees, to shade the pleasure seekers.

Late one evening, sitting on the gingerbread veranda of a houseboat on the moonlit disc of Dal Lake, I felt the slight shiver of an earthquake, a tremble in the belly of the Himalayan peaks. Shouts of alarm carried from the distant shore.

The tremor sent a single dark ripple whispering across the silvery water, like a scalpel through silk.

Cobra Road

I did not see Kashmir again for a dozen years. When I returned, it was as if malignant gods had considered its beauty and had apportioned bitterness to match it. There was no escaping a permeating melancholy. The place was corrupted and brutalized by political mischief, militancy, terrorism, insurgency and military occupation. In the space of a few years more than fifteen thousand people had been killed. Srinagar lay sullen under the gun. The last ball had long since been bowled at the lovely cricket ground and the pavilion was occupied by troops whose shirts and trousers were hung out to dry in the windows. Few people ventured out after sunset. In any case, the cinemas adored by a film-loving people were shut. The tourist business which had been a significant part of Kashmir's economy had shrivelled. Most of the hotels were closed. Posters showing smiling honeymoon couples walking carefree in the Mogul gardens were torn and faded. The holiday houseboats on the lakes and waterways, symbols of Kashmir's sybarite years, lay forlorn and sagging. The paint was peeling from their names, High Luck Flower, Queen of Heaven, King of Kashmir, which had once seemed so jaunty. The land that lived by hospitality had lost its purpose. And, more than that, the very lakes and water lanes, now polluted and tangled by weeds, were shrinking. It was easy enough to believe that Kashmir was accursed.

Kashmir lies within the Himalayan ramparts where the edges of India, China and Pakistan rub together. It had ancient traditions of a snake cult, Buddhism and worship of the Hindu god Shiva. A legend tells that Christ survived crucifixion and made his way to this valley and died here. It came under Muslim rule in the fourteenth century and was absorbed into the Mogul empire of Akbar the Great in 1586. The Afghans conquered it in 1753. They were driven out in 1819 and Kashmir was absorbed into the Sikh empire of Ranjit Singh. When the British

The Poisoned Garden

defeated the Sikhs in 1846 they sold Kashmir and the neighbouring southern territory of Jammu to a Hindu chief for £750,000. For the next 101 years the people of Kashmir, nine-tenths of whom were Muslims, lived under a Hindu dynasty. In the main, they were the poor at a distant gate, misgoverned and excluded from schools, the administration and the armed forces.

When the subcontinent was partitioned in 1947 the Maharaja of Kashmir had to choose between India and Pakistan. Pakistan expected that because of Kashmir's overwhelming Muslim majority it would join Pakistan's own Islamic entity. But the indecisive Maharaja hoped that somehow his state could remain independent. As he fiddled, thousands of Pathan warriors from the North West Frontier rushed in to Kashmir with the intention of seizing it for Pakistan. They might have done so had they not wasted time plundering and raping. They were close to Srinagar when the hapless Maharaja opted to join India and fled the capital in his fleet of Rolls-Royces. Indian troops arrived just in time to save Srinagar from the invaders. After battles between Indian and Pakistani forces, Kashmir was left divided along the line where the fighting stopped in 1948.

That was the first Kashmir war. The second was in 1965 when Pakistan tried and failed to annexe the state. In particular, it coveted the heartland, the fertile Vale of Kashmir, ninety miles by twenty-five, whose climate and 5,000 foot altitude were always part of its allure. This is where the Moguls luxuriated in their gardens, where the British came for relief from the plains and where the Indian middle classes came to play. Jawaharlal Nehru, the descendant of Kashmiri Hindus, adored it.

Kashmir is the child of angrily divorced parents. The quarrel over its custody carries a serious risk of war. India will never let Kashmir go. Pakistan will never possess it. But the matter does not end in this apparent stalemate. At the heart of things lies the fact that both countries define themselves in the feud over Kashmir.

The conflict also nurtures a mutual suspicion that dates from the eighth-century Muslim conquest of western India and which continued through more than six centuries of Mogul rule and had its tragic and vicious dénouement in Partition. Pakistan was created as a homeland for the subcontinent's Muslims. It sprang from a belief in Hindu–Muslim incompatibility, the idea that Muslims could not live with Hindus in one country. Although, down the centuries, Hindus and Muslims had established a fairly tolerant way of living together, many Muslims feared that independent India would be a Hindu India in which they, the Muslims, would be unprotected second-class citizens. Jinnah and other Muslim leaders did not believe in Nehru's concept of Indian secularism. They did imagine, however, that India and Pakistan could exist in a perfectly civilized fashion.

Pakistan was an invented country, a by-product of India's long struggle for independence. As an idea, it took shape only in the few years before Partition. On separation, two-fifths of India's Muslims remained in India. Muslims today form less than one-eighth of the Indian population, but since India has around a billion people and even small ratios represent huge communities, there are more Muslims in India than there are in Pakistan. Millions of Hindus and Muslims do indeed share one land. India considers that Kashmir is, irrevocably, Indian territory. It is also the only Indian state with a Muslim majority; and to Indian minds it demonstrates the fact of a secular India. It is therefore an integral part of India's identity. With its Muslim majority, Kashmir-in-India seems to ask: what was Partition for?

In a way, Pakistan remains stuck in 1947. Since its birth, debate about what it should be has formed a central part of its

The Poisoned Garden

short history. Rather than enjoying a positive identity it has had to labour with the negative of being not-India, of identifying itself in respect of India. Islam did not bind it: the eastern wing seceded in 1971 and became Bangladesh in defence of Bengali culture against the attempted domination by western Pakistan. This was the cause of the third war with India. Pakistan has had long periods of army rule. Its diverse component territories do not co-exist easily. But its people find common cause in Kashmir. Pakistan nurses the grievance that it was robbed in 1947. The grievance is itself part of Pakistan's identity, a unifying focus, the beloved wound. By complaining about India's treatment of Kashmiris and showing that Hindus are rough on Muslims, Pakistan asserts the justification for Partition. For their respective audiences both Pakistani and Indian leaders have to demonstrate that they are 'tough' on Kashmir.

Estrangement is complete. Trade between the two countries is negligible. No air service links their capitals. The border is always tense. In Kashmir there is a permanent grumbling small war of mutual artillery bombardment. As for the line of the border itself, India and Pakistan are keenly alert to 'cartographic aggression' and both have specialist teams who examine every atlas, encyclopaedia, guide book and magazine for inaccuracies and will stamp them saying the maps are not correct. Sometimes maps will be excised, like pornography. CDs may be rejected outright because they cannot be electronically labelled as inaccurate. Such is the sensitivity of the Kashmir issue that for foreign politicians even to utter the word is to risk having contumely heaped on them. From time to time, people strike up conversations on trains or planes and ask: 'So what are your views of the Kashmir situation?' I long ago learnt to avoid giving an answer. They do not want an opinion, only a pretext to pick at the scab. They have a way of trying to draw one into the lobster-pot of 1947 and the minutiae of a bilious family quarrel.

Cobra Road

Kashmir is more than a chronic sore in the dealings between India and Pakistan. It is an unstable element in the larger matter of the co-habitation of Hindus and Muslims in India, a relationship central to subcontinental affairs.

Apart from anything else, this relationship is notable for the ignorance that marks each community's view of the other, the misunderstanding of the other's beliefs and opinions. The Hindu asks: is he a Muslim first or an Indian first? There is a vague suspicion that Muslims are a fifth column and are not wholeheartedly for India. 'It's easy to smear a Muslim. Just call him a Pakistani agent,' a businessman said. Several times I have had the experience of sitting with a group of Hindu men, decent and intelligent on the face of it, and have heard them argue that although Hindus outnumber Muslims by more than eight to one, Muslims are planning to outbreed and overtake them. 'They can have four wives, you see.' And they repeat this mantra of prejudice, apparently unaware of its absurd proposition that there is a vast and outnumbering population of Muslim women, enough to provide Muslim men with four brides each. Yet this nonsense plays to atavistic fears and is part of the assertion that India is a besieged Hindu island in a hostile Islamic sea.

Trivial as it seems, Hindu nationalists complain that Indian Muslims cheer for Pakistan during Test matches, that they hand out sweets when a Pakistani scores a century. Such stories encourage the demonizing of Muslims. My friend Kuldip Nayar told me he was out walking with his ten-year-old grandson and they fell to talking about cricket. At that time, Pakistan were playing better than India.

'That', said the boy, 'is because the captain of India is a Muslim and not a Hindu.'

'Good God,' his grandfather said, 'who told you that?'

'They talk about it at school,' the boy said. 'Everybody says it.'

The Poisoned Garden

Kuldip was distressed. He is an old-school liberal. He saw the violence of Partition, the bodies and the mobs shouting for more blood, and fled to Delhi from Punjab. He grew to believe passionately in the Nehruvian ideal of secular democracy and has worked and written for many years in the cause of Hindu-Muslim reconciliation.

Because Kashmir is a Muslim state adjacent to Pakistan, every suspicion concerning Muslims looms larger. The journalist Tavleen Singh noted that the first political remark she ever heard about Kashmir was: 'All Kashmiris are traitors.' There is barely any trust at all, though there is not much appetite among Kashmiris for joining Pakistan. Some Indians sound positively colonial as they grumble about the supposed failings of the people of Kashmir, gratuitously bestowing on them such ethnic characteristics as guile, greed and cowardice; and, of course, they bleat about Kashmiri ingratitude.

In the 1980s, Delhi's mismanagement of Kashmir steered the state towards disaster. Mrs Gandhi threw out its elected government and brought Kashmir under Delhi control in keeping with her belief in strong central government. Statesmanship and wisdom retreated like thawing snow. The rigged election of 1987 was a watershed that created a strong sense among Kashmiris of being cheated by Delhi. The slide could not be stopped. Militancy grew, and with it separatist demands. The authorities' hard line and the arrest of moderate Kashmiris made extremists of many people. The collapse of order led to occupation by military and paramilitary forces. Pakistan exploited India's difficulties by arming Kashmiri militants. Often using the plentiful weapons left over from the Russian–Afghan conflict, Pakistani and Afghan warriors crossed the mountains to join the fighting, declaring the cause of Kashmir an Islamic holy war. Most of the Pandits, the Hindu minority of 150,000 people, fled to the south, their houses left empty or ruined, their temples silent. India was in for a long haul and waged a ruthless war which, with its instances of indiscriminate killing and disappearances, increased Kashmir's alienation and humiliation.

❖

I took a taxi from the airport to Dal Lake and Mr Butt's compound. I remembered the plane trees, the lawn stretching to the lake and the view of the mountains. In spite of the troubles, Mr Butt has kept his houseboats open. The British built these pleasure arks to circumvent a maharaja's edict forbidding outsiders to own land in Kashmir. A style developed: long boats made of cedarwood, tricked out with fretwork and carved balconies, handsomely finished with local walnut and pine, the furnishings and red plush sofas and pictures just teetering on the edge of kitsch. As I recalled, the cooks, apart from preparing local dishes, also served roast and two veg and treacle pudding.

In his office, Mr Butt clasped me to his bosom.

'Hello, my dear,' he said, with his slightly sad smile. 'Welcome back.'

Whether he really recognized me after a dozen years I could not tell, but he made a show of it. I had stayed in his houseboats in the days of peace, when they were always full, and the lake was busy with shikaras. Boat-borne pedlars with cargoes of shawls, papier-mâché, silverware, carvings and carpets swarmed aboard and murmured, even as you tapped your boiled egg: 'Sir, buy this carpet and enjoy eternal beauty in your England home.'

Mr Butt decided it was time for a nostalgic interlude and ordered up tea and biscuits and brought out his visitors' books, as he always used to. These ledgers were inscribed with tributes to Kashmir's tranquillity, to its hospitable people and, above all, to the comforts of Mr Butt's ornate houseboats. Mr Butt shook his head sadly as I read these dispatches from long ago, the last letters from Shangri-La.

Still, he was pleased to see me and to have my business, though he knew I was back for the wrong reasons. I was on assignment and would not have been there but for some trouble. In one of his houseboats were David and Jenny Housego, a British couple who had been trekking in the mountains when their sixteen-year-old son Kim and David Mackie, a fellow walker, were seized by Islamic guerrillas. These men believed that the kidnapping of Europeans would alarm and embarrass the Indian authorities and publicize the Kashmir crisis abroad.

Rather than leave everything to the Indian authorities and British diplomats, the Housegos and Mrs Mackie decided to stay in Kashmir and, if possible, contact the guerrillas. They drove into the mountains, to Pahalgam, a town once busy with tourist business, now deserted and run down. They walked up and down the main street and distributed leaflets asking for information. People crowded around them. Some were sympathetic and said it was a crime for a son to be stolen from his father. Others spoke angrily about the harshness of the security forces. 'My son of fourteen has been tortured by the army.' 'The soldiers have raped our girls.' 'We have had the army killing us for six years and the world does nothing – but two Englishmen are kidnapped in the hills and the world takes notice.'

Housego was calm and persistent and told the people he would stay in the district for three days, saying that anyone with information could approach him in confidence. The next morning, while he was talking to people in the street near a police station, a man slipped through the small crowd, pushed a note into his hand and hurried away.

The note was in English. 'Respected Mr David,' it began. It urged him to drive at once to a house in Anantnag, a town thirty miles to the south of Pahalgam. Housego did not hesitate. I went with him. On that tortuous mountain road thirty miles seemed a long way. We waited an hour at the address we had been given and a man arrived, clad in white, a large, smiling and avuncular figure, with a meticulously groomed beard. He introduced himself as Dr Qazi Nisar. We learnt later that he was a respected cleric. When people spoke of him they said he was a good man. He made it clear to us that he would be our intermediary.

'Come with me.'

All three of us squeezed into a scooter-rickshaw and buzzed through narrow alleys to a large house. Dr Nisar took us to a room upstairs, asked us to sit down and went out, saying softly, as he closed the door: 'Please wait. They will come soon.'

We waited more than an hour. In a melodramatic flurry, the door flew open and Dr Nisar entered followed by four men in grimy shirts, baggy trousers and worn sandals. The small room was suddenly full. The men's faces were masked by scarves that made them look like bandits in an old black-and-white Western. Two of them carried Kalashnikovs. After some hesitation and keen hard looks, they all shook hands with us. The tallest of them spoke English well and did all the talking, leaning forward on a couch, his dark eyes intense, his breath puffing out the black silk of his mask. He was nervous and sweat gleamed on his brow. He said he and his companions had risked death to come to this meeting and we had no doubt he was right. He complained bitterly about the Indian army's recent bombardment of a village in the hills. He was plainly irritated by Housego's leafleting action in Pahalgam and ordered him not to do any more of it, to go back to Srinagar to wait for news. Housego said he would. We agreed on a telephone code word so that we would be sure that any message was from this group.

At last, the leader rose and said: 'They will be released soon. God forbid that any harm is done to them.' The four shook hands with us and left.

The Poisoned Garden

Some of the tension subsided. Dr Nisar asked us to keep secret his role as a go-between. 'I only wanted to help,' he said. He grasped our hands and embraced us both.

The next time I saw him, three days later in the oppressive heat of the afternoon, he lay on a makeshift bier on the open back of a lorry. Large blocks of ice had been placed close to his body. His murderers had shot away half his face and I supposed that this was to make his death more horrific for his family. Around the lorry, as it drove slowly through Anantnag to the burial ground, thousands of people screamed, wailed and chanted. Women stood in windows and on balconies, their shoulders shaking with sobs. Later, I asked why Dr Nisar had been murdered. People shrugged. Maybe he was shot simply for acting as an intermediary, someone said. A warning to others, perhaps. But in Kashmir's snake pit, no one could be sure.

The guerrillas kept their promise. Seventeen days after the kidnapping, the Housegos got their son back, and Mrs Mackie her husband. Mr Mackie had shaved before his release. His captors had brought him a razor, but as they made clear to him, they preferred him with whiskers. The luxuriance of their own beards, they indicated, attested both to their manliness and the vigour of their beliefs.

❀

The next kidnapping was more savage. Five Western tourists were seized and villagers found one of them, a young Norwegian man, with his head cut off. In Srinagar people said this proved that the murderers were not from Kashmir. It was too brutal an act for a Kashmiri, they said, too alien, like the bayoneting of a baby. It must have been done by one of the foreign groups fighting for Kashmir's 'liberation'.

This time I did not stay aboard one of Mr Butt's houseboats.

Cobra Road

I had a room in Ahdoo's Hotel in Srinagar. It was in the centre of town on Residency Road, closer to news sources and with fewer flies than the hotel across the lake. The taxi drivers who hung about outside were patient men with hopeful looks. Correspondents brought them a welcome addition to an income that had become meagre. They knew the addresses of the key players, the political and religious figures, the militants, the sages, who gave us their views and titbits of news over cups of sweet tea and sugary biscuits.

Ahdoo's was scruffy and the rooms dimly lit. The power failed often and the fans clanked to a stop. But there was always hot water and the staff were helpful, seeming quite glad to have something to do in these difficult days. At five in the morning I heard the whine that loudspeakers make when they are switched on. A muezzin called people to the first prayer of the day. As often as not, though, I was already awake because of the zing of mosquitoes and the barking of dogs in the streets. These sad and awful creatures roamed in small packs, skinny and starving, with desperate eyes and horrible open sores on their backs, the dogs of hell. The city had a poisoning programme to reduce their numbers and had killed hundreds of them, though not, unfortunately, those which ranged the streets near the hotel. I wished, for the sake of the animals, that the poisoning were more efficient.

Below my room, on the path beside the brown river, armed patrols walked by, the men's khaki uniforms covered with flak jackets like sandwich-boards. A waiter brought tea and toast and the four-page morning papers, the *Greater Kashmir* and the *Mirror of Kashmir*, with their regular catalogue of killings, pictures of bodies and allegations of torture. They complained frequently about the filth in Srinagar. An article about stinking rubbish in the streets was headlined 'Welcome To The City Of Garbages'. An editorial about sewage complained that there

The Poisoned Garden

was no safe and hygienic way of dumping excreta, that it was shovelled into the lake or simply left in heaps near the roads. It concluded sadly that although Kashmir was a beauty spot there was a 'a foul smell emanating from the land because it is smeared with faeces . . . the stinging smell is abhorring'.

From time to time the telephone rang in my room. I picked up the receiver. Silence. There was no one there. There never was. The telephones were a motif for Kashmir itself, a disconnected place, isolated in its own troubled world. You could spend a day trying to telephone Delhi and hear only a recorded voice, the murmur of a sleepy woman, saying over and over: 'Please dial after some time.'

One day, a government minister arrived from Delhi to open the new 12,000-line telephone exchange in Srinagar. With official fanfare and the press looking on, he made the inaugural call. After that the exchange did not function at all. The Srinagar newspapers reported that even the telephones in town that had actually been working before the minister's arrival had mostly fallen silent. Officials in the telephone headquarters whose job it was to deal with complaints were no longer troubled by the public. On the grounds of security, people were kept out of the headquarters by armed guards, and nobody could get through on the telephone. It was total victory for the bureaucrats.

As I was about to leave Ahdoo's one morning, a grenade exploded across the street. The hotel guard quickly shut the steel gates. The grenade was aimed at a passing police jeep but missed. I saw an old man being helped away, blood pouring from his leg.

The government held a press conference every afternoon and gave news of attempts to deal with the kidnappers and their demands. The conference was sometimes a rowdy and disputatious event at which Kashmiri journalists harangued officials with fierce passion, rising to their feet, demanding answers. Once, a reporter stormed out theatrically in protest. The uproar subsided very quickly, as things do in the subcontinent, and the correspondents and officials, who had been shouting and arguing, then chatted amicably over tea and sweet cakes.

Every evening I slipped out of Ahdoo's gate and walked half a mile to an office where there was still a treasured working telephone. Since hardly anyone was out after sunset and the taxi drivers had gone home, the street was not only dark but also deserted. I did as I had been advised. I walked slowly and stayed in the middle of the street. I held a torch on my chest, shining the beam on to my face to identify myself, to show that I was a foreigner. As I walked, I heard the jeeps of the police and paramilitary forces slowing behind me and the gears being changed. The jeeps followed for a while and then slowly pulled out and passed me. I saw the shiny faces of men staring out of the back, tense and suspicious, their fingers grasping their guns. At last I left the street and went into the office where the telephone sat on a desk. I was given tea and waited to make my call, dialling repeatedly until I got through. Afterwards, an hour or so later, I retraced my steps to Ahdoo's, the torch beam on my face, a pungent smell of drains in the air.

Srinagar was a city of whispers. Words passed down a chain and messages arrived by mysterious means. Rumours bubbled up like gas and found their way through narrow alleys where shopkeepers squatted in the dusty shafts of sunlight. They floated around the carved wooden buildings of the old part of the city and filtered through the hot and noisy streets which smelled of turds and spices and were crowded with cows, horses, foals, dogs, cars, trucks and scooter-rickshaws.

At Ahdoo's, these rumours and fragments of information seeped from the first floor to the second, in and out of the dark rooms. I associated the theories with the smells of food, for they

The Poisoned Garden

were often aired in the shadowy restaurant over unleavened bread, lentils and grilled chicken. One morning, a new rumour said that the unfortunate Norwegian hostage had been beheaded in an argument over Salman Rushdie; but how could anyone possibly know such a thing? Some of the tales told in Srinagar were like the sentences I saw on a computer screen in the town, the words wobbling as if written on water. There was fevered talk about the possibility of commando action. Detectives from Scotland Yard flew to Srinagar to give advice on negotiating with kidnappers and, after the story had been through the editorial mincer, a local newspaper reported the arrival of 'commandos from Scotland'.

One morning there was a knock on my door. A man whispered that armed guerrillas had occupied the hotel restaurant. I went down to have a look. Six thin bearded men, their eyes glaring like those of angry eagles, stood against a wall, toting automatic rifles. In front of them sat six others, three with masked faces, and one of these read a statement to some assembled correspondents. When this was done, the armed men wrapped their guns in a homely red tablecloth and vanished into the streets. Later that day there was another knock at my door and a man said he had some photographs. They showed men teaching children to fight. The men wore masks and struck the familiar, clichéd warrior poses, holding up their guns. The boys in the photographs were aged about ten or twelve. The guns were too large for them, but they raised them to their shoulders and squinted down the barrels. When I mentioned this to a local politician he said that the Kashmir quarrel was transmitted through the genes.

One Friday I joined the crowds streaming in their thousands to the Hazratbal mosque on the banks of Dal Lake. Here there was kept a sacred relic, a single hair of the Prophet, preserved in a glass tube. I had never seen it but was told that a cleric would

Cobra Road

draw it from his coat with a dramatic flourish and display it to the faithful. A large force of police was there that day and there was a feeling that tempers might easily flare. It was hot and the atmosphere was edgy. It was impossible to get into the inner part of the mosque. Once the prayers started, however, the atmosphere grew calmer.

Next day I returned to the mosque and walked into its garden. I had not gone far when I was surrounded by half a dozen young men. They were all hostile and one of them was certainly menacing, moving nervously, eyeing me. I knew he had a gun.

'Not allowed in mosque,' one of them said, pushing me. 'Only for Muslim.'

I walked down a narrow lane to the lake, past sweetshops and butchers' stalls, and watched glistening men cook rounds of bread as big as bicycle wheels in vats of boiling oil. I squeezed through the press of people at the lakeside and hired a canopied shikara and had myself paddled down to Mr Butt's for tea. Mr Butt flung out his arms. 'Welcome back, my dear,' he said, thumping my shoulders in his embrace. He forgave me for staying at Ahdoo's and not with him.

All along Residency Road armed policemen stood in front of the shops and stalls, one man posted every few yards. On my way to meet a friend, I passed a policeman stationed on a corner. About two minutes later I heard a gunshot. A youth had walked up behind the policeman, pulled out a gun and shot him through the neck. The policeman died on the pavement. On the way back to the hotel I walked past the crimson puddle.

At Ahdoo's the staff flicked cloths at the dust in a desultory way. The telephone rang in my room. I picked up the receiver, but there was no one there.

11

To the Spinning Water

'CALL ME THAMPI.' He pronounced it Tumpy. 'It is enough. First and second name both. Complete south Indian name is too much of mouthful for you.'

He laughed. 'Too much of mouthful even for south Indians.'

He met me at the airport in Cochin, on the south-west coast. He was a square and merry-eyed man, his mouth always on the edge of a smile, his face framed by luxuriant wavy hair and a strong black curly beard. A dab of sandalwood paste on his brow indicated that he had been to the temple that morning.

He was bursting to tell me about his recent trip to Shanghai where his striking appearance had made him a curiosity. 'While I was taking stroll, these Chinese people were staring,' he said. A woman had tugged at the thick hair on his forearm and, like some daring teenage pop fan, had pulled at the tuft showing over the V of his open collar.

'I said: "Madam, please, I am human being." But, of course, she had never seen a man in her own country with such hair and such lush beard.'

Most of the outsize suitcases and roughly taped cardboard boxes on the baggage carousel had started their journey in the Gulf states. Kerala long ago built its bridges to the wider world and has had the west in its eyes for centuries. For many years its young men have crossed the Arabian Sea to the Gulf to seek their fortunes as cooks, drivers, construction workers and servants, returning with cash for land and houses and an enhanced status as prospective bridegrooms. A planeful of them, slight, dark and moustachioed, dressed in new clothes and shoes, jostled around the carousel. They summoned up porters to manhandle their prizes on to carts, and then, framed in the airport doorway, they savoured their triumphant appearance before their welcoming families and the appraising eyes of earmarked brides and prospective fathers-in-law. These were not battered airport trolleys they pushed, but venturers' caravels laden with treasure and the symbols of success: video-recorders, cameras, stereo systems and electric food mixers.

'For every one person arriving, forty waiting to greet,' Thampi laughed, helping me push through the throng of heroes and out to a waiting Ambassador.

The driver eased into the hooting herd.

'You must be knowing', Thampi said, 'about our indecent driving in India, our helter-skelter traffic.'

I was swallowed into the swelter of Cochin and felt the first rill of sweat on my back. We dropped my bags at a hotel and drove to the waterfront where a small boat with an outboard engine rocked gently at a jetty. Thampi had arranged a trip, partly for the pleasure of a breeze but mainly because a boat was the most rewarding means of exploring a water city of low green islands. The outboard kicked into life and its fumes mingled with the harboury smell of salt water and oil.

In a few moments we were far away from Cochin's push and shove and had become part of its defining element. This is India's fourth-largest port, the country's southern naval base, threaded together by bridges and beetling ferries, hemmed by godowns, wharves, cranes, storage tanks and stacks of boxes. Freighters and frigates manoeuvred to their berths. Container

To the Spinning Water

heavyweights oozed in from the blue ocean, like fat men entering a bar. Long cargo boats with a few fingers of freeboard slipped by on the lazy swell, drawn by sails fashioned from fertilizer bags stitched into a ragged patchwork. Dolphins broke surface in sudden exuberant flashes. Stork-legged men fished from black canoes among drifting rafts of water hyacinths. A sinewy ferryman rowed a heavy boat, an image of toil, fourteen passengers crammed in the stern and their bicycles heaped on the bow. The evocative Chinese fishing nets, the spindly stars of Cochin postcards, their technology unchanged for more than two thousand years, stood waiting to be dipped into the tide. Ashore on the sand, beneath the palms, fishermen repaired their narrow boats, suturing the planks with tightly drawn thread spun from coconut fibre, then waterproofing the hulls with a slippery emulsion of egg yolk and cashew oil.

Cochin harbour, in its modern form as a major deep-water port, is the achievement of Sir Robert Bristow, who was chief engineer here between the world wars. He directed the digging of channels and created an artificial island of dredged mud and named it Willingdon in tribute to the Viceroy. Sir Robert has not been forgotten in Cochin. Apart from the harbour, his chief monument, there is a Bristow Road and, in the Cochin museum, a waxwork figure of him sitting at a desk, bald-headed and bespectacled, in a dark suit and bow tie. Cochin harbour was another epic of imperial engineering, like the construction that went on simultaneously at the other end of British India, the building of the Khyber railway. Like his counterpart in the Khyber, Sir Robert suffered a breakdown under the strain of his task and was sent to England to recover.

Sir Robert built and occupied the first house on Willingdon Island. It was pleasant enough, though plagued by crows and rats. As he related in his own account of the Cochin harbour project, he developed a kind of pidgin to communicate with his servants. When his butler complained about some transgression by the cook, Sir Robert summoned the cook before him.

'Now, cook. You know you were wrong, and now you are very rude. Therefore Master very angry. Government saying Masters not beating any servants, so Master saying this: will cook be fined eight annas or will cook have three hits with stick backside?'

'Master, please I having three hits.'

The butler placed the cook across a chair and Sir Robert raised a light cane. As the stick fell, however, the cook changed his mind and turned over so that the blow fell on his knee. Next day the cook grumbled to the butler about his bruised knee and the butler asked Sir Robert what he should say.

'Tell cook', Sir Robert said, 'Master only hitting place where plenty soft meat: same place where ayahs smacking too much naughty babbas. Not hurting very much. But cook, he turning over, and stick hitting place where no meat, only bone. Therefore cook very silly, and if any more trouble I fining eight annas.'

There was, Sir Robert reported, no more trouble.

❂

This was not my first visit to Cochin. I had been here briefly with my wife fifteen years before. With some flourish, I remember, an effusive hotel manager had installed us in the honeymoon suite. It was an enormous high-ceilinged room. To our right, as we stood on the threshold, was a dark brown cocktail bar without a single bottle or glass or glacé cherry. In the distance, to our left, were two narrow beds, hard enough, we later discovered, to suit penitential monks. Between the bar and the beds stood a ping-pong table. In the dining room that evening, a tuxedoed band had played Thirties ballroom jazz and, to a roll of drums, the bandleader announced a cabaret. A comely girl had emerged, wearing an expression of boredom and a harem costume of floating veils and a jewelled brassière. To an exotic saxophonic sound, she twirled slowly, like an underpowered ceiling fan, while most of the diners ate their fish curries, seemingly indifferent to her dance. They were middle-aged, middle-class hotel restaurant people; and perhaps they knew, as we did not, what would happen. After some minutes, the dancer allowed a couple of veils to drift to the floor and, finally and tantalizingly, removed the glittering brassière, revealing a larger jewelled bodice beneath; then, her modesty and mystery intact, she had rustled swiftly away.

❦

Thampi was an official of the Spices Board of India and was to take me on a tour of plantations, spice groves and pepper factories. First, we had lunch in the Spices Board canteen – and how could it be anything but one of the world's better curry houses? It was a delicious meal; a soup of lentils and tomato and tamarind; rice, and dishes spiced with fenugreek, chillis, curry leaves and asafoetida. There was fried mustard, boiled beans with gourd, grated coconut and pepper; omelette and curd; sweet balls of gram, sugar, cardamom and clove; and dainty bananas. Naturally enough, everyone around the table was a spice enthusiast and proclaimed the life-enhancing virtues of spices. Take this as an anti-allergen, take that as an anti-oxidant, take another to prevent flatulence. There was excited talk about the research in medical laboratories into the disease-fighting properties of certain spices. And, of course, there was hardly any need to mention that some of these roots and berries were fabled aphrodisiacs.

Thampi took me to a freeze-drying plant where green peppercorns, picked late in the day and transported from the hills overnight to preserve their freshness, were painstakingly sorted. Each peppercorn was examined, one by one, by women standing at several tables in teams of a dozen. They discarded every blemished or undersized berry. 'All of these ladies', the manager explained, 'are divorcees and widows sent to us by a charity which cares for women from broken homes, educates their children and finds them work.'

Pepper is the greatest spice of all. The trade in it, like the trade in wine in Europe, is part of history's foundations. The Malabar coast, which includes the modern state of Kerala, was for many centuries the world's only source of pepper. Today, still, India is the world's largest producer. In ancient times pepper and other spices were carried from here to Arabian ports and thence by way of the Red Sea to Egypt. They were also transported overland and by sea to the Indus river; and from there were hauled by camel train to the Silk Road which stretched westward from China through the Pamir mountains and branched down to the Mediterranean. When she entered Jerusalem, the Queen of Sheba had in her procession spices and sandalwood brought from Ophir; and Ophir, scholars have speculated, was a port on the Malabar coast, although some opinions place it further north. The Greeks imported Indian pepper and the physician Hippocrates used it in his prescriptions. The port of Alexandria, built by Alexander the Great, grew into a significant spice market.

The Romans adored pepper. Magnates hosted peppery banquets, drank heavily spiced wine and craved Indian gems, ivory furniture and expensive silks. Courtesans demanded Indian jewels and rare essences in payment for their services. Men and women reeked of unguents pressed and infused from Indian spices. Nero had his palace decorated with pearls and ivory and, copying a friend, ordered his plumbers to install gold and silver

To the Spinning Water

pipes delivering fragrances on tap. A Roman gourmet composed ten books of recipes using pepper and other spices. The Senate rumbled with complaints about the ruinous price of pepper. Indeed, the Romans loved it so extravagantly that their spending on it undermined the imperial economy.

The key to the early trade with India was an understanding of how the wind blew in the Arabian Sea. Arab navigators and traders in Gujarat were the first to understand the patterns of the monsoon: the word comes from the Arabic *mawsim*. In the first century, however, Hippalus, a Greek merchant, demonstrated the consistency of the south-west and north-east monsoons. With the secret cracked, the pepperholic Romans sent their own spice fleets to India, making the round trip within a year. Cochin and other parts of the Malabar coast were drawn into Rome's commercial orbit. As far as is known, the Romans did not build in India, but they sent soldiers to protect their pepper trade near Cochin; and hoards of Roman gold coins, sent out to pay the bills, have been unearthed.

By the fifth century, the taste for pepper had spread to the barbarians beyond the northern fringes of the Roman empire. The Gothic invaders who appeared before the ramparts of Rome in 408 demanded a tribute of gold, silver and three thousand pounds of pepper to call off their siege; though two years later they overran the city anyway.

Pepper reached northern Europe and the Baltic along the trade routes that spread from Constantinople from the fourth century. Baltic merchants freighted it to England and bartered it for wool. During the Crusades of the eleventh to thirteenth centuries, English soldiers discovered Indian spices in the dishes of Palestine. The journals of sixteenth-century travellers refer to kari, a Tamil word meaning a spicy sauce, and during the British Raj generations of soldiers and administrators learnt to enjoy Indian cuisine and discovered why Bombay Ducks do not quack. Curry recipes began to appear in Europe in the early seventeenth century. The Salut-e-Hind, the first Indian restaurant in Britain, opened in Holborn in 1911 and the famous Veeraswamy in Regent Street in 1927. In the 1960s curry moved into the mainstream, becoming as British as roast beef, and Taj Mahals and Stars of India opened in every High Street. Now numbering more than eight thousand, these restaurants employ more people than the coal and steel industries.

A pepperers' guild, forerunner of the Grocers' Company and ancestor, too, of the apothecaries who made medicines from spices, was founded in London in the twelfth century. Most animals were slaughtered at the onset of winter because supplies of grass and other fodder were too meagre to last until spring. Pepper and cinnamon were used to preserve meat, or at least to hide the smell of decay and alleviate the wretchedness of winter. For many years peppercorns were valuable enough to be counted out like coins to pay rents and fees; and well-to-do fathers gave bags of pepper as their daughters' dowries.

The European craving for pepper inspired advances in shipbuilding and ocean navigation and the founding of empires. One evening, Thampi and I drove along winding lanes to a beach hamlet near Calicut called Kappkadavu. It means 'the place where the ship came in'. Among the palms and peach-coloured cottages stood a stone marking the spot where in 1498 the Portuguese adventurer Vasco da Gama scrambled ashore. He was the first European to find the sea route to India by way of the Cape of Good Hope. After victualling on the east coast of Africa, his three ships sailed to this place in Kerala in twenty-three days; and on this beach da Gama sniffed the air of a sensuous Eden.

At that time the spice trade in Europe was controlled by the Sultan of Egypt and the merchants of Venice. Their heavy duties rankled. Vasco da Gama was sent to open a new sea route

To the Spinning Water

and challenge the arrogance of these pepper lords. He also went to make a Christian challenge to the power of Islam. He was a ruthless man and in India his bad name endures. His savage conflicts with Muslim traders and local warriors sealed a reputation for brutality. Nevertheless, his three voyages to India and the hugely profitable cargoes he and his successors brought home broke the hold of Venice and Egypt on the spice trade. He died in Cochin in 1524 and was buried there in St Francis's church, the first Catholic church in India; and his tombstone can still be seen. His bones were exhumed by his son fourteen years later and reburied in Portugal. There the inscription on his tomb saluted him as the Great Argonaut, Admiral of the East Indies and their Famous Discoverer.

The Great Argonaut sailed to India in the hope that he would bring to it all the benefits of Christianity. He was astonished, therefore, to find that Christian pioneers had preceded him by fourteen centuries; and Portuguese dismay deepened when these long-established Christians refused to accept the authority of the Pope.

Indian Christians believe unshakeably that St Thomas, Doubting Thomas, arrived near Cochin in AD 52; and the small Jewish community which still exists in Cochin insist that their ancestors were already in residence when Thomas got off the boat. The existence of these early Christians of India played a part in the legend of the enigmatic Prester John, who supposedly ruled a Christian empire beyond the Islamic lands. Over the centuries, and under the broad label of Syrian Christians, numerous congregations developed with varying beliefs and practices. Later, the establishment of the Roman Catholic and Anglican churches added to Kerala's rich religious stew and to the large number, variety and beauty of its churches. Today more than a sixth of Kerala's people are Christian.

The Christian influence helped to modernize and develop the

state of Kerala, challenging and breaking down caste and feudal systems and creating an appetite for education. Dr M.G.S. Narayanan, an historian I met one evening in Calicut, pointed out that Kerala had never been a remote southern enclave. It was, from ancient times, outward-looking, with connections to a broader world. The Western influence that began with the pepper trade with imperial Rome became permanently established through Christian traders, and this modernization was strengthened later by the large-scale migration of Keralans to the West. Kerala was clearly part of Hindu India, but the long contact with other cultures, Roman, Arab, Portuguese and British, made Keralans less defensive and more tolerant of different ways of life, inculcating an adaptability and aptitude for innovation that became a hallmark of the Keralan character.

During the construction of Cochin harbour, Sir Robert Bristow stood on a pipe while a deep channel was being dredged, and felt through his feet the vibration of showers of coins rattling through it, sucked up from the wrecks of ships from the Portuguese and Dutch eras. The fortunes made by European merchants were regarded enviously by the Danes who decided that they, too, would like a spice colony in India. Theirs is a curious story. In 1620 Danish merchants arrived on the Coromandel coast in Tamil Nadu, bought the village of Tranquebar from the Raja of Tanjore, fortified it and set up in business. The colony did not prosper, however, and the few cargoes sent to Copenhagen failed to make much money. After 1639 no ship arrived from Denmark for twenty-nine years. The colonists waited patiently and their numbers dwindled. Indeed, by the time another ship sailed in, there was only one Dane left. But the colony survived until 1845 when it was absorbed by the British.

To the Spinning Water

Thampi's spice tour continued. We drove out of Cochin on the road to Madurai. An advertising hoarding announced: 'This TV Is Intelligent Unlike Many Of The Programmes On It'. A tailor offered 'Suits Highly Satisfying For The Male Ego'. Many of the lorries we passed were painted a bright turmeric yellow and sported large boards over the cabs with names like Michael, Jesus, Sherly, Heetee and Christ. One truck was adorned with a graphic painting of the martyrdom of St Sebastian, although the artist's enthusiasm for arrows left the poor saint looking like a porcupine.

Indicative of Kerala's religious eclecticism, shop windows were full of devotional figures. Christ and the Virgin stood side by side with Kali and Ganesh. Slogans of another faith – 'Saluting Comrade Lenin's Glorious Birthday Anniversary' – were painted on walls. Kerala voted in the world's first democratically elected Communist government in 1957.

We had been travelling only a few minutes – 'Reach Home In Peace Not In Pieces' – when we came upon a crowd gathered around a crash. I braced myself for horror, but it was not bad. Around the wreckage of a rickshaw and a scooter the two slightly bloody drivers were arguing and the bystanders were energetically taking sides. 'What they must do', Thampi said, 'is to agree a price quickly, before the police come. If the police are there they will want a cut of any deal.'

A mile farther on we saw a police bus at a builder's yard and a dozen constables in khaki uniforms hovering around. Thampi took in the scene at a glance. 'Even those who talk of honesty and straightforwardness are themselves guilty of cheating and other wrongdoing. This contractor fellow has been illegally mining sea sand. The police are confiscating it. He will be fined 20,000 rupees, but since he has made so much money illegally, the fine is peanuts only.'

Our route took us across the Cardamom Hills. Tea bushes

stretched over the slopes like the wales of green corduroy. Pepper vines with their little shiny pearls of berries entwined themselves around jackfruit and coconut trees. Coffee beans ripened on their bushes. A farmer living in a small pink house told me that he made a decent enough living for his family with his four cows, coffee bushes, pepper vines and a few rubber trees.

Peppercorns dried on bamboo mats beside the road. Traditionally, the mats were covered with cow dung to create a clean surface, but the practice created a difficulty for spice wholesalers because Western markets demanded high standards of hygiene and did not want spices that had been dried on dung. The farmers, though, had dried spices like this for centuries and, since the cow is sacred to Hindus, would hardly regard the dung as a pollutant.

'We had to persuade farmers that while cow dung is holy for us in India it is not so holy for customers abroad,' Thampi said. 'We showed them that different drying methods bring better prices. Younger farmers are better educated and some have been abroad and have no difficulty understanding this. They are brought up with the new hygiene. Now peppercorns are dried on bamboo mats or polythene sheets coated with fenugreek paste.'

A wholesaler said that future growth in the spice business would depend partly on finding solutions to the diseases of the rich. 'We will produce spices that suit a lifestyle, that are developed as health cures, cancer fighters, natural products to make war on disease. We used to believe wholeheartedly in pesticides and laughed at the environmentalists' warnings. But now we know that people don't want to buy spices that have been treated with pesticides. So we grow in a more organic way and develop disease-resistant crops while our researchers find ways of fighting pests naturally, setting natural predators against them.'

To the Spinning Water

After a night in a forest guest house, we breakfasted early on potato curry and puris and walked through a plantation where cardamom bushes grew beneath a canopy of tall trees. We watched the plantation girls arriving for work in bright saris, with fresh blossoms tied in their blue-black hair. There was a heavenly aroma from long black pods of vanilla drying on blankets in a garden. Then we committed ourselves once more to the steep and rutted forest roads where the jeeps are driven with reckless verve.

In Tamil Nadu we seemed to pass through vivid green seas of rice. We stopped to stretch our legs in a long avenue shaded by tamarind trees and Thampi, ever the supplier of nutkins of knowledge, said: 'In south India it is believed that when a woman starts asking for tamarind seeds it is a sign that she is pregnant.' The seeds are valued for a tang that contributes to the distinctive flavour of Worcestershire sauce. They are also recommended as soothers of sore throats. The most celebrated tamarind tree in India grows in Gwalior, over the tomb of Tansen, a sixteenth-century poet and singer, for twenty-seven years a favourite at the court of the Emperor Akbar. Singers still travel to the tree to pluck the leaves and brew them up as gargles, hoping for sweeter voices.

We stopped at a pan stall and Thampi had the pan-wallah make him a quid with some sweet and sour flavouring. 'Sometimes', he said, 'ganga is put in for the extra kick.' He chewed at the wad, squirrel-cheeked, and smiled a blood-red smile.

Streaming towards us along the road, thousands of pilgrims made their way to the temple at Sabarimala, in the rainforests where Kerala and Tamil Nadu meet, to worship the god Ayyappan. There are fashions in gods as in anything else. Their popularity waxes and wanes in a country where the power and variety of religious expression shows no sign of abating and the number of gods and invocable saints seems only to proliferate. Ayyappan, known as a protector of villages and slayer of demons, has enjoyed a growing popularity in recent years, as the crowds heading for Sabarimala demonstrate. Many of the pilgrims we saw wore orange lungis and had been garlanded by their families. When they reached the temple they would break a coconut at the bottom of its eighteen golden steps, each step representing a vice that pilgrims are meant to renounce. Strict devotees would roll three times around the temple. During the forty-one days of the pilgrimage, men abstain from sex, shaving, liquor, meat and eggs; and the pilgrims are mostly men because the temple is forbidden to women in their menstruating years.

We had lunch at an agricultural college and as we drank coffee afterwards, a professor remarked: 'You know, my generation in India has been too patient. We believed that the politicians and administrators should be given time to deal with the country's problems. I think our younger people are less patient with these fellows than we were, and rightly so. They demand change. Look at education. It is a complete scandal and one of the reasons is a disgraceful lack of political will. Education was meant to be compulsory for everybody up to the age of fourteen, but this has been achieved only in Kerala and Goa. Because they are educated, people in Kerala understand politicians better and have a horror of one party being in power for too long. So the Communists have power for a while, then they are kicked out and the others are voted in, and then they are kicked out, too. This keeps politicians on their toes and limits the extent of corruption. But the truth is that some political interests like their followers to be illiterate. That way they are easier to control. But I am optimistic. The end of the Nehru dynasty has been a good thing. We are now in transition, rather as England was after 1832.'

To the Spinning Water

Back on the road, Thampi gestured to the south and said: 'There's a poor village over there where mothers kill a newborn girl by pushing a blade of rice plant into the throat so that very quickly and gently the baby chokes to death.' At times, among the millions of very poor, hard-pressed to find food, drinkable water and work, another female mouth to feed is simply too heavy a burden.

For some reason the traffic on our approach to Madurai was particularly unruly and we came across several wrecks. When we stopped for a snack in a restaurant, I saw a driver and his mate enjoying slugs of whisky, diluting it with beer, filling their glasses to the brim. As we waited at a railway crossing a truck smashed full tilt into the back of a bus waiting beside us, throwing the passengers forward like bundles of laundry.

Madurai looked miserable and down-at-heel in the grey light and drizzling rain. Gutters ran with dirty water. The tall gopurams, the wedge-shaped towers of the Meenakshi temple, were looming masses in the murk. Because of the rain Thampi and I decided to visit the temple the following day. Thampi felt, unnecessarily, that I should be entertained. When it was dark and the rain had stopped he took me to the town's old palace for a *son-et-lumière* performance. At best this is a third-rate art form. Here the *son* was a deafening screech and the *lumière* just fitful flashes. Thampi looked relieved when, after ten dire minutes, I nudged him and we fled to dinner.

Our hotel was a modern concrete structure and I could see immediately where the architect or builder had cut corners. One of the staircases had so little headroom that I had to duck well down to descend it. A piece of carpet was pasted on the concrete beam to prevent skull fractures. In my room was a notice which, I assumed, arose from the management's experiences and gave an idea of the way some visitors behaved.

Dear Guest, it said, Please try to co-operate with us in maintaining the property and avoid spoilage/missing of articles. If it happens, the concerned guest will be responsible and the rate for that article will be added with the bill. The rates are as follows: Single bedsheet Rupees 250, Window curtain 1,000, Dressing table 150, Chair leg 400, Window glass 500, WC (whole fitting) 2,500. Please avoid use of bed for dining purposes.

It was difficult to believe that a guest might steal a whole water closet, but in India so many things are possible.

The temple at Madurai is one of the most gorgeous in India, the flowering of the city's most brilliant period, between the sixteenth and eighteenth centuries. Seeing the formidable gopurams in sunshine I felt I could be a traveller arriving on another planet. The towers are decorated with tier upon sumptuous tier of carvings, with thousands of exquisitely formed figures in vivid carnival colours. Gods, saints, genies, sprites, demons, cobras, elephants and mythical beasts dance, pose and cavort in a riotous celebration of Hindu art and legend. These swelling gods and goddesses are crowned, belted and bebaubled, their breasts, bellies, thighs, cheeks and chins suggesting extravagant celestial banquets. They are figures in a fantastic dream that have been let out to play.

Below the towers, ant-like crowds milled in the streets and flowed in and out of the temple precincts. Inside, I wandered dark corridors lit by faint light. The air was thick with the smell of candle smoke, incense and homely fried food. Bare-chested priests clad in white lungis, their foreheads dashed with the three horizontal stripes of the followers of Shiva, walked the cloisters, their canticles echoing around the passages and pillars. Worshippers prostrated themselves in shrines and alcoves, and smeared coloured powder on their foreheads and touched their beards and chests. Out of the shadows young men emerged with faces daubed a startling yellow. Pilgrims

To the Spinning Water

bathed their hands in the heat of flames flickering in front of the images of gods. A crowd pressed round a bronze figure of the goddess Kali and after their prayers they bought small pellets of butter, kept in a tub of cool water, and hurled them at the figure, coating it in melting butter. Kali was dancing, and her devotees threw the butter to keep her cool. Meanwhile, worshippers wandered the temple shops and ambled back and forth from the passageways of prayer, as the tide washes in and out of a cave. The weary curled up and slept on the stone floors polished to a sheen by the feet of the years. A sign kindly advised: 'Have Worship On Mondays When Goddess Meenakshi Is Adorned With Diamond Crown'.

❁

I used to wonder what would happen when MGR died. Driving through Tamil Nadu I could see that the old star lived on in a way. Statues of him by the roadside, complete with the hat and concealing dark glasses he always wore, were painted in bright colours.

In Madras I visited the imposing MGR memorial on the promenade overlooking the Bay of Bengal and, like everyone else, took off my shoes when I entered the gates. The memorial was a black cube under the curve of white lotus leaves and bore the surprisingly modest epitaph 'Diligence Earns Eminence'. M.G. Ramachandran was a celebrity phenomenon, a film star politician who became Chief Minister of Tamil Nadu and a god of sorts; so adored that when he fell ill a number of devotees committed suicide, offering their lives to the gods in exchange for his. When he died in 1987 several people burned themselves to death and others cut off their fingers and toes in mourning. The stars, directors and scriptwriters of the film business have dominated Tamil politics. It was they who founded the DMK party to resist the domination of northern India and the superiority of the Brahmins, and they reached the people primarily through films. MGR frequently played the poor boy who climbed to success, gained access to upper-caste women and triumphed over his enemies; and his screen persona and the real-life politician merged.

He was also the mentor of the remarkable Jayalalitha who shrewdly used his fame to enter politics herself. As a starlet she was admired for her voluptuous figure and fair skin but her film past was a complicating factor in her rise. A man may use screen celebrity to leap into politics, but a woman cannot. South India takes a Victorian view of actresses and assumes they give favours to studio bosses. Jayalalitha buried her screen past and a biography of her contained no reference to it at all. She reinvented herself as a mother-goddess, wearing voluminous gowns over her ample figure, and became a sulky cult figure, known variously as the Visionary Lady, the Divine Mother and the Pillar of Strength. She became a Tamil empress, Chief Minister of the state, ruling nearly sixty million people. On her forty-eighth birthday, the arms of forty-eight devotees were tattooed with portraits of her, and forty-eight cockerels were sacrificed at a temple. As a tribute, one of her admirers declared himself dead and had himself carried in a funeral procession, though stopping short of cremation. Later, Jayalalitha emerged as a bizarre, manipulative and outrageous figure in national coalition politics, living in a state of permanent tantrum, a subcontinental Violet Elizabeth Bott.

❁

I returned to Cochin and drove down the coast to Alleppey to board a converted rice boat. It was sixty years old and built of teak. The sleeping cabin and saloon had a roof of bamboo and

To the Spinning Water

wattle fashioned in a distinctive hump. A group of rice boats appeared like a convocation of armadillos. A crew of four looked after me, the captain, the cook, the engineer and the guide; and the craft was powered by bamboo poles and a small outboard. The boat's library consisted of a paperback copy of Dickens's *Hard Times*, so I had Mr Gradgrind for company.

Much of the spirit of Kerala lies in its waterlands, the rivers, lakes, canals and shallow fens sluiced by more than forty rivers running down from the hills. For three months each year the monsoon rains drench everything and the land bursts with a brilliant fecundity; and to my ear the language, Malayalam (a palindrome), has the sound of gently bubbling water.

The rice boat whispered through a skein of creeks and jungled islands, an unobtrusive platform from which I observed the seamless lives of amphibious people as they fished and planted and endlessly washed themselves, their babies and their bright garments. We became part of the traffic of canoes heaped with coconuts, cattle fodder, bricks and purple mounds of freshwater mussels. On their islands, thick with bamboo and banana, people worked the gardens of pink cottages, men tying and retying their lungis in the characteristic fidget of the south. Boatmen poled ferries filled with people, bicycles and chickens. Fishermen stood motionless in the shallows, with arrows set ready in tight bowstrings. Kingfishers dived in electric flashes and egrets studied the heads of buffaloes, picking off ticks in the manner of attentive valets.

Late in the afternoon we stopped at a creek-side toddy shop, a hut with wooden benches on an earth floor. Four men, shoulders shaking with excitement, played a game with mussel shells on a board scratched in the earth. The pot-bellied barman hoisted a plastic can of toddy, the fermented sap of the coconut palm, and dribbled it through a strainer into glasses. It tasted rank and undrinkable. My guide tossed it back with relish. In

Cobra Road

the hour before dusk the boat was anchored in a broad lagoon and I heard the distant pulse of a temple drum. The crew lit oil lamps and cooked a fish curry with coconut and rice, followed by pineapple and banana fritters. I stretched out on the foredeck mattress in the cool breeze and had a short session with Mr Gradgrind. Strings of lamps flickered on fishing nets, mechanical herons, a legacy of Kerala's ancient trade with China, like the cooking woks and the conical hats of boatmen. I rose at five o'clock to watch the sunrise. The crew jumped over the side for their bath, then brought tea and a peppery omelette.

❂

I headed south again, through Trivandrum, the capital of Kerala, and on to Kovalam which was thick with small hotels, fish restaurants and sunset-facing bars. There were numerous ayurvedic centres offering the oil massage for which Kerala is renowned, and I submitted myself to a stocky and jolly scrum-half of a man who showed me a pot of oil which, he said, was a traditional recipe with his own herbal additions. The colour of dark honey, it looked and smelt rather like the Virol my mother used to spoon into me. I had been told to ensure that the masseur prayed, for without prayer his work would not be effective. He closed his eyes and his lips moved and then he sprang into action, vigorously rubbing oil into my scalp, neck, shoulders, back and thighs. He tugged at my ankles and wrists and when, after forty-five minutes, he bowed his head and set me free, I felt like the Boneless Wonder.

Since the ever-graceful and always evocative coconut palm is a motif of Kerala, I called at the Coconut Research Station for an education. Three scientists there were delighted to see a foreigner, set me up with a coconut to drink from, showed me their plantation and extolled the coconut's glories. I was surprised to learn that there are no wild palms. All are owned and are an important source of wealth.

'They grow to between fifty and a hundred feet,' said the first scientist. 'And a coconut palm planted at your birth will last all your life and give a hundred nuts a year.'

'It is called the tree of heaven,' said the second. 'Every part is useful. The trunk is used for roof rafters, doors and furniture, the leaves for thatch and fuel, the fibre of the nut for coir rope and matting, the shell for handicrafts and charcoal.'

'Coconut water is a healthful drink and can be used to feed infants and is pure enough to be dripped into the veins,' said the third. 'The oil is used in making medicine, in cooking and soap. It is a skin tonic and famous for making the hair strong and healthy. What remains after extracting the oil is fed to cattle.'

'The coconut grove', said the first, 'provides a microclimate and shade for other plants like pepper vines, cocoa, pineapple and banana.'

'The nut is the most popular offering to the gods and the flower is used at marriages,' said the second.

There did not seem much more to say. The scientists thought for a moment. 'Climbing the trees teaches village boys agility,' said the third.

'And the coconut husk is used to scrub elephants,' they all said. 'It is the elephant's loofah.'

I set off for the far south along a dappled road, through an Accident Prone Kilometre, in and out of the villages with their Catholic shrines and abundant hammer and sickle flags, past the Tea and Coffle House, the Needle Fight Tailors, the shops selling Hardwares, Footwears and Underwears, the One Stop Shopping For Delicious Desires, and the Department Store – Get All Under One Roof Without Bore Or Yawn. People walked in single file along the edges of the road, men with mattocks on their shoulders, girls with hibiscus and jasmine in their hair, and children with satchels bound for the Kids Oxford Matriculation School.

Cape Comorin, the first and last place in India, was hot and dazzling. The little cape town itself, Kanya Kumari, was hardly pretty, a straggle of unattractive concrete buildings and stalls selling glittering plastic bracelets, keychains, seashells and pieces of coral. I tried the town museum, wishing more than anything else to escape the heat for a while. Among the paltry exhibits were statues and rusty swords, a few stuffed birds, one of them capsized, and a snake so inexpertly stuffed that it resembled a lumpy Christmas stocking. As if desperate to fill one of the grubby glass cases, the curators had found coloured plastic models of the human heart and urinary system.

Nevertheless, the town had a seaside cheerfulness; and, standing on the most southerly point of the cape that I could find, I thought it all exhilarating. It sang with the appeal and drama of all land's ends. To the east across the Gulf of Mannar lay Sri Lanka and to the west the Arabian Sea. Beyond the offshore rocks, the blue wildness of the Indian Ocean stretched uninterrupted all the way to Prydz Bay in Antarctica.

Half a mile off the coast, a flotilla of lateen-rigged fishing boats, speckled sails taut and brave, their nimble crews drenched, tacked their way across the rough water and raced the scudding clouds. Ashore, the polite and formal palms nodded in agreement with the seas.

There was no mistaking the significance of this place. In the mountains of the north I always imagined the country unrolling southwards to this final punctuation. Here, though, I saw India having its beginning, emerging magically from the rock pool at my feet and expanding phenomenally, reaching northwards for 2,000 miles across all those dusty furlongs and teeming acres to the massive gables of the Himalayas. The rocky cape suggested the substance of India, its diversity. The crowds

To the Spinning Water

in the streets and temple precincts had journeyed from many parts of India, and with their different languages, their styles of dress, their skins shaded from pale to dark, they were a sample of its bewildering variety. A professor I had recently seen in Delhi told me that he had counted 4,634 communities or castes among Hindus, Muslims, Sikhs, Christians and Jains, and that India had ninety-one cultural zones of which eighty-nine were different, one from the other, in shades of belief, ritual, values, styles of dress, cuisine, agricultural practices and art. India grows ever more varied and supple.

The cape itself spoke eloquently of belief. It is a holy place and always full. Legend says that when the goddess Sati was sliced into pieces and fell to earth, this was where her back came to rest. The chief temple is dedicated to Kumari, the virgin goddess, and worshippers crowded in to pray at her image. A man stood outside, holding a pot for gifts of money, his face painted yellow, his lolling tongue penetrated by a sharpened stick, like an arrow. Ferries full of pilgrims bucked across a channel a couple of hundred yards wide to a rock surmounted by a temple. The rock looked a little, but not much, like St Michael's Mount in Cornwall. This was where Swami Vivekenanda, who first popularized Hinduism in the West, meditated before deciding to take his version of enlightenment to America. The cream-washed church of Our Lady of Good Counsel rose handsomely from clustered pantiled houses, a reminder that Christianity secured its foothold in southern India in the very early years of the Christian era. Gandhi journeyed here to meditate; and here, too, some of his ashes were cast into the tide.

Stone steps led down to the pool. It was walled from the sea by smooth brown rocks on which the spinning waters broke in clouds of spray. Scores of men, women and children picked their way down the steps, pressed their hands in prayer and, depending on their build and temperament, strode or waddled into the sea. They held their noses and submerged themselves and came up spluttering. Shining and refreshed, they ascended the steps and held out lungis and saris at arm's length to billow and dry in the hot wind. Around the steps a dozen holy men squatted on cloths and dispensed blessings, and, here and there, beggars performed their eternal holy function of receiving alms.

12

In the Carnatic

THE EXTRUDED SHAPES OF the hills to the west of Bangalore were rendered even more theatrical in the low-angle play of the dawn light. We were passed by an Ambassador with a swank-sign on its rear saying: 'Air Conditioned Car No Hand Signals'. Drivers commonly brighten up their Ambassadors by affixing a Western logo to them; Mercedes-Benz, perhaps. Or they paint the words Power Brakes, often spelt Power Breaks, on the boot. The Ambassador I was travelling in had the logo Isuzu 1800 stuck to the dashboard.

'With these fellows,' a friend once remarked, 'it is a wishful think only.'

A couple of hours after leaving Bangalore I was on the Cauvery River, at Seringapatam, the palace, fort and deathplace of Tipu the Tiger.

'No freedom-loving Indian', said the inscription beneath his portrait in the palace, 'can forget the history of the heroic self-sacrifice of Tipu Sultan, who fought like a tiger for the freedom and for maintaining the prestige of our country. He has won immortal fame for showing to the world that Indian men are not merely house husbands, but also warriors.'

These last few words were rather touching. Tipu and his father, the great general Haidar Ali, resisted the encroachments of the British East India Company in the late eighteenth century. They turned Bangalore into a military base and arsenal where, among other weapons, they manufactured rockets with iron casings, which at that time the British military did not possess. Haidar Ali had a corps of twelve hundred rocketeers. While he and Tipu were active they were the chief threat to the British domination of southern India. Once they were removed there was little to impede the British advance.

The story of Haidar Ali and his son is told partly in the vivid murals at the palace in Seringapatam. One shows Haidar Ali riding to war 'in royal dress, clean shaved, imperturbably smelling a rose in his right hand'. Another shows the carnage of battle where, as the inscription notes, there were 'heads without bodies, and vice-versa'.

Tipu first accompanied his father on an expedition of war at the age of thirteen and spent most of his forty-eight years fighting the British intruders. As Sultan of Mysore, he could have become a vassal of the East India Company like other rulers but he much preferred to fight and risk death before such dishonour. In his time the concept of India that emerged in the following century did not exist: Tipu's fight was for his own independence and not for that of India at large. Nor was he as shrewd and wise as his father. He was rash and erratic. But he was an authentic warrior and undeniably fierce and brave. The British branded him an obstacle to civilization's progress, a fanatic and a 'perfectly savage' monster. The bitterness of this opinion sprang partly from the acute British suspicion of Napoleon, the fear of a French attack on India and the fact that Tipu had French advisers and French-trained troops.

Tipu's final scene was played out in 1799 when British forces besieged Seringapatam, his well-fortified capital. A brigade of these troops were led by thirty-year-old Colonel Arthur Wellesley, the future Duke of Wellington. Tipu's forces gave him

In the Carnatic

a punishing time of it, using their rockets as well as muskets. A dozen British infantrymen were taken prisoner and had a horrible end: some were strangled by a wrestler and the others had nails driven into their skulls. In the last stages of the fighting, Tipu was shot in the head by a British soldier who was trying to steal the jewellery he wore. The body, short and tubby and dressed in white linen with a crimson cummerbund, was still warm when Arthur Wellesley saw it. He tried and failed to find a pulse.

In the Kannada language tipu means tiger and Tipu was always portrayed as one. 'Better to live two days as a tiger than two centuries as a sheep,' he would say.

The tiger was the emblem of his state. His throne was studded with ten gold tiger heads and covered with sheets of gold and was borne on the back of a carved tiger. After his defeat, the gold was peeled off and distributed among British officers. Arthur Wellesley, who lived in Tipu's palace after the siege, sent his brother Richard Wellesley the grotesque toy that Tipu so enjoyed. This was a mechanical life-size wooden tiger sinking its teeth into the throat of a prostrate red-coated officer of the East India Company. Its eighteen-note pipe-organ, cranked by a handle, produced appropriate roars and screams. It was brought to London nine years after Tipu's death and is now in the Victoria and Albert Museum. Tipu's sleigh-toed slippers, part of the Indian booty accumulated by the family of Clive of India, are in Powis Castle in Wales.

Tipu came to be hailed as a martyr for Islam and lies honoured in the painted hall of a domed mausoleum. His tomb, which is next to that of his father, is covered with a tiger-stripe cloth.

When I emerged from the gate of the mausoleum a young man approached. 'I am guide,' he said. 'I will take you to Tipu Sultan tomb.'

Cobra Road

'I have just seen it.'

'This is not tomb. Tipu is at other place. I will take you.'

I held up Murray's guide, the unassailable arbiter. 'This is the tomb. This book says so.' The man was unabashed.

'Book is correct. Tomb is here. It is at other place also.'

Leaving him with the last word, we drove out of Seringapatam and headed through eucalyptus groves and a string of villages to Coorg, a land of plantations, forests and shapely hills, about sixty miles by forty. Rather like Scotland, some of the old British planters used to say. No, no, said others, more like Wales. Anyway, its prospects please and since much of it is at four thousand feet it has a refreshing climate. It is not only beautiful but retains a sense of what it once was, a hill kingdom, a place apart. Its people are distinct, tall and relatively fair. In their own language, which is not written, they call themselves Kodavas. Their ancestors arrived here in the sixth century, perhaps driven by upheavals in the north, and over the centuries the Coorgs became a proud nation, devoted to their traditions. Their women, for example, have always enjoyed a higher status than that of their Hindu sisters.

At a time when the British liked to categorize whole peoples under certain characteristics, the Coorgs were marked as one of India's martial groups. They were also regarded as mannerly. In any case, they certainly had a strong idea of who and what they were. Both Haidar Ali and Tipu Sultan ravaged the land but did not conquer it. Christian missionaries enjoyed little success in converting the people of Coorg. Brahmins never persuaded the Coorgs, who are nominally Hindus of the warrior caste, to defer to them.

However, the Coorgs enthusiastically learnt English and allied themselves to the British in the fighting against Tipu. In the 1830s they were ruled by a mad and murderous king who, to their relief, was deposed in 1834. The British Resident asked

In the Carnatic

them how they would like to be governed and they said: By the British, please. Thus was Coorg annexed and it lived peacefully and fairly profitably under the Raj for the next 113 years. The disgraced king went to London with two of his wives and died there in 1859. The Coorgs were loyal to the British during the rebellion of 1857 and were consequently exempted from the legislation of 1861 prohibiting Indians from bearing arms.

A genuine pride in the military strain endures. 'You must see the statue,' I was told when I arrived in Mercara, the chief town of Coorg; and I was taken to the fine memorial raised to Field Marshal Konandera Cariappa, perhaps the most famous of all Coorgs, the first King's Commissioned Indian officer, 1919, and the first Indian Commander-in-Chief of the Indian Army.

Mercara was a busy place of winding, slightly dishevelled streets and little shops. The thick grey walls of its hill-top fort encompassed a broad campus of government offices, a jail, a church and a library where swotters nodded in the leaden heat and dozers slumped on the tables. Books crumbled in glass-fronted shelves: Graham Greene, Wordsworth and Oscar Wilde turning to dust. Worthy *Reports on the Backward Castes* were disintegrating into a chalky powder. There is a certain smell to books in India. At home, I have only to open a volume bought in an Indian shop to feel myself for an instant back in Bombay or Bangalore. Reading an old history of Coorg, I learnt that it once had numerous pythons and cobras and also two unlikely serpents, one which grew two heads and the other which crowed like a cock.

I climbed to the top of the ramparts and looked down into the yard of the jail. A group of men were playing volleyball while others were sleeping or lounging in the shadow cast by the high wall. Half a dozen were washing their clothes in a cement trough and a few, clad in brown vests and pants, soaped and washed themselves. Seeing me, they waved and I waved back. A warder in a khaki uniform, his feet in flip flops, sauntered up and down, trailing a bamboo cane. I wondered if these men were serving sentences or whether they belonged to the wretched class of remand prisoners, known in India as undertrials, who often wait years for their cases to come to court, so long in fact that the evidence and the details of the crimes – and the men themselves – are often forgotten.

In the hotel restaurant that evening I asked for a bottle of mineral water.

'Cold or warm?'

A disco tape was played at Maximum Thunder level. Since I was the only diner, I asked one of the waiters to turn it off. He looked astonished. For five minutes there was peace, but the waiters were decidedly unhappy. The music returned, seeping in at first, then bursting through like a wave. It was as if the waiters had a fear of calm or silence.

Next day, Rama, a junior manager of a coffee plantation, arrived to show me the sights. He was a Coorg and spoke English, Kannada, Tamil, Hindi and, of course, Coorg. 'In this part of the world you have to know at least three languages. But Kodalu, the Coorg language, is what we speak at home. There are 400,000 of us but there is no doubt that we are beginning to lose our identity and that makes us sad.'

Coorg used to belong to the old Mysore state. When the boundaries of many Indian states, including Kerala, Tamil Nadu and Andhra Pradesh, were redrawn on linguistic lines in 1956 it became part of the Kannada-speaking state of Karnataka. A certain animus against Hindi in the south springs from fear that efforts to make it the national language would undermine the minorities. Hundreds of languages and thousands of dialects are spoken in India, and Indian banknotes give an indication of that variety by carrying an inscription in fifteen of them, each representing an ancient culture. Although widespread in the

In the Carnatic

south, Hindi remains a minority language. Many Kannada-speakers would rather have English than Hindi, seeing English as an opportunity rather than a threat, and the teaching of Hindi is often neglected.

We drove through forests to the place where the Cauvery meets two other rivers. The Cauvery is sacred and this confluence is especially so. Several barbers squatted, wielding cut-throat razors, giving a ritual tonsure to baby boys held in their mothers' arms. They also shaved the heads and faces of half a dozen men who had travelled here as part of their mourning following the death of a parent. Afterwards, these men tied white lungis around their waists, bathed in the river and squatted in a circle on the bank to say prayers.

We drove higher into the hills to see the temple and tank at the source of the Cauvery. Water drawn from here is used in ceremonies of blessing and healing. I climbed the hundreds of steep steps to the top of the hill in the company of a crowd of wiry and determined old ladies. We all gazed out at the forested slopes and valleys.

Coorg is one of the finest places anywhere for growing coffee and produces a third of India's crop. In the plantations I saw near Pollibetta the berries grew as red as cherries in the company of poinsettia and bougainvillaea beneath the branches of silver oak, rosewood and dadap. Coffee had its origins in Ethiopia and the berries were carried to Arabia and eventually reached Holland from the Gulf port of Mocha. A traveller took coffee seeds to India around 1600. The first coffee houses in London opened in the seventeenth century: one of the most renowned was The Cheshire Cheese in Fleet Street. The first cafés in Paris opened in the 1670s. In India, cultivation spread to Goa and Mysore. British settlers arrived in Coorg in the 1850s to plant coffee and created a life of plantation, bungalow, club and sport. The memorial I saw in Pollibetta church to

William Davies, a planter for fifty years, called him 'a kind man and thorough sportsman', an epitaph that seemed to speak, too, of the agreeable life of Coorg.

In the billiard room in the Bamboo Club, the old planters' rest, hung a photograph of twenty-year-old Lieutenant William Robinson, born in Pollibetta, who in 1916 won the VC for shooting down a Zeppelin over England, the first airman to do so. The hero was himself shot down in 1917 and taken prisoner. He died of influenza in 1918. By his photograph were some framed fragments of wood and wire from the Zeppelin.

The driver of the car I had hired did not know his way around Coorg, but as soon as he reached the outskirts of Bangalore in the late afternoon he felt more at home. He grew more aggressive. In Coorg he had been decent and careful at the wheel. In his own territory he was a ruffian. What was it that an Indian acquaintance had remarked recently? 'The lack of humanity in our country continues to distress.'

'Slower,' I said to the driver, and saw him frowning at me in the mirror. I began to hate him for his callousness, the way he swung past women and children with inches to spare.

We were brought to a sudden halt. A bullock cart was stranded in the middle of a junction, completely blocking it. The driver got down and whacked the animal hard across its flanks and shouted. A policeman strode over and bellowed. A boy pushed at one of the wheels and another pulled at the bullock's head. Finally some men pitched in. In a flurry of pushing and whacking and shouting, the floundering animal got under way.

❂

After they defeated Tipu Sultan, the British stayed only a few years in 'the pestiferous atmosphere' of Seringapatam before the mosquitoes did what Tipu could not, and drove them out.

In the Carnatic

Bangalore, at three thousand feet, was much more salubrious, as the grave of a general in one of its churches suggests. He died at ninety-two after seventy-five years as an India hand. Bangalore was already a prosperous textile town and from the military point of view well-sited for overseeing southern India. The British constructed a cantonment so vast that men had to ride their horses from one place to another. On Clapham Street, Myrtle Lane and Richmond Road they built spacious bungalows with decorated bargeboards, fretwork canopies and deep verandas, all embroidered by roses and shaded by jacaranda and rain trees. Bangalore has renamed some of its roads but has avoided a wholesale effacement of its history; and Brigade Road, Cavalry Road and Infantry Road bear witness to some of its saga.

The cantonment had been established for more than eighty years when Lieutenant Winston Churchill of the 4th Hussars arrived in 1896. With two other officers he shared a pink and white bungalow where, before dawn, servants came to their bedsides, lifted their chins from the pillow and lathered and shaved them before helping them into their uniforms so that they were on parade by six. Such was the heat of the sun, wrote Churchill, that 'long before eleven o'clock all white men were in shelter'; and after lunch at half-past one they slept until five when they mounted up for polo, which, as Churchill remembered, was 'the serious purpose of life' in the cantonment. After dinner, the officers smoked in the moonlight – the end of 'the long Indian day as I knew it; and not such a bad day either'.

Churchill, it is said, used to read newspapers on the veranda of what is now the Victoria Hotel on Residency Road. It is still a refuge and rather more necessary than it was. Bangalore styles itself 'the garden city' and, although it has fine parks and many of its trees have escaped the developers, the city's streets have become like most in India, a reeking pandemonium of traffic.

Breakfasting on the veranda one morning, I read of a snake

catcher who had been bitten to death by a cobra in a village near Bangalore. In the opinion of another snake catcher the man had paid the price of over-confidence. 'His technique was all wrong,' he explained. 'He approached from the front and caught the snake with his bare hands, instead of with a pronged stick. He worked with his heart and not his head.' It seemed clear, too, that the unfortunate snake catcher had difficulty in grasping the cobra. His hands had only the stumps of fingers because it had been his custom, whenever a snake bit one, to cut the digit off at once.

I had been put in touch with K. R. Ramachandran, a retired civil servant, and we met for coffee at the hotel. He had been the Collector of Hyderabad, the head of the civil administration in that city. He was educated at the universities of Mysore and of Wales, and had happy memories of his years in Aberystwyth in the 1940s. 'How is Aber these days?' he asked eagerly. He was proud to have retained some fragments of Welsh and recalled the student tradition of walking the promenade beside Cardigan Bay and kicking the steel railing at the end of it.

'The Bangalore of my boyhood', he said, 'was a paradise. There was little traffic, of course, and no pollution; and the presence of three thousand British troops in the cantonment gave it a definite British flavour. Manners were better. Today there is a marked material improvement in people's lives and even the very poor are better off, but manners have declined. You know, we used to regard northerners as more boorish than us, but I have to say a certain coarseness has seeped into the south, too.'

In his retirement he did good works. He took me to see a charity nursery school in which he had an interest. Its pupils were seventy slum children and they were sitting on the floor of a classroom when we arrived. As well as the rudiments of education they were given breakfast and lunch. Pregnant women and nursing mothers joined them for their midday meal and were also taught to make clothes for their children. The children were immunized against polio and diphtheria. Because part of the ethos of the school was the teaching of respect for nature and animals, a variety of trees had been planted in the grounds and there was a duck pond and a compound for rabbits.

The school shared its site with a dogs' home. Stray dogs were rounded up in the streets by a lasso-wielding dog catcher and the females were brought to the home and spayed before returning to a life of scavenging in the streets. I was about to ask the school head if it would not be better to kill the dogs humanely, when he said: 'Of course, some people would object, on religious grounds, to exterminating them.'

I asked him how successful the school was. 'The trouble is', he said, 'that when these children go on to primary school there is a very high drop-out rate. They are their parents' labourers and are taken out of their classes to tend the goats and the buffaloes. We meet parents and encourage them to keep their children in school and they say school is a good idea, but who will look after the animals and the younger brothers and sisters? Some parents say to us: why not teach the kids at night? But the fact is that many parents get drunk at night and are not interested in educating their children anyway. We give free uniforms and free scholarships, but we find it hard to make progress. We reach a dead end. India is so large and our school is a drop in the ocean. What to do?'

He shrugged. It was a hard question to answer. Schools like this do make a difference. Education charities, volunteers and literacy movements have taught thousands of children. But the state fails to do so. Just over half the people are literate and the literacy rate is among the lowest in the world.

The constitution of India states that education should be free and compulsory for all children up to the age of fourteen; but spending on education has been steadily reduced since independence. India actually spends less on schooling as a proportion of its income than a very poor country like Tanzania. The majority of primary schools are inadequate. Three-fifths have only one teacher, hundreds of thousands of them have no drinking water and most have no lavatories. Under half of the children aged from six to fourteen go to school. The drop-out rate, as the head in Bangalore said, is high, and is particularly so among girls. The point was made to me several times in my travels that some politicians find it much easier to lead and manipulate illiterate people and have an interest in keeping their constituents unlettered while simultaneously complaining about poor education. Manufacturers would lose their cheap child labour if education were compulsory. While many people look on failures in education and the state's virtual abandoning of its responsibilities as a scandal, many more are indifferent. For the bulk of the people of India, for those who need it most of all, education is a lost cause.

Mr Ramachandran took me to meet his friend Professor Ramaswamy, director of the Centre for Action, Research and Technology for Man, Animal and Nature, which emerges acronymically and appropriately as Cartman. The professor was at his desk. He looked like every Westerner's idea of an Indian guru. He had a bald domed head, a long white beard and a ready smile. 'As you can see,' he said, making a well-practised joke, 'my head tells a story of India: none where it is needed, plenty where it is not.'

He sat back in his chair. 'It may be unfashionable to say it, but I am pleased that at a particular point in history the British met the Indians and fed their British ideas into the Indian consciousness. It was a collision, but on balance it was a happy and profitable one, certainly profitable for India, though many of the British came only for enrichment.'

The professor, I soon learnt, was a prolific and ubiquitous

In the Carnatic

writer and lecturer on social and environmental causes. One of his chief projects, he said, was to modernize that timeless symbol of the Indian countryside, the bullock cart. Its technology has hardly changed in thousands of years, but there are sound economic reasons for improving it. Indeed, the bullock cart in India belongs to the twenty-first century as much as the jetliner.

Reeling off figures, the professor made his case. Eighty-four million draught animals plough more than two-thirds of the land and carry 25 billion tonnes of freight a year, a lot of it grain. Only a minority of farmers own bullocks. They are too expensive for most cultivators who must rent them from others. To replace bullock-power with mechanized power would take millions of tonnes of petroleum; so bullock-power saves the country a huge amount of money, makes a significant contribution to the economy and generates hundreds of thousands of jobs.

'But', said the professor, 'the carts are idle for four-fifths of the time and the animals have to be fed and maintained. They should be used more efficiently as transport in the off-season, earning more money for their owners.'

That could be achieved by improving draught animal power (DAP in the beloved Indian language of initials) by replacing TCs (Traditional Carts) with ICs (Improved Carts). The TC is inefficiently built of timber and its weight places a strain on the bullock's neck. Its capacity is low, less than a tonne, and its iron-rimmed wheels damage the roads. The IC, on the other hand, is of light steel, has wheels with roller bearings and pneumatic tyres, and beams and yokes designed to relieve the strain on the bullock. A bullock in the shafts of an IC can carry heavier loads more efficiently and could earn four times as much as the traditional cart.

Professor Ramaswamy told me about another of his campaigns. He wants to end the commonplace brutality in slaughterhouses. In many abattoirs, he said, a buffalo calf awaiting killing is prevented from moving by having one of its front legs broken, and the leg is swung around and placed on top of the neck behind the ears. Slaughtermen make cattle fall by breaking their legs with blows from iron bars and beat them on the skull with heavy hammers. Cattle are goaded into the slaughter areas by sticks thrust into their anuses and are often butchered in the presence of other animals awaiting their turn. Pigs are dropped from a height to break their legs and immobilize them and are often beaten to death. Most slaughterhouses in India were built by the British. The professor said: 'I think it is time they were modernized.' He wants humane stunning to be introduced.

'Our indifference to cruelty is an aspect of a more general brutality in our society,' he said. 'The government has little interest in the suffering of animals and to many people animal welfare is about kissing pet dogs and cats.'

He looked up from his desk. 'At which hotel are you staying?' I told him.

'Now,' he said, 'if it is all right with you I would like you to shift today into the Bangalore Club where I am a member. You will be more comfortable. We can meet there for a drink and for dinner and I will introduce you to some friends. I shall arrange everything.'

Such kindness is not unusual in India and I enjoyed being taken over. The professor summoned his clerk and driver and soon I was packed and on my way to the Bangalore Club, to a suite with a sitting room, bedroom and bathroom. The club was a six-acre haven, with tennis courts and a large library. I soon found my way to the blue swimming pool where gents were patiently doing their lengths. 'Ladies', said a notice, 'Are Requested To Put On The Cap Before Entering The Water'.

In the front hall of the club, the light streamed over a marble

In the Carnatic

floor, brown leather sofas and a stuffed leopard. There were portraits of Sir Mark Cubbon, the administrator for Bangalore and Mysore for twenty-seven of his sixty-two years in India, and of Sir Thomas Munro, the Governor of Madras. Munro was an enlightened administrator who insisted that it was a British duty to educate and improve Indians so that they would be able to run a free and proper government. He proposed that Indian officials should be well-paid, advice that remains ignored to this day.

A glass case in the front hall contains the minute book of the club subcommittee meeting of June 1899 that approved the writing-off of the debts of seventeen officers, including Winston Churchill, who owed thirteen rupees, a sum that would have bought a few dinners. Other matters were decided, too:

1. The subcommittee sanctioned the purchase of six dozen napkins.

2. An application from Assistant Scavenger Sweeper Maduraswamy for increase of pay is considered. The subcommittee see no reason for an increase of pay.

Poor Assistant Scavenger Sweeper Maduraswamy. What lower form of humanity could there have been? What stiff fellows they were, not to give a few more annas to the wretch who daily cleaned their thunder-boxes.

Mr Ramachandran took me to lunch. He indicated a man and woman sitting at a table across the room. 'A good man. He married a divorcee and that is quite a brave and decent thing to do in a society like ours which is still fairly formal.'

I walked in the streets for a while. An almost irresistible tailor's sign said: 'Enter A Nobody, Exit A Gentleman'. The sign in Mahatma Gandhi Road which warned that: 'Urinating, Spitting And Littering In Public Places Will Attract

Administrative Charges' did not seem very threatening. And the pious 'Avoid Bad Health And Environmental Turmoil' was barely a tug at the sleeve.

The circular central library rose in redbrick majesty in a rose garden in Cubbon Park. I read for an hour and noted that the Office of the Commissioner for Public Information had set its resident McGonagall to work.

> Food for Thought
> Plenty we have got.
> We cater to reader's hunger
> Without getting a bit of anger.

I had a drink at a table on the lawn with Professor Ramaswamy. 'When people see our leaders taking money,' he asked, 'what is the ordinary man to do? No one is ever dismissed in the public sector because dismissal is not in the culture. Instead, a man is transferred. You know, only fifteen per cent of the money allocated for development in rural areas reaches the people it is intended for. The rest is swallowed by bureaucrats and politicians.'

The only pubs in India are in Bangalore. The city boasts about them and I thought I should give them a try. At the first, I got through the door but could not make it to the bar because of the roar of music. A sign outside another pub said: 'Buy A Drink, Shoot Another Down Your Throat'. I decided to do so in the civilized atmosphere of the Bangalore Club.

There I settled to read a little book of advice for railway travellers. The author described a kind of war in which passengers were at constant risk from shoe stealers, baggage thieves, hustlers, pimps, conmen, crooked policemen, fake policemen, necklace snatchers, gamblers, cheating clerks, dishonest ticket collectors and criminals offering drugged food. For baggage thieves, he warned, 'a few seconds of diversion is enough – for example when someone is looking voyeuristically at the thunder thighs of Raveena Tandon on the film magazine's cover on the station book stall'. He remembered a woman on a train who had had her bag stolen and who told him: 'Fortunately, we are newly married, otherwise my husband, a military officer, would have banged me for the blunder.' Offering a warning about prostitutes, he wrote: 'Remember, a whore can never substitute for a homely wife who oozes warmth and affection. For bachelors a visit once in a while is pardonable. It is certainly more virtuous than eyeing the neighbour's wife or a friend's sister.'

❂

In the newspapers at the club I saw that the sandalwood bandit of Mysore was still at large. He had been classified by the press as Public Enemy Number One. It was an intriguing story. Through murder and terror and the chopping off of heads he had gained control of much of the profitable trade in one of India's sacred trees.

The white sandalwood is prized for its fragrant roots and heartwood which are used in religious rituals. The wood is burnt as incense in temples and sandalwood paste is applied with the right thumb as a mark, the tika or tilak, on the forehead. It signifies a blessing or an anointing. Sandalwood was traditionally used in cremations and has formed the pyres of all Indian leaders; but it has become so rare and expensive that even at the cremation of the wealthy only small chips of it are used. Its fine grain is perfect for carving and craftsmen make it into combs, beads and statuettes of gods and elephants. The smell lingers for years. The oil is an ingredient of perfume, soap and candles, and the paste is rubbed into the skin to make the complexion clearer and to cure rashes. Thousands of people toil in small incense factories, rolling sandalwood paste on to bamboo spills. No part of the tree is wasted. People scent their clothing with sachets of sandalwood powder, and shavings are sold to be thrown on to fires to produce an aromatic smoke.

Sandalwood is the distinctive scent of the attractive city of Mysore. It wafts from workshops, markets and temples. I went there to find out more about the bandit. His name was Veerappan and photographs showed a thin man with an exceptionally large and curled moustache. The lurid stories described a ruthless killer. He had certainly murdered more than fifty men. His way with suspected informers was to exhibit their heads in their villages. It was also said that he employed a pet monkey to taste his food.

Ever elusive, he roamed 4,000 square miles of forest east of Mysore, an enduring humiliation for the authorities. It was part of the melodrama that politicians made extravagant and quotable promises – 'We will get him even if he is hiding in the womb of his mother' – and that vainglorious police officers publicly swore to catch him. When a certain superintendent, known as Rambo, vowed to bring him in, Veerappan raised a taunting banner over a village street saying: 'Come and get me if you have the guts.' Sure enough, Superintendent Rambo led a force of police in buses along a forest track. Veerappan blew up one of the buses, killing twenty-two men; and Rambo, flung high into the air, was one of the few survivors. A senior Mysore officer, who had publicly vowed to get Veerappan, was lured into ambush with five of his men and the bandit left a message by the bodies: 'I give you bullets, not medals.'

No sandalwood tree may be privately owned. Even if it grows on private land it belongs to the government. Veerappan started as an apprentice ivory poacher in the Cauvery River forests and killed hundreds of elephants. When the government banned

In the Carnatic

ivory trading, he moved into the sandalwood business. He organized felling and transport and bribed and threatened forest staff to get their co-operation. He could hardly operate without some official connivance. He terrorized local people into silence and killed his rivals. The papers said that his very name made people shiver. Indeed, when I asked about him in a town on the edge of the forest forty miles from Mysore, people looked nervous and would say nothing. The authorities had put a huge price on his head, a reward so fantastic that it served only to make him more legendary.

13

The Centre of the World

AT MY APPROACH THE guard in the colonnaded portico of the palace at Kawardha braced his spine and stood taut and splendid. His right hand gripped a long spear. He wore a scarlet coat with gold facings and a turban of palest rose. His brambly white beard was fashioned into a fork and his smile disclosed teeth like battered redoubts.

His name was Kaur Singh and he sprang from a tribe of minstrels in Madhya Pradesh. Many years before, he had made it plain to his family that he would work nowhere but at the palace. Any other position lay beneath his dignity. As I learned later, he had what some men would consider an ideal matrimonial arrangement. He had two wives and one of them cooked while the other did the housework. The only dark clouds in his life arose when he displeased one or other of them, as he did occasionally, and they united to throw him out of the house. Whenever this happened he volunteered for night guard duty at the palace, muttering that there was 'a bit of trouble at home'. When he was forgiven and restored to their affections, his wives gave him a leg massage, one wife to each leg.

The cream stucco palace was on the modest side as Indian palaces go, although it had a darkly cavernous durbar chamber beneath a dome. The palace was built in the 1930s by the last maharaja to reign over the old kingdom of Kawardha, a remote district six hours by road from Jabalpur in Madhya Pradesh.

This central region of India is the homeland of the Gond people, the largest among the numerous aboriginal tribes of India. They ruled much of this huge swathe of the country and gave their name to it: Gondwana. The kingdom of Kawardha was founded in 1751 by a branch of the Gonds known as Raj-Gonds. The gods of this family handed them an ample allowance of misfortune. The worst blow fell in 1865 when the family's honour was tarnished by the maharaja's misconduct and maladministration. The British reduced his status, a demotion and exemplary punishment that caused enduring chagrin to his successors who prostrated themselves pathetically in an effort to regain their former position.

In 1909, the Kawardha family wrote to the Viceroy: 'Your Excellency's humble memorialist submits his prayer in the same manner as a child to its parents, for it is no mean boast to say that the Raj-Gonds have always looked with affection to the British Raj and to it have remained staunch . . .' They reminded the Viceroy that they had raised a statue of King Edward VII. The Viceroy was unmoved and replied stiffly that nothing could be done.

Two years later, with a new Viceroy in office, the family tried again and pleaded perfectly reasonably that 'the delinquencies of a single member should not be made the grounds of condemnation of an ancient family'. Again, the Raj loftily rejected the petition.

In 1914, the family petitioned yet again and cited a 'heart-burning discontent on account of the deaf ear being turned to them by His Majesty's Government. All well-wishers of the Raj hope that this case which is as clear as daylight will receive the kind consideration of the benign British Government which is noted for justice.' Far from being benign, the British remained

The Centre of the World

pompous and unbending. Nevertheless, as a note in the family file points out, loyal little Kawardha sent thirty-eight men to fight for the Empire in the Second World War.

At the time of the unfortunate demotion in 1865, the family already laboured under a curse. In the early nineteenth century, Ujjiar Singh, the ruler of Kawardha, visited the temple at Bhoremdeo, some miles from his home. Like the better-known temples of Khajuraho, farther north, Bhoremdeo dates from the eleventh century and, as I saw myself, celebrates human exuberance in some fine carvings of sexual capering, the male fertility figures enjoying the exaggerated features of the giant at Cerne Abbas in Dorset.

In one of the temple rooms is a statue of Hanuman, the monkey god. Ujjiar Singh ordered this to be removed to a temple at Kawardha. Hanuman, however, appeared to him in a dream and warned him not to do so. When Ujjiar Singh ignored the warning, Hanuman appeared again to utter a curse that no sons would be born to the family while it ruled Kawardha. As it happened, no more boys were born to the ruling family for four generations. Instead, the second sons of another branch of the family were adopted and placed on the throne. In 1932, however, a prince, Vishwaraj Singh, was born to the family and it was assumed, in the rejoicing, that Hanuman's curse had been lifted. But events were to demonstrate to the superstitious that the curse still had some force. When India became independent all of the princely families ceased to rule; and Vishwaraj never reigned.

His son, Yogeshwar Raj Singh, planned to be a tea planter but was drawn back to his roots. Like others in his position he had no power, but among his family's former subjects he enjoyed some residual status. He also had land and a palace and a good education. He had been a pupil at the Raj Kumar College in Raipur, one of the schools founded by the Raj for the sons of princes. He planned a political career and also started schemes to improve the health and education of tribal people. He set about maintaining his palace by turning hotelier and taking visitors on treks in the hills, an enterprise he shared with his companion, Margaret Watts-Carter. I stayed with them for a few days. Yogeshwar, known by the diminutive of Yogi, was tall, slim and courtly – I thought there was something of the Rajput about him – and Margaret was vivacious with a merry laugh. She was half-Indian and half-English, born in south India to an English missionary's daughter. Her mother was raped as a schoolgirl and Margaret was the outcome. She was adopted as a baby by an English couple and raised happily in Sussex.

Yogi and Margaret were keen to take me to a place called the Centre of the World. It was a settlement of the Baiga tribe who, like the Gonds, were among the original Indians, established long before the first Aryan nomads reached India around four thousand years ago. There are about four hundred tribes today, about seventy million people in all, mostly living in the forested parts of the country. The Aryans did not arrive with a portmanteau religion and many of the gods and godlings that crowd the Hindu pantheon were already worshipped among the animist tribals. Tribals believe that almost everything has a god or spirit and consider, for example, that a sneeze is a manifestation of the sneeze goddess. Ganesh, the elephant-headed god, and Hanuman were presumably tribal gods long before the Aryan migrations. Many tribal people worship cobras and, to the Gonds, lightning is a cobra's daughter leaping from a box.

The experience of tribals has varied widely and has something in common with that of most aboriginal peoples in the world in their contacts with invading cultures. The newspaper stories I read about tribals in Madhya Pradesh told how they were 'pitted against powerful political interests' and 'bore the brunt of police excesses ... kept in cells without water' and how they were swindled out of their wages. The government of India, however, has a constitutional commitment to improving the condition of tribals and operates a policy of positive discrimination, awarding them seats in Parliament and in state legislatures and marking out quotas for them in government jobs and schools.

In some ways, the tribals have passed through the experience, well-known to American Indians, of being demonized and romanticized, neglected and reinvented, the playthings of the media and of academia. There is endless official and academic argument over whether they should be persuaded to move into the developed modern mainstream or encouraged to live apart within their traditional cultures, or a bit of both. In popular Indian cinema they have often been depicted as head-hunting savages and cannibals and it has suited directors, too, to show them as earthily sensual dancers. They are popularly seen as both innocents in the forests of Eden and as incorrigibly criminal participants in savage feuds.

'Hurry,' says one tribal to another in a newspaper cartoon, 'hide the video – the anthropologists are coming.'

'The trouble is that no one ever asked the people themselves what they think,' Yogi said. 'They have always been told what is good for them and they have suffered because they are trusting people, not cunning or devious. The Baigas, for example, don't like confrontation, and when they are thrown off buses they just accept it.'

The three of us set off in a jeep for the Centre of the World on a road which wound through fields of lentil and the remains of mango groves. 'They have been cut down for fuel, taking away the shade and damaging the land,' Yogi said. 'All over India the destruction of forests is on a tremendous scale.'

Certain trees are not often felled. The peepal, one of more than eighty varieties of Indian fig, is perhaps the most highly respected, worshipped as an abode of gods and known to Buddhists as the bo tree under which the Buddha attained nirvana or enlightenment. For this reason Hindus and Buddhists will not cut it down or trim it. The banyan is another fig, loved for its immense size and its shade, and is considered as the husband-tree of the peepal. Banyan is really a nickname, given to the tree by Europeans who saw shopkeepers, or banyas, doing business beneath its branches.

But, overall, trees are cut down with little concern for the long-term damage this does. Greed is part of the problem. Forest officials and politicians are among those involved in the vast business of illegal felling and timber smuggling. The rules are readily circumvented. There is a widespread indifference to the plunder of natural resources. India's forests are shrinking by four thousand square miles every year, and since they are the sponges that supply streams and rivers, the looting of them is one of the causes of the growing menace of drought. At the same time, the mismanagement of reservoirs and irrigation schemes also causes drought, flooding and soil erosion which lead to the spread of desert. The area of land prone to flooding has increased threefold in twenty-five years. India has enough land to grow all the food it needs, but as the land becomes degraded people move into the forests, felling and clearing. A growing awareness of the dangers is more than matched by a growing exploitation of woodland. Many afforestation schemes look impressive but are plantings of fast-growing trees like eucalyptus, pine and teak, short-term projects which do little to conserve the soil.

We turned off the main road and took a narrow tributary lane into the hills. This in turn became a steep and rutted track hacked out by hand, so severe a test for the jeep that we got out and walked. But at last we reached a plateau and drove to a cluster of mud-walled houses with roofs of brown tiles, the

The Centre of the World

home of a hundred and sixty people. I could see why it was called the Centre of the World. In every direction there were entrancing views over the thickly wooded Maikala Hills and not another habitation in sight, no power lines, no telephone wires, no fences, no roads, no barbed wire.

The village was given its name by a tribal leader, a shaman, or holy man, called Bakru. Thirty years earlier, he had been living in a village on the plain but had wearied of being cheated, pushed around and derided as a primitive, the commonplace treatment of many tribals. Like some minor Moses, he led a group of his people to this hill and directed the building of houses. Every family had land on which they kept chickens, pigs and cattle and grew millet and tobacco. They sometimes caught rats and birds to eat, too.

Bakru had a bearded and rather noble face. He spoke with Yogi in the tribal language. Some of his people had criticized him, saying that to take up cultivation was a betrayal, a scratching of the face of mother earth. 'But we cannot live in the past and stay completely apart from the rest of the world,' Bakru said. 'That would be unrealistic. We have to integrate and educate our children. We have a schoolroom and a teacher who comes up every day. We can do all of these things and still keep our customs.'

There was some good news, Bakru said. A tiger had recently come to live in the jungle on the outskirts of the village. There had not been a tiger there for years and its absence suggested that the gods were angry and had deserted the district, perhaps because too much of the forest had been cut down. A tiger was to be feared, of course, but on the other hand its presence was evidence that the gods were in a more favourable mood.

We went to one of the houses to see the preparations being made for our dinner. Two young men pounded herbs and spices and cut up vegetables. A jungle fowl, imprisoned in a corner,

Cobra Road

watched and awaited its fate. We walked half a mile down the hill to the village well and a plantation of bananas, jackfruit, papaya and limes. Women and children pumped up the water, filled their pots and carried them on their heads up the hill. We sat on iron-brown rocks on the hillside and watched the sun go down, listening to the chatter of monkeys and parakeets and the bells of the cattle being driven home by small boys.

As we walked back, Yogi identified plants and trees. He stopped and pointed to the path. We looked down.

'Hyena poo,' said Yogi.

Bakru held court outside his house. Men squatted on their haunches smoking pipes and bidis. One of his sons entered the compound and knelt, touching his father's feet three times with his fingertips. Children stood, listening to the adult talk. Women stayed indoors. One of the villagers set up an old candelabra and lit candles. Yogi, Margaret and I sipped whisky while Bakru and Yogi talked. The stewed jungle fowl arrived and we ate it with chapatis. And we had another glass of whisky.

Three charpoys and bedding were set out for us on the veranda. I awoke a couple of times in the small hours. The first time, I heard bells bonging gently as the cattle shifted in their byre. I imagined the new tiger prowling in the forest not far away, the denizen of a diminishing domain. The second time, the night was slashed by vivid lightning, the cobra's daughters leaping from their boxes, dancing frenetically across the indigo sky.

❂

Yogi arranged a jeep and a driver to take me to Raipur, six hours away to the south. Reaching the centre of the town, I saw people crowded around some stalls beneath a clump of trees. The buzz of excitement, the way the crowd spilled into the road, sug-

The Centre of the World

gested an accident, a crushed bike or a capsized rickshaw. The proprietor of a soft drinks shack was passing colas from his ice box into a thicket of upstretched rupee-waggling fingers. Like his neighbour, squeezing the juice out of sugar-cane, he was doing good business.

The driver stopped the car and said 'Look', and I saw why. A man was impaled face down on the high spiked iron railings behind the stalls. He had been there for a while, the body horribly contorted, the blood on the railings dark and congealed. Probably the police had been told and had seen that there was nothing they needed to do in a hurry. The spectators were drinking their pop and juice, chattering and staring. Small boys were wide-eyed. Before I could get him to move on, the driver went to find out exactly what had happened. My first thought was that this was a suicide, that the man had killed himself by jumping from the grubby office block that rose behind the railings. The driver returned and said no, the man had been working high on a ladder which had slipped.

I went to the State Bank of India to change money and was given a pay form to take to the cash desk. Behind his wire grille, the cashier was ready to sport with his victim. He looked at me insolently, leaning back in his chair, flicking his hand dismissively at the proffered pay form.

'Not possible to pay now. Come back after some time.'

'How long?'

'Half hour, one hour. Come back in afternoon.'

'I'm afraid I cannot wait that long.'

'You see,' he lectured, leaning forward, his voice rising, 'you are not understanding internal workings of bank.'

Again, the wrist flicked in dismissal. 'Come back after some time.'

This was a challenge. Man versus Babu. There can be no victory in this war, for the weight of centuries and custom are with the lord of inertia and obstruction. But sometimes a skirmish can be won. I went to the bank manager. He rose at once from his desk to meet the challenge, strode to the cashier and stood over him. He shouted, enjoying his authority, and the cashier was dust beneath his chariot wheels. Reluctantly, the wretch opened his cash drawer and counted out soiled notes, none too quickly. Fixing me with a scowl, he pushed the smelly little heap through the grille.

❖

I drove up to the national park at Kanha. The swathe of land in this part of Madhya Pradesh is called Kipling country in some guide books because it is the setting of the Jungle Books, the stories of Mowgli and his extended family of forest creatures. The nearest Kipling got to it were glimpses of the countryside from a train during his last visit to India in 1891, a journey of four days and four nights from Ceylon to Lahore, in which he 'could not understand one word of the speech around me'. His imagination supplied all the colour.

A sign at the entrance to the park said 'Blow No Horn', an unusual instruction in India where the horn often appears to be wired to the throttle of every vehicle. Beside the gate stood a green-painted wooden office with a sign stating that it was the Doubt Clearance Cell. Inside, a forestry official in a khaki uniform was writing in a ledger.

'What is the Doubt Clearance Cell?' I asked.

'It is to clear up doubts.'

I must have looked puzzled, for he added helpfully: 'It is for answering questions, for assisting.'

'So you could tell me how many tigers there are in the national park?'

'Yes. More than a hundred are there.'

The Centre of the World

'Will the tigers survive?'

'Yes.'

'How do you know?'

'There is no doubt.'

I saw the deep scratches that tigers make on trees to mark their territory, but I did not expect to see a tiger in Kanha. I had seen them years before in the Corbett national park on the edge of the Himalayas; and it is true that the first sight of a tiger is unforgettable. Here in Kanha, I was happy enough travelling the dusty tracks through the rolling meadows and the forests of sal trees, tall and skinny hardwoods which grow pale yellow sweetly perfumed flowers. Silk-cotton trees were in brilliant vermilion bloom and there were plenty of orioles, bee-eaters, rollers, peacocks and racquet-tailed drongos. A pack of red-brown jungle dogs were rapidly reducing to bones a deer they had brought down, diving into the carcass with bloodied muzzles while vultures waited their turn. One morning, however, from the back of an elephant, I saw a tigress in a thicket. She did not look her noble best, not a picture of awful symmetry. She lay deeply asleep on her back, her head out of sight in the leaves, her hind legs splayed apart, suggesting her opinion of jungle tourism.

It is hard to know whether to be optimistic or pessimistic about the future of the tiger. Its numbers are small. A few years ago the efforts made by the Indian government and private individuals seemed to give the tiger a good chance of survival in the national parks. Later, the pendulum swung to pessimism. Now the future of the tiger is in the balance. The threats to it are so serious that, sadly, it might become an oddity in a small corner of India, like the lions of Gir, or go the way of the Indian cheetah, which was last sighted in 1968 and is doubtless extinct.

When you look around princely palaces and see the profusion

of tiger skins and mounted heads you might conclude that India has stuffed its last tiger. There are more than enough of these trophies in the aristocratic halls of Britain, too. Sahibs, brown and white, killed enormous numbers. The rulers of Udaipur and Surguja shot at least a thousand each. But a greater threat to the tiger has been the spread of farming into the jungles, the pressure of population and the demand for space, and the shrinking stocks of game for tiger to feed on.

Every now and then, an old, crippled or toothless tiger eats a villager or two, and fellow-villagers call on the authorities to shoot the tiger. A national park warden I know remarked: 'It's not the sort of thing you can say publicly, but there is a terrible shortage of tigers and more than enough of us Indians.' In any case, healthy tigers avoid contact with people. Villagers who know the habits of tigers are not afraid to go out and tend cattle in tiger country. A man-eater is a rare beast, but 'Tiger Eats Man' always makes news. 'Snake Kills Man' rarely does, although snakes kill about twenty thousand people a year in India.

Apart from the shrinking of its habitat, the tiger's chief enemy is the poacher. These men are killing a tiger a day. In most reserves, the protection of tigers has almost broken down because too many people, including forest officials and policemen, benefit from the profits of poaching.

The tiger pays a high price for the flaccidity of Chinese men. It is killed primarily to meet the demands of potion-makers who use pieces of tiger in their quack remedies, especially those bought in the belief that they enhance the libido. Tiger bone pills and tiger bone wine are popular in China and elsewhere. I have seen the bones and claws of tigers on sale in street markets in Shanghai. China banned the trade in tiger parts in 1993, but the demand has not abated and smuggling remains profitable. Perhaps the only hope for the tiger is a cure for impotence which is both reliable and very cheap.

The Centre of the World

In the Himalayan passes, on the merchant routes between India and China, there is a two-way trade, with the organs, bones and skins of tigers and leopards heading for China, and the expensive, rare and therefore highly prized hair of the chiru, the Tibetan antelope, being transported into India.

This hair is shahtoosh, literally 'king's wool'. It is exceptionally fine, much thinner than a human hair, and has for many years been woven by a number of families in Kashmir into shawls of extreme lightness and warmth. They are coveted everywhere. In India they may form part of a bride's dowry. In India and the West they are sold in expensive boutiques. The trade in this material is, however, illegal under an international convention. Police call for a fairly simple laboratory analysis that proves that the hair comes from the Tibetan antelope. These creatures are not true antelopes but goats. They inhabit the high Tibetan plateau and, for the sake of fashion and beauty, are ruthlessly hunted – trapped and shot – by nomads and poachers.

The romantic story that shopkeepers tell about shahtoosh is that it grows on the necks of goats and is snagged on thorn bushes and carefully harvested by peasant women. The truth is that the only way to get the hair, the undercoat, is to kill a chiru and rigorously comb or shear the hide. The hair is mostly dun coloured or grey but a more valuable white hair grows around the throat. Hunting is carried out in winter when the coat is at its thickest. Tibetan nomads carried shahtoosh hair for centuries and its source was a secret; even the merchants and spinners in Kashmir did not know the animal it came from. Now, the hides and sacks of hair are gathered at border towns to be traded and smuggled, often through Nepal, concealed in trucks and mattresses. Profits are large and, as with the tiger, police and officials are involved. It costs about twenty times more than the hair shorn from another species of goat which makes pashmina shawls. The chiru used to move in vast herds across the highlands, in tens of thousands. The hunters, if they are not stopped, will make them extinct, just as Buffalo Bill and his friends cleared the plains of the American bison.

❋

My skull was soon sore from hitting the roof on the rutted road to Jabalpur. Pathways of red earth veined the sage-green hills and the slopes were spotted with whitewashed houses and herds of white and brown cattle. 'Forest Is Temple Of God' said a large sign at the roadside. Skinny women ran by at a trot, heavy bundles of firewood suspended from each end of a springy stick balanced on their heads. Nine-tenths of Indian homes use wood for cooking and the daily inhalation of its smoke, the equivalent of many packets of cigarettes, damages the health of millions of women.

A long bridge crossed the shining Narmada. In Hindu belief the river sprang from the body of Shiva, the Creator and Destroyer, and is one of the seven most sacred streams. As such it is abundantly served by temples and bathing places. A portion of Gandhi's ashes was immersed in the Narmada. Local people loyally hold the Narmada to be more sacred than the Ganges. You have to bathe in the Ganges to wash away sins, they say, but it is enough simply to gaze on the Narmada to be cleansed. Indeed, the goddess of the Ganges herself comes here every year in the form of a black cow and departs snow white, scrubbed of her sins. A number of holy men spend years, even their entire lives, wandering its banks. The river rises fifty miles north of Kawardha and flows westward for eight hundred miles through central India to the Gulf of Cambay, north of Bombay. A pilgrimage from the mouth to the source and back along the other side, sixteen hundred miles of purposeful wandering, gains high merit on the heavenly scoreboards.

The Centre of the World

The Narmada is one of India's significant internal frontiers, the line between north and south, between Hindustan and the Deccan, between the lighter skins of the north and the darker of the south. In the sepoy uprising of 1857 it marked the southern limit of insurrection. For a while, the British lost control in the north, but they always maintained it in the south. This heart of central India was for centuries isolated and mysterious. Civilizations rose and decayed and left little trace. The Gonds ruled largely undisturbed. To reach the south, the Moguls travelled down the western side of India and only nibbled at the edges of the thickly forested centre. By and large the relationship between Hindus and Muslims is easier in the south. The Mogul empire did not penetrate deeply into the south where Muslims arrived as merchants rather than invaders.

This heartland was not effectively invaded until the sixteenth century, the time of Akbar the Great. Asaf Khan, a Mogul noble, was excited by the stories he heard of this mysterious Gond kingdom: it possessed legendary herds of elephants, its people paid their taxes in gold and it was ruled by an exceptionally beautiful woman, Durgavati, widow of a Gond prince. Asaf Khan invaded in 1564 and defeated Durgavati's forces near Mandla. He took as loot her stud of fourteen hundred elephants and 101 iron cooking pots brimming with gold. But he did not get Durgavati. She had an operatic end. Wounded by arrows, she plunged a dagger into her breast and toppled from her elephant. Nor did Asaf Khan get her female entourage for his harem: the women burnt themselves to death. After that, the history of the region became the usual tangle of treachery, patricide, fratricide and the everyday strangling of nephews.

The forces of the British East India Company seized Jabalpur in 1817 and made it the chief military base of the Central Provinces and the site of a large gun carriage factory. Part of the legacy is a city of numerous handsome colonial houses. The game of snooker had its origins in the game of black pool played in an officers' mess here, although it was perfected at the southern hill station of Ootacamund. The British spelled the name of the city Jubbulpore, but in 1930 the deputy commissioner argued that much time and energy were wasted in writing out the ten letters of Jubbulpore and proposed the use of Jabalpur. The commissioner, however, said it would be too expensive to change the rubber stamps. They compromised, each agreeing to spell the name as he wished.

❁

The manager of the Samdariya Hotel in Jabalpur wore a striped cravat in the military style. The marble lobby was large and airy. All of this was a façade. Halfway up the staircase a large marble tray was filled with decorative gravel that looked like cat litter; and, indeed, a cat had left a black spiral in the middle of it. Upstairs, shabbiness prevailed. The carpet of my room was a murder scene of betel spittle. The pillows had been used by a man with a heavily oiled head and the bedsheets were ragged and dirty. The room boy cheerfully changed them for sheets that were ragged but clean.

I went out to find a taxi and met Rahoo, moving sluggishly in the torpid air. He seemed to have been born without smile muscles. When he fastened his sunglasses to his big face he looked sinister. When he removed them he revealed a shifty glance. He kept a wad of pan in his mouth and spat red gobbets of juice. We agreed terms. He settled wearily behind the wheel and drove me to the railway station to check the times of trains. As soon as we stopped, a youth approached the car and knocked on the window. He did not look like a beggar.

'What does he want?'

The Centre of the World

I saw one of Rahoo's eyes enter the corner of the rear view mirror and give me a calculating look.

'Parking tax. It is five rupees only.'

From the station he drove me to a clinic to meet a doctor whose name I had been given. The doctor, neat in a snuff-coloured safari suit, was affable and courteous. He sat me down in his surgery and sent for tea. Smoke curled from an incense stick and moved like a stealthy serpent among the books and paperweights. A mosquito settled to feed on his bare arm. He wrote out the names of people I should see, made a few telephone calls to arrange appointments and gave directions to Rahoo.

Rahoo's cheek bulged with his betel quid and a dribble of juice overflowed his lips. The doctor spoke to him, evidently telling him to go outside to empty his mouth. Rahoo went out to spit.

'These fellows,' the doctor said, 'they are using so much pan, which is why there is so much of mouth cancer.'

The doctor told me he was a Christian and held high office in the Bharatiya Janata Party, the Hindu nationalists. 'Most of India's problems', he said, 'arise from the wars with Pakistan and from insurgencies, fighting which has led to poverty. Somehow we would like all of these places to be one, Pakistan, India and Bangladesh, but since Partition is a fact of history it will be most difficult to merge them into one. We say that religion is very important and that anyone who is without religion cannot rule with honesty and moral values. But whatever religion you are born into, you must be free to worship. The BJP does not interfere in the worship of Muslims or Christians and we expect them to be kind to other religions. This is crucial. I am critical of Muslims because I have lived in Muslim countries and I have seen how bad and cruel they can be.'

In the early evening I set off with Rahoo to see the chief spectacle of Jabalpur, the falls on the Narmada and the gorge of the Marble Rocks. He had gone a mile or two when he stopped the car and a scruffy boy appeared at the window.

'What is this?' I asked.

I saw Rahoo's eye in the corner of the mirror. 'Give two rupees.'

'Why?'

'It is visitor tax only.'

I laughed and gave the boy the money.

I hired a boat rowed by three men and steered by another. In the canyon the white limestone cliffs gleamed coldly in the light of the rising moon, as ethereal as icebergs. Here, say the stories, the monkey legions of Hanuman leapt over the gorge on their way to destroy the demon king of Ceylon. And here, a young British officer drowned when he was forced to seek refuge in the river when the notoriously bad-tempered bees that live in the cliffs swarmed around his boat.

In the hotel restaurant that evening I asked the waiter for a beer.

'Beer is not possible.'

'No?'

'In room only. Not in restaurant.'

'Why's that?'

'This is pure veg restaurant. Beer not possible in pure veg restaurant.'

After the meal a waiter gave me a book in which to write an opinion. The three columns were headed: Comment, Birthdate, Wedding Anniversary. In the Comment section a previous diner had written 'No Comment'; and another had admonished 'Service to improve'.

Next morning I asked for an omelette.

'Omelette is not possible.'

'No?'

'Omelette is not possible in pure veg restaurant.'

The newspapers I read over my vegetable cutlet said that used surgical needles were being collected from hospital scrap and repacked, unsterilized, in small workshops and resold. Another report said that police had tried to disperse two rival mobs of striking workers with bamboo canes, but when this failed, they opened fire and killed two men. There is always a limit to police patience. There was much, as usual, about the tangle of politics, but only three paragraphs were given to a gun battle between police and a hundred Naxalites – rural Maoist militants – in which five Naxalites and one police officer were killed.

Rahoo was lying on the back seat of the car and was startled when I tapped on the window. He rose and spat a tablespoonful of betel gore.

'How long for your trip?'

'Two hours.'

'Two hours is not possible. Three hours' minimum.'

'Two hours.'

'Sir, I am telling you, three hours is minimum. That is Jabalpur rule.'

'Two hours.'

He exhaled wearily and started the engine. The rear seat gave off the smell of his morning nap.

A newspaper report on the forthcoming Holi holiday in Jabalpur said traders were doing well as people stocked up. 'Mad rush in the market prevailed due to the sound pocket condition of the buyers who have received their salaries a few days back.' Magistrates had banned guns, swords, axes and explosives and warned that 'cops will keep a hawk eye'.

Holi is a major festival, chiefly celebrated in the north, a celebration of the end of winter, with echoes in the carnivals of the West. It is an explosion of exuberance and licence, of bonfires, drums and larking in the streets. On Holi itself I did not venture out. I watched boys and young men – women stayed indoors – running up and down the streets, hiding and ambushing each other, rubbing coloured powder into their victims' faces and hair, squirting them with large syringes. In its gentler forms, Holi is a time when neighbours and friends put a little colour on each other's faces as a mark of goodwill.

The following morning, as I walked to the State Bank to change money, the streets had something of the aftermath of battle. Cows with horns painted red and blue and green, their hides splashed with dye, resembled licorice allsorts. Many of the people were dazed, the boys glassy-eyed, their hair red and blue, shirts saturated with dye, and the streets and whitewashed walls of houses were splashed with paint and powder.

As I turned into the State Bank gaggles of smiling men embraced each other, dipped their fingers into little plastic bags of powder and daubed each other's faces. The Foreign Exchange Department was upstairs, a large and dingy room filled with desks that seemed to come from a jumble sale, scarred green filing cabinets, piles of dog-eared ledgers and groups of rubber stamps. A notice said 'Listen To Your Customer He Is The Source Of Your Progress'. Its message was lost on the few men in the room who looked up from their desks and, seeing me, at once averted their gaze.

More men came in, their faces garish with colour. They shook hands with the others and embraced them and painted their cheeks and foreheads with powder. At last, a clerk approached me reluctantly and asked what I wanted. When I said I wished to change money he looked astonished. He went away and returned with a form for me to complete. After ten minutes, he came back and took it away.

The room gradually emptied, though a senior figure, a manager of sorts, stayed at his desk in a corner and studied a ledger. Some minutes passed before another man appeared. He

The Centre of the World

took an incense stick from a packet, lit it and waved it slowly in smoky circles over the portrait of a goddess under a glass plate on a desk. He moved from one desk to another, casting his wreaths of grey smoke over the portraits of gods and goddesses secured under sheets of thick glass. As a final touch and benediction, he passed the incense over a box of rubber stamps.

Three clerks emerged into the room, faces painted with stripes of mauve, yellow, green and red, their hair bright. Approaching the manager in the corner, they bowed low and placed their foreheads on to his hands.

At last, a man came to the counter bearing the Foreign Currency Notes Transactions Register. This was about two and a half feet wide. The details of my transaction were written into it and rubber stamps banged. Now this immense tome was transported to the manager who pored over it for several minutes before rising to go to the washroom. He reappeared after some minutes, drying his hands, and carefully inserted himself into his seat. In a slow and stately manner he signed a paper. This was ferried to me with his signature and some drops of washroom water. I was free now to go downstairs to the cash desk.

Behind the counters there was the noise of merriment, raucous laughter, and clerks with grinning faces bright with colour. 'You see,' said a clerk at the cash guichet, 'it is festival in India, like a thanksgiving.' While he counted out the rupee notes his colleagues approached from behind and rubbed powder into his face and hair.

I walked through the town to the High Court and wandered its cloisters and grove of palms. Attracted by the building's Victorian grandeur and touch of Disney, I framed a photograph as an aid to memory. It was Saturday and there was no one in sight. But the noise of the shutter was like a pistol shot. Busybodies are a special caste in India and, sure enough, from the emptiness, a thin man came running towards me shouting and waving his arms.

'Sir, photograph of High Court not permitted.'

As I drifted away I heard his refrain echoing through the cloisters. 'Not permitted, not permitted.'

A few minutes later, out in the street, a gang of wild-eyed youths circled me. It was too late to flee, and in any case there was nowhere to go. Suddenly, they were upon me, yelling. One grabbed me round the waist, another by the shoulders, another by the hair. I felt their fingers forcing dye into my eyes and rubbing paint into my scalp. They attacked with such force that we all fell in a ruck into a sweet stall, knocking a pan of boiling fat which splashed and sizzled. The commotion brought out the Sikh owner and some other stall keepers who shouted and threw punches. The attackers fled. But, as so often in India, a crowd had erupted from the dust itself and fifty men and boys jostled around the Sikh's stall, eyes wide in expectation.

The Sikh dusted me down and gave me one of his sugary sweets, like a yellow bird's egg.

'They are well-known bad men,' he said, 'not enjoying Holi but liking to make trouble and damage. You see, it is holiday. But violence is there.'

I returned to the hotel to wash, thinking myself conspicuous, and in the mirror I was confronted by a vision as colourful as a monkey's backside, but of course my face was as red and as blue as almost everyone else's. There were three boys in my room. Two were making the bed. The third, with his back to me, was finishing the remains of the pure vegetable cutlets I had had for breakfast, winkling out dobs of tomato ketchup from the bottle with his little finger which he sucked contentedly.

I called on Dr M.C. Choubey, a physician, who had written a book of historical sketches of Jabalpur. British historians, he wrote in the preface, suffered from a colonial hangover and it was necessary to compile an unbiased story of the past. 'People here are not at all aware of their history. You have to teach it. That is my mission. You British came as strangers, but you made us understand our history.'

Dr Choubey was an admirer of the Cornishman Sir William Sleeman, the destroyer of the cult of Thugee, whose members had murdered thousands of travellers in central India. 'What was interesting was the way he went about it,' Dr Choubey said, 'the extent to which he steeped himself in the culture of Thugee and set out to understand it. He knew that if he was going to be able to destroy these stranglers he would have to know as much about them as they knew themselves. That was his genius.'

The origins of Thugee are obscure but their activities were certainly reported in the thirteenth century. The Thugs worshipped Kali, the goddess known as the destroyer who wears a garland of skulls around her neck and a belt hung with the severed heads of enemies. They also worshipped Bhowani, the smallpox goddess. They killed for pleasure, in the name of Kali, because they believed it was their destiny and sacred obligation to do so. One of the curiosities of the cult was that both Hindus and Muslims were members of it, their differences buried in the cause of murder. It was financed by rich men as a service to the goddess. Membership was hereditary and the induction of a son, his first killing, was a cause for celebration. Thug means deceiver and the stranglers' method was to join groups of travellers and behave as ideal companions, always ready with music and songs. And while the travellers relaxed and sang around a fire the Thugs suddenly pounced and throttled their victims with scarves of yellow silk, Kali's favourite colour, with a coin tied in one corner for purchase. They plundered the bodies and buried them in graves dug with a pickaxe, regarded as Kali's tooth.

Sleeman, the son of a customs officer, joined the East India

Company at the age of twenty, bought a sword from Henry Wilkinson in Ludgate Hill, and sailed for India in 1809. In 1830, with a strong sense of Christian mission, he began to break the Thug network. More than anything else, his was an intelligence operation, a matter of assiduous inquiry, in which Sleeman, based in Saugor and in Jabalpur, learnt the private language of Thugs, compiled detailed maps and encouraged captured Thugs to inform on others. In ten years he broke the cult. One of its members confessed to strangling 931 travellers and spoke of the joy of doing so. Sleeman hanged and imprisoned many Thugs but also opened a reformatory school in Jabalpur for young Thugs, some of them children, so that they would have an occupation other than killing for Kali. They made carpets among other things and wove a large one for Queen Victoria, which was laid at Windsor Castle. The school later became the Jabalpur Polytechnic.

'Thugee' Sleeman was Commissioner at Jabalpur in the 1840s. He married in the city's Anglican church and a memorial there records that he died at sea while homeward bound after forty-seven years of unbroken service in India. The town of Sleemanabad, north of Jabalpur, to whose destitute farmers Sleeman gave some land, remembers him with gratitude.

Sleeman, says Dr Choubey in his book, befriended the local people; and other British officials are remembered for the heroic work they performed during a famine. But the disagreeable attitudes of some British administrators have also been catalogued by Dr Choubey. The insults they handed out have not been forgotten. For example, Sir Joseph Fuller, Commissioner of Jabalpur in 1897–8, 'was a diehard bureaucrat and always insulted the natives whenever he got an opportunity'. He became a Lieutenant-Governor of Bengal and 'there he continued to hold animus and disrespect against the native population'.

The Centre of the World

An official called I.J. Bourne also gets bad marks in Dr Choubey's book. 'The British sent many District Officers who would take sadistic pleasure in hounding people. I.J. Bourne took charge of Narsinghpur in 1918 and instantly engaged himself to crush the National movement. He was a typical imperialist, ruthless, arrogant and imbued with an air of racial superiority. He collected 100,000 rupees for the war fund from the impecunious proletariat, although the world war had ended. In 1924 he arranged to throw human excreta on the members of the district conference. He was so enraged with [an Indian official] that he composed a dubious limerick in Hindi . . . "I would rather be a mango than a member of your caste".'

The account ends simply and without any comment: 'Mr Bourne was devoured by a tiger in the forest of Betul.'

14

The Road to Panagarh

'Panagar,' I said to Rahoo.

His eyes widened and assumed a look of disbelief. He lowered his head to one side and allowed a copious stream of spittle to fall from his mouth. It seemed to linger suspended in the air for a moment, a shining scarlet rope, as if drawn from deep inside his body, before it splashed into the dust. He wiped a sticky driblet with his hand.

'Panagar is outside Jabalpur. Is extra.'

I did not argue. We joined the flowing river of traffic heading north on the Murwara road, past the Blooming Buds English Nursery School, the log market and the temples, the hideous concrete blocks of government housing and the National Council for Weed Science. Rahoo gave no more than a few grudged inches of clearance to some schoolgirls on their bikes. They were twelve or thirteen, neat in their uniform white shirts and matching pigtails, satchels slung over their backs, as crisp and clean as idealized nurses on a battlefield. Intrepid and seemingly fearless in the scrum, they were in the vanguard of India's bright hope. A bunch of smaller children, in the uniform of a primary school, huddled like chickens in a cart drawn by a bicycle. At the roadside, much less fortunate than they, a boy who looked about ten used his hands to shovel cow dung into a plastic bag.

Rahoo reached into his shirt pocket and pulled out some grimy dollar bills. His leering left eye came into view in the corner of the mirror, like a yellow moonrise.

'Change dollars. How much you give?'

'Nothing. I don't want dollars.'

He asked several more times and then gave up and spat out of the window.

We left the city behind. The land on both sides of the road assumed a familiar pattern of fields and dusty trees, weedy ponds with egret sentries, tractor workshops and tea stalls, straggles of gleaming brown goats, circling kites, women sticking pancakes of dung on to walls to dry.

In November 1857 British cavalry patrols rode up and down this road in pursuit of rebellious Indian soldiers. There were numerous skirmishes. The following year, with the uprising suppressed, the Commissioner for Jabalpur issued an order to his officials that was in keeping with the new and ugly mood among the British in India, the terrible mixture of retribution, arrogance, missionary dogma and racial prejudice: 'I shall feel obliged by your fully making it known to all your native Government Servants that when they meet a European Gentleman it will be considered disrespectful and treated accordingly if they do not make the customary salaam . . . the act will conduce much towards healing the wounds.'

I supposed that some of the trees shading the edges of the road were the remnants of those originally planted by William Sleeman, the Thugee-buster, for he was a lover of trees and an enthusiastic planter of them. When he was in charge of the Jabalpur district he created an avenue of peepal, banyan, mango and tamarind for ninety miles along this highway and ensured that other roads were similarly shaded. In the early years of the Raj the planting of such avenues was as much a feature of the administration as the roads themselves.

The Road to Panagarh

Panagar was only ten miles out of Jabalpur. It bustled with carts, bicycles and crowds of shoppers. There was a pink clock tower, built to celebrate India's independence, and beneath it an archway leading into a bazaar where awnings shaded the fruit and vegetable stalls and shops selling cloth, rope, spices, paint and steel pans.

The most important building in town was the Panagar Municipal Corporation, a white bungalow dated 1910, standing in a courtyard set back from the main street. The door led directly into the office of the Chief Municipal Officer. A broad-shouldered and magisterial man, with a thick moustache, sat at a large desk furnished with a cream telephone, a bell, an in-tray, a closed ledger, a rack with four gold-coloured pens and a sign bearing his name. A fan turned overhead, cooling his brow. He motioned to me to sit and called his clerk to bring tea. While I waited, a steady traffic of men entered the office and handed him notes and documents. Some went around his desk to bob down and touch his feet. Others conferred briefly with him. He looked at papers, signed them, rang his bell and called an assistant. When I told him my business he nodded, picked up the telephone and spoke briefly.

'I will tell you about Panagar,' he said, as we sipped tea. 'It is about two hundred years old, perhaps more. It is true that at one time the name had an "h" at the end of it, but this fell away over time. According to the census there are 21,458 persons here. You should know that Hindus and Muslims help and respect each other and celebrate each other's festivals very co-operatively. They are cordially living.'

'A peaceful town, then.'

'Why not?'

By now several men had come into the room. They darted around the desk to touch the feet of the Chief Municipal Officer. After a few minutes, the President of the Municipal Council arrived, dressed in a freshly ironed ivory-coloured shirt and trousers, a dab of vermilion on his forehead. More tea was fetched. We talked for a while and then I told my story, quite slowly, and the Chief Municipal Officer translated the sentences as I spoke. Years ago, I said, when I was a small boy, I lived in a village in England. My father's house had a name – I made a theatrical pause – and the name of the house was Panagarh. In those days I did not know where Panagarh was. I only knew that it was far away in India. But I told myself that one day I would travel there.

'And now I am here.'

The men nodded as they digested the story. One of them rose from his chair and stepped forward to shake my hand. The others did the same. The President also clasped my hand and made a short speech. The Chief Municipal Officer translated: 'He says that they are all honoured that the name of this city was the name of your father's house. They say that their city is now your city also.'

The President of the Municipal Council explained that the name of Panagar meant that it was a place where pan, the betel vine, grew. The Chief Municipal Officer nodded. 'Actually,' he said, 'it was very famous for betel leaves at one time. But today it is not so famous for it. In fact, growing of betel is not on a large scale nowadays.'

Dr Choubey, the historian I had met in Jabalpur, had told me that a very old stone had been found in Panagar with an inscription saying that it was a place where betel vines grew. The *Imperial Gazetteer* for Jabalpur published in 1908 noted that Panagar meant 'betel fort', and that it was indeed celebrated for its pan – or betel leaf – gardens, several of which extended along the banks of a large reservoir on the outskirts of the village.

The betel gardens of old Panagar were shady groves. The betel vine is like its cousin, the pepper vine, and winds itself around tree trunks, thriving only in sheltered places. In many areas the growing of betel leaves was reserved for certain castes. The cultivators ritually washed themselves before starting work in the gardens and forbade menstruating women to enter. Betel gardens were temples of a sort, often sacred and mysterious and associated with cobras and the worship of cobra gods.

The bright green leaf of the betel vine varies in flavour. It may be aromatic or pungent. But the leaf is only the beginning of the story. On to it is smeared a paste of slaked lime made from powdered chalk, seashells or coral. A sprinkle of the third essential ingredient follows: chopped or sliced pieces of the areca seed harvested from the tall, slender and unmistakable areca palm of southern India. This is the so-called 'betel nut'.

The leaf and its ingredients are folded into a little purse or quid, often secured with a clove. It is always taken whole and never nibbled. It is placed between the gum and the cheek so that the juices slowly seep into the system, sometimes for hours. Some addicts go to sleep with a quid in place. The reaction of the areca with the lime paste and the oils of the betel leaf is responsible for a mild buzz, a dizziness and a feeling of gentle euphoria. It has been likened to the effect of nicotine. Some betel-chewers say it gives them a burst of energy and others merely a feeling of well-being.

The chewing stimulates a flow of distinctively red saliva. The redness is augmented by catechu, or katha, a paste containing tannin made from the heartwood of a species of acacia tree, which lends the mixture a certain tartness. The hard pieces of areca seed are not swallowed and have to be spat out, hence the red bursts of spittle that stain pavements, stairwells and walls, inside and out, everywhere, from the Himalayas to Comorin, and attest to the passion for the trinity of betel, lime and areca.

The mixture has been chewed for at least ten thousand years. The custom was widespread across South-east Asia, Indonesia and Micronesia and reached India about two thousand years ago. Arabs recommended it as a medicine, but in some parts of the Islamic world it has been placed in the same category as alcohol and forbidden.

Betel leaves are often offered to gods but, curiously, they are an earthly pleasure and are not available in heaven. Traditionally, pan was a social sacrament, offered to guests arriving and departing, and part of the ritual of setting the seal on agreements. Making pan was, and remains, an art. It was a social grace taught to women, an accomplishment with echoes of the elaborate tea-making ceremony practised by geishas in Japan. It had a role in the intricate customs of court. It was an honour for a traveller or envoy to be given a pan from the king's own box; and, in some parts of Asia, a ready-chewed quid from the ruler's own mouth. The equipment included exquisite betel boxes, sometimes decorated with gold or silver, with compartments for the ingredients, a spittoon and a hinged sharp-edged cutter for slicing the areca nuts. The cutters, as may be seen in the collection of Samuel Eilenberg of New York, are often as ingenious as they are beautiful; elegant and sometimes amusingly erotic.

Today, the areca nut is usually chopped mechanically and a pan may be bought ready-made. But a good pan-wallah is admired and builds a loyal clientele. He sits in his wooden stall with his pastes and nuts and special ingredients and the leaves that are always kept moist. Connoisseurs favour the leaves from certain regions and some like a leaf that has been buried for a while to improve its flavour. Into the basic pan, the pan-wallah may put flavoured or scented chewing tobacco, cardamom, cumin, ginger, melon seeds, syrup, mint or menthol. In the south the pan may be sprinkled with grated coconut. In the north it may be luxuriously coated with silver sheet, beaten so thin as to be eatable, as it is in the making of desserts and sweets.

The Road to Panagarh

Ancients saw pan as a cleansing and strengthening drug. It is still taken as a digestive. Old Indian writings mention its ability to expel wind, to suppress body odour and to kill worms. Interestingly, the chief alkaloid produced by chewing pan is arecoline, used as a worming agent by veterinary surgeons. Among Hindus, pan is on a list of the chief pleasures of life, which includes women, music, flowers and aromatic oils. It is forbidden to ascetics and widows. A quid of betel has always been considered an aphrodisiac as well as a relaxant. Many pan-wallahs produce a quid popularly known as 'the bed-breaker'. Sometimes, for those who can afford it, a dash of crushed pearls is added to the pan as an aid to lust. According to old stories, a bride, while being bathed by her maidservants preparatory to her wedding night, would sit on a stool covered with betel leaves which were made into a quid and despatched to the quivering groom.

❦

The *Imperial Gazetteers* were the remarkable Domesday Books of British India, compendious records of districts covering their history, physical features, flora and fauna, mineral resources, climate, minute details of cattle ownership and crops, wages, land revenue, descriptions of the people, their health, castes and superstitions, and the disasters, like famine and earthquake, that befell them. The 1908 gazetteer for Jabalpur recorded that Panagar was a place of some antiquity. It was on the East Indian railway, had a large cattle market, a population of about four thousand, a Church of England Mission with a hospital, a Christian orphanage, a police station, a school, a post office and a military camping ground. The records of the Church Missionary Society show that a mission was established in Panagar in 1857; and a dispensary was opened in 1902 and named after Miss Eleanor Buchanan, a missionary who died of cholera while nursing a patient in 1900.

Panagar, then, was typical of thousands of unremarkable small Indian towns where British people set up schools and missions and police stations and played their small parts in education, medicine and administration; and I supposed that the house where I lived as a boy was given the name of Panagarh by a teacher or doctor or police officer who spent time there.

The Chief Municipal Officer found a guide to show me the modest sights of Panagar. He was a cheerful man, a partner in a textile shop in the bazaar, and happy to give me an hour or more of his time. He took me through the streets and showed me an old temple whose stones were crumbling. 'It is very old and not used, but you can see there is a knob on top of the dome. It is gold, at least three hundred years old. But no one will steal it. All the people know that if they dared to do so, they would receive a terrible pain in every part of their body.' He took me to the Jain temple and up the steps to the top from which there was a view over the town, its jumble of roofs and red tiles, the railway line, the women washing and carrying water jars, and distant low hills.

In the inner sanctum of the temple he showed me an ancient image, the seated figure of a white marble god, behind which there rose a protecting cobra with a flared hood and seven heads.

At the end of the tour he took me to his shop in the bazaar and motioned to me to sit on some cushions. Then he sent a boy to fetch coffee from a stall. I had asked for black coffee and when it was brought I refused sugar. The boy watched me drink it and wrinkled his face. 'He has never seen it drunk like this,' the shopkeeper said. 'He thinks you are strange to have coffee so.'

I thanked him for his generosity and said goodbye. It seemed fitting, in this place named for, and once famed for, its betel

The Road to Panagarh

leaves, to buy a pan. I soon got rid of it but I was left with the areca, gritty and sharp, worse than raspberry pips, lodging everywhere in my teeth and gums and under my tongue. I started to spit out the fragments. Rahoo watched, bemused, wondering why a man had come from the other side of the world to walk the streets of this nowhere place called Panagar. I began to feel a slight lightness in the head. Doubtless it was the heat, or simply India itself.

I felt I was spitting out chaff. There was a slight curl to Rahoo's lips.

I moved towards the car. Rahoo expectorated a red betel gobbet. He looked up and moved his vampire mouth.

'Leaving Panagar?' he said, hopefully.

'Yes,' I said, finally, 'leaving Panagarh.'

❋

This book was with the printer when I received a letter from Mrs Christine Virgin who lives in Saskatchewan, Canada. She emigrated from Hayling Island, my boyhood home, in 1947. In her letter she said she had just returned from a trip to Manitoba where she visited a friend who also had connections with Hayling Island. While Mrs Virgin was at her friend's home she chanced upon a copy of the *Hayling Islander* newspaper, sent out by her friend's nephew. As luck would have it, that particular edition carried a note in which I asked if anyone could tell me why the house in which I had lived had been called Panagarh. Yes, wrote Mrs Virgin, her father, Captain Christopher Duckham, had been based at Panagarh with the Royal Engineers. When he returned from service in India in 1945 he moved into the house and it was he who gave it its intriguing name.

Index

Abdur Rahman, Afghan ruler, 12
Afghanistan, 12, 16–17, 21–9, 44, 49
Afridi tribe, 15–16, 17–18, 43–4, 49
Agam, Afghanistan, 25
Ahmadabad, Gujarat, 138–40
Akbar the Great, Emperor, 166, 193, 239
Alang, Gujarat, 133–5
Alexander the Great, 31, 40
Ali, Subedar, mahout, 86
Alwar, Rajasthan, 84–5, 88–9
Amritsar, Punjab, 55–67; Bhandari's Guest House, 57–8; Golden Temple, 61–3, 66–7; Jallianwala Bagh, 58–61
Asaf Khan, Mogul warrior, 239
Aurangzeb, Emperor, 125
Avitabile, General Paolo, governor, 13
ayurvedic massage, 200
Ayyappan, god, 193–4

Babur, Emperor, 31, 95
Bachchan, Amitabh, film star, 73–5
Baiga tribe, 228, 230–2
Bangalore, Karnataka, 213–20; Bangalore Club, 218–19, 220; pubs, 220
Bangladesh, 169, 241
banking, 13, 233–4, 244–5
Bayley, Victor, engineer, 45–7, 49, 183
beggars, 96, 102–3, 204
betel chewing, 101, 193, 240–1, 243, 251, 255–7, 259
betel cultivation, 254–5
Bharatiya Janata Party, 99–100, 125, 148, 241
Bhasin, Raja, writer, 156

Bhindranwale, Jarnail Singh, 65–6
Bhoremdeo Temple, Madhya Pradesh, 227
Bhowani, goddess, 247
Bhuj, Gujarat, 105; Mirror Palace, 108
Birla, Ghanshyam Das, industrialist, 159
Blood, General Sir Bindon, 34
Bombay, Maharashtra, 93–103; architecture, 100–1; Elephanta Island, 94–6; Gateway of India, 94; Gymkhana Club, 101; politics, 99–100; population, 98–9; poverty, 98; St Thomas's Cathedral, 94; shanty towns, 98, 99–100; traffic, 102
Bourne, I. J., district officer, 249
Bristow, Sir Robert, engineer, 183–4, 190
British East India Company, 205–6, 239–40, 247–8
British Raj, 59–61, 78–9, 82–4, 109, 117, 136–7, 146, 148, 151–2, 154–6, 187–8, 208–9, 211–14, 216, 219, 226–8, 240, 246–7, 248–9, 252, 257–9
Buchanan, Eleanor, missionary, 258
bullock carts, 217
bureaucracy, 118, 122, 136, 145–7, 177, 220, 233–4, 244–5
Burt, Captain Seymour, 131

Cape Comorin, Tamil Nadu, 202–4
Cariappa, Field Marshal Konandera, 209
caste, 63, 110, 112, 129, 140, 161, 203, 255
Cauvery River, Karnataka, 211, 222

Index

Cavagnari, Sir Louis, administrator, 44
cemeteries, 33, 37, 44, 213
Chakdarra Fort, Pakistan, 39–40
Chanwa Fort, Rajasthan, 76
Charsadda, Pakistan, 37–8
chiru, 237–8
Choubey, Dr M. C., historian, 246–7, 248–9, 254
Churchill, Winston S., 34–6, 39–40, 60, 97, 142, 213, 219
cobras, 2, 97, 131, 144, 166, 196, 209, 213–14, 228, 232, 255, 258
Cochin, Kerala, 181–5, 187, 189–90; harbour, 182–3, 190
coconuts, 7–9, 116–17, 124, 130, 194, 199–201
coffee-growing, 211–12
conservation, 90–1
Coorg, Karnataka, 208–12
Coronation Durbar (1911), 83, 137, 151–2
Coryton Mayne, J.W., headmaster, 117
cricket, 85, 91, 94, 102, 117, 143–4, 165, 166, 170
crime, 53, 75–6, 129, 144, 148, 209–10, 220–3, 247–8
Cubbon, Sir Mark, administrator, 219
curry, 187–8
Curzon, Lord, Viceroy, 83

Daily Telegraph, The, 35–6, 40
Daman (Union Territory), 127; Indian invasion (1961), 127–8
dancing bears, 42–3, 160
dancing monkeys, 144–5
Darra, Pakistan, 40
Davies, William, coffee planter, 211–12
Delhi, 83, 143, 149–52, 157–60; Birla house, 158–60; Coronation Park, 152; Gymkhana Club, 149–50, 152, 154; Lodi Gardens, 157–8; pollution, 150–1
Denmark, 190
Deogarh Fort, Rajasthan, 76–7
Diu (Union Territory), 127–9; Indian invasion (1961), 127–8

driving, 15, 52–5, 73, 102, 111–12, 139, 149, 182, 191, 205, 212, 251
Dufferin, Lord, Viceroy, 12, 154–5
Durgavati, warrior, 239
Dyer, Brigadier-General Reginald, 10, 58–61

Economist, The, 128
education, 101, 113, 117–18, 121–2, 136–7, 148, 194, 214–16, 219, 227–8, 231, 251
Ellis, Mollie, hostage, 43–4
Elphinstone, Mountstuart, administrator, 13
Emergency (1976), 84–5

film industry, 74–6, 197–8
Fincastle, Lord, 35
fishing, 95, 101–2, 123–4, 183, 200
forestry, 97, 229–30
Fuller, Sir Joseph, administrator, 248

Gama, Vasco da, 188–9
Gandhi, Indira, 64–6, 84, 154, 158, 171–2
Gandhi, Mohandas Karamchand, 37, 61, 109–11, 120, 138–42, 148, 153, 203, 238; Ahmadabad ashram, 138–41; assassination, 126, 140, 158–60; education, 117–18; influences on, 132–3; Mahatma title, 118–19; salt march, 109
Gandhi, Sanjay, 65, 147
Ganesh, god, 97, 125, 228
George V, King, 83, 151–2
Ghazni, Mahmud of, 125
Ghosh, Dr Kamla, schoolteacher, 162
Gill, K.P.S., police officer, 66
Gir Forest, Gujarat, 121–3
Gobind, Sikh Guru, 63–4
Godse, Gopal, 126
Godse, Nathuram, assassin, 125–6, 140, 159–60
Gond tribe, 226–7, 228, 239
Gondal, Maharani of, 119–20
Greenwood, Lieutenant, 13

Index

Griffiths, Sir Percival, administrator, 41
Gujarat, 105–40, 187

Haidar Ali, 205–6, 208
Handyside, Eric Charles, police officer, 41–3, 151
Hanuman, god, 125, 227, 228, 242
health, 113, 135, 147–8, 150, 238, 241, 243, 257
Hearn, Colonel Gordon, 45
Henty, G.A., author, 34
Hindu nationalism, 99–100, 125, 126, 148, 241
Holi festival, 243–5, 246
Housego, David, 173–5
Housego, Kim, 173, 175
Hyderabad, Nizam of, 79

Illustrated London News, 36
Imperial Gazetteers, 19, 254, 257
Indian Express, 99–100

Jabalpur, Madhya Pradesh, 239–47; Marble Rocks, 242; Narmada Falls, 242
Jahangir, Emperor, 165
Jains, 130–2
Jaipur, Maharaja of, 89–90
Jaisalmer, Rajasthan, 90–1
Jallianwala Bagh massacre, 10, 58–61
Jayalalitha, politician, 198
Jinnah, Mohammed Ali, 153, 159
journalism, 34–6, 40, 93–4, 143–4, 148, 176–8, 179, 228–9, 243

Kali, goddess, 197, 247, 248
Kanha National Park, Madhya Pradesh, 234–5
Kanya Kumari, Tamil Nadu, 202
Kappkadavu, Kerala, 188
Kashmir, 71, 165–80
Kashmir, Maharaja of, 167
Kawardha Palace, Madhya Pradesh, 225–6
Kerala, 181–94, 198–201; Christianity in, 189–91; waterways, 198–200

Khan Abdul Ghaffar Khan, Pathan leader, 37–8
Khushal Khan Kattack, poet, 38
Khyber Pass, Pakistan/Afghanistan, 3, 11–12, 28, 31–3, 45, 49
Khyber railway, 45–9
kidnapping, 173–6, 177–9
Kim, 3, 4, 11
Kipling, Lockwood, 155
Kipling, Rudyard, 3, 11–12, 33, 60, 79, 155, 234
Kitchener, Lord, 45
Kohat Pass, Pakistan, 40–1, 42
Kohat, Pakistan, 44–5
Kovalam, Kerala, 200
Krishna, god, 161, 162–3
Kumari, goddess, 203
Kumbha, king, 80–1
Kumbhalgarh Fort, Rajasthan, 81
Kutch, Gujarat, 105–9; Great Rann, 105–6; Little Rann, 108–9

language, 210–11
legal system, 147, 209–10
lions, 120–3

Macaulay, Thomas, historian, 101
Mackie, David, 173, 175
Madhya Pradesh, 225–59
Madras, Tamil Nadu, 197
Madurai, Tamil Nadu, 195–7
Maffey, Sir John, administrator, 41, 42, 43
Malakand Fort, Pakistan, 38–9
Malakand Pass, Pakistan, 34–6, 38
Malam, Ramsingh, craftsman, 108
mangoes, 51–2
marriage, 65, 85–90, 161, 162–3, 219
Masters, John, 19, 20, 31, 33
Mehta, Rajchandra, poet, 132
Mercara, Karnataka, 209–10
Mishra, Om Prakash, Collector of Diu, 128–9
Moberly, Lieutenant-General Sir Bertrand, 44–5
Moraes, Dom, writer, 123
Morning Post, 60
Munro, Sir Thomas, administrator, 219

262

Index

Muslims, 57, 99–100, 125, 126, 131, 159, 166–71, 179–80, 239, 241, 253
Mysore, Karnataka, 222

Naipaul, V.S., 145, 146
Narayanan, Dr M.G.S., historian, 190
Narmada River, Madhya Pradesh, 238–9
Naxalites, 243
Nayar, Kuldip, writer, 71, 160, 170–1
Neemrana Fort, Rajasthan, 73–4
Nehru, Jawaharlal, 52, 128, 146, 167
Nisar, Dr Qazi, cleric, 174–5
North West Frontier, Pakistan, 1–2, 3–4, 11–12, 15–21, 31–49, 70; tribes, 15–21, 45–6, 49

opium, 76, 137–8

Pakhtunwali, 11, 17–20, 27–8, 46
Pakistan, 21, 37, 71–2, 167–72, 241
palaces, 107–8, 119–20, 135–7, 225–6, 235–6
Panagar, Madhya Pradesh, 6, 253–9; Municipal Corporation, 253–4
Panagarh, Hayling Island, Hampshire, 1–2, 4, 6, 254, 258, 259
Partition, 37, 57, 69–72, 153, 159, 167–71, 241
Pathans, 16–21, 33, 37–8, 39, 40–4, 45–6
Pennell, Theodore, missionary, 18, 19–20, 46
Peshawar, Pakistan, 3, 9–14, 21–2, 45; cantonment, 12–13; Dean's Hotel, 10–11, 22, 30, 45, 48; museum, 14; Street of the Storytellers, 21
Peter the Great, 147
pilgrimage, 114–17, 129–31, 161, 163, 193–4, 196–7, 202–4, 211, 238
poaching, 222, 236–8
pollution, 81–2, 96–7, 135, 150–1
population control, 113, 147–8
Portugal, 127–8, 188–9

poverty, 98–100, 108–9, 112–13, 135, 147, 163, 195, 219
princely families, 76–81, 82–5, 87, 88–9, 107–8, 136–7, 226–8, 235–6
Prior, Melton, war artist, 36
prohibition, 109–11, 128
Punjab Frontier Force, 44–5
Punjab, 11, 13, 52, 58, 65–7, 69–72
Pushtu, 16, 25

Raipur, Madhya Pradesh, 232–4
Rajasthan, 73–4, 76–84, 90–1
Rajputs, 76, 79–81, 82–5, 89–90
Ramachandran, K.R., administrator, 214, 219
Ramachandran, M.G., politician, 197–8
Ramaswamy, Professor, reformer, 216–18, 220
Reading, Lord, Viceroy, 42
religion, 8–9, 61–4, 95–6, 113–17, 124–5, 129–31, 161, 163, 179–80, 189–91, 193–4, 196–7, 203–4, 211, 221, 228, 238, 241
Roberts, Field Marshal Lord, 44
Robinson, Lieutenant William, airman, 212
Ruskin, John, 132
Russian-Afghan War (1979–89), 16–17, 21–30, 171

Sabarimala, Kerala, 193–4
Sadullah (Mad Mullah), 34, 39
Salazar, Antonio, 127–8
sandalwood, 221–3
Sati, goddess, 115, 203
Satrunjaya, Gujarat, 129–31
Scott, Paul, author, 56, 145
Seringapatam, Karnataka, 205–8
ship-breaking, 133–5
Shiv Sena Party, 99–100
Shiva, god, 8, 9, 115, 116, 166, 196, 238
Shute, Nevil, 2
Sikhs, 34, 58, 61–7, 154, 166–7
Simla, Himachal Pradesh, 154–7
Singh, Ambika, 85–9
Singh, Brijendra, tiger expert, 85–8

263

Index

Singh, Jitendra, 84–9
Singh, Kaur, palace guard, 225
Singh, Khushwant, writer, 151, 152–4, 160
Singh, Maharaj Dalip, 76
Singh, Maharaja Sir Jai, 84–5
Singh, Maharana Sir Fateh, 82–4
Singh, Ranjit, King of Punjab, 13, 70–1, 166
Singh, Rawat Nahar, 76–8
Singh, Sir Sobha, 152
Singh, Sujan, 152
Singh, Tavleen, journalist, 171
Singh, Ujjiar of Kawardha, 227
Singh, Yogeshwar Raj of Kawardha, 227–9, 231–2
Sitwell, Ensign W.H., 44
slaughterhouses, 217–18
Sleeman, Sir William, defeater of Thugs, 247–8, 252
snooker, 144, 240
Somnath, Gujarat, 123–6
Spate, O.H.K., geographer, 31
Spectator, The, 128
spice trade, 128, 185–9, 190, 192–3
Srinagar, Kashmir, 165–6, 175–80; Ahdoo's Hotel, 176–7, 178–9, 180; Butt's houseboats, 172–3, 180; Dal Lake, 165, 172–3; Hazratbal mosque,179–80
Starr, Lillian, nurse, 20, 43–4
Stead, W.T., 2
Swat Valley, Pakistan, 39–40

Tagore, Rabindranath, 61
Takht Sinh, Thakor of Utelia, 136–8
Taliban, 16–17, 20
Tamil Nadu, 190, 193, 195
Tansen, poet, 193
Thackeray, Bal, politician, 99
Thampi, P.S.S. (Spices Board), 181, 182, 185–6, 188–9, 191–3, 195
The Slave of the Khan, 3–4, 6, 12
Thugee cult, 247–8
tigers, 85, 86, 100, 107, 119–20, 152, 207, 231, 232, 234–7, 249
Times of India, The, 35, 123
Times, The, 5–6
Tipu Sultan, 205–8, 212
Tolstoy, Leo, 132
Torabora, Afghanistan, 25–6
tourism, 91, 111, 122, 145, 235
Tranquebar, Tamil Nadu, 190
Trevor, Michael, author, 3
tribals, 228–9

Udaipur, Rajasthan, 80–4; Pichola Lake, 81–2; Shivniwas Palace Hotel, 81–2
University of Wales, Aberystwyth, 214
Utelia Palace, Ahmadabad, Gujarat, 135–8

Veerappan, bandit, 221, 222–3
Virgin, Christine, 259
Vishnu, god, 116
Victoria, Queen, 36, 71, 82, 248
Vivekenanda, Swami, 203
Vrindavan, Uttar Pradesh, 161–3

Wade, John, staying on, 56–7
Wagah sunset ceremony, India/Pakistan border, 67–9, 71–2
Wankaner Palace, Gujarat, 111
Watts-Carter, Margaret, 228, 232
Wellesley, Colonel Arthur (1st Duke of Wellington), 206–7
widows, 161–3
Willingdon, Lord, Viceroy, 152, 183
Wilson, Field Marshal Sir Henry, 60